GREAT PERFECTION

GREAT PERFECTION

Outer and Inner Preliminaries

by the Third Dzogchen Rinpoche
Foreword by The Dzogchen Ponlop Rinpoche
Translated by Cortland Dahl

SNOW LION PUBLICATIONS
ITHACA, NEW YORK • BOULDER, COLORADO

Snow Lion Publications
P.O. Box 6483
Ithaca, New York 14851 USA
607-273-8519
www.snowlionpub.com

Copyright © 2007 Cortland Dahl

All rights reserved. No portion of this book may be reproduced by any means without prior written permission from the publisher.

Printed in Canada on acid-free recycled paper.
Designed & typeset by Gopa & Ted2, Inc.

ISBN-10: 1-55939-285-1
ISBN-13: 978-1-55939-285-3

Library of Congress Cataloging-in-Publication Data

Nes don Bstan 'dzin bzaṅ po.
  [Rdzogs pa chen po mkha' 'gro sñiṅ thig gi khrid yig thar lam bgrod byed śiṅ rta bzaṅ po. English. Selections]
  Great perfection : outer and inner preliminaries / by the Third Dzogchen Rinpoche ; introduced by the Dzogchen Ponlop Rinpoche ; translated by Cortland Dahl.
    p. cm.
  Includes bibliographical references and index.
  ISBN13: 978-155939-285-3 (alk. paper)
  ISBN10: 1-55939-285-1 (alk. paper)
  1. Rdzogschen. I. Title.
BQ7662.4.N4713 2007
294.3'444—dc22
                                                                    2007029454

Table of Contents

Foreword by The Dzogchen Ponlop Rinpoche   vii
Translator's Introduction   xiii

The Excellent Chariot: A Vehicle for the Path to Liberation

Homage and Pledge of the Composition   3
How to Listen to the Teachings   5
The Lineage History   7
Empowerment   13
The Common Preliminaries   17
  1. The Precious Human Existence & Refuge   19
    The Freedoms and Endowments   19
    Taking Refuge   27
      The Practice of Taking Refuge   30

  2. Impermanence & Bodhichitta   37
    Death and Impermanence   37
      Qualifications of Teacher and Student   37
      Contemplating Impermanence   44
    Compassion and Bodhichitta   57
      Aspiration Bodhichitta   57
      Application Bodhichitta   60
      Bodhichitta in Practice   60
      The Benefits of Bodhichitta   61
      [Developing Bodhichitta]   61

  3. Karma & the Three Vows   63
    The Principle of Karmic Causality   63
      The Ten Virtues   67
      The Ten Forms of Vice   70

Virtue and Liberation	72
The Four Immeasurables	73
The Six Perfections	74
Karma and Samsara	75
Karma and Nirvana	76
The Three Vows	77
The Vows of Individual Liberation	77
The Bodhisattva Precepts	79
Samaya Vows	84
4. The Suffering of Samsara & the Practice of Vajrasattva	**91**
The Suffering of Samsara	91
How to Listen to the Teachings	91
Contemplating the Suffering of Samsara	93
The Meditation and Recitation of Vajrasattva	112
Confession	116
5. Liberation & the Mandala Offering	**127**
The Benefits of Liberation	127
How to Listen to a Teaching	127
Contemplating the Benefits of Liberation	129
Mandala Offering	135
Gathering the Accumulations	135
6. Faith & Guru Yoga	**141**
Faith and Liberation	141
The Nature of the Teacher	141
The Nature of the Student	142
Qualities Needed by Both Teacher and Student	143
Faith	144
The Guru	156
The Practice of Guru Yoga	162
Concluding Verses	171
Abbreviations	173
Glossary	177
Notes	229
Texts Cited	235
Bibliography	243
Index	249

Foreword

IN THE TIBETAN BUDDHIST tradition, the most profound and commonly practiced teachings are those of the Vajrayana. Within this powerful system of skillful means, the supreme view and most potent methods are found in the teachings and practices of Dzogchen, the Great Perfection. These instructions are regarded as the pinnacle of the teachings and as the most direct path to realizing the nature of mind and the reality of the world.

The instructions of the Dzogchen lineage are used to directly point out the nature of mind and bring the experience of enlightenment into our ordinary life. These teachings are known as "pith instructions," the pure, quintessential knowledge that cuts through all confusion and gets straight to the point. There is a saying, "Don't beat around the bush," meaning, "Get to the point." That is Dzogchen.

In many ways, these teachings go beyond scripture and the formality of spiritual techniques. These two do have their place, since it is important to study scripture and meditate in a step-by-step manner. Yet, at some point we also must connect directly with the nature of mind. We have to strike the crucial point, the enlightened state, and leap directly into experiencing and realizing the true nature of our mind.

The term "Dzogchen" can be translated into English in different ways: as the Great Completion, the Great Perfection, and the Great Exhaustion. It is called the *Great Completion* because the nature of mind is endowed with all enlightened qualities and everything is complete within it. Everything is complete within this path, within these instructions. If we relate this to our individual path and practice, it means that the mind itself is completely awakened right from the beginning. It is full of the genuine qualities of buddhahood. There is nothing missing.

It is called *Great Perfection* because the nature of mind and the nature of the world is perfect from the beginning. There are no impurities in the true nature of mind. All incidental stains are temporary. The true nature, or reality, of mind is perfect; it is inherently pure. In Dzogchen language, this nature is called *original purity*—you don't have to look beyond your immediate experience to find some other thought or emotion that is more sacred, more pure.

It is called the *Great Exhaustion* because, first, from the point of view of the fruition of the path, all the mind's impurities are exhausted and consumed; and second, from the point of view of mind's true nature, these impurities have never had any true existence. In reality, they have no true essence. They are just the confused appearances of our thoughts. From the positive side we say they are originally pure, and from the point of view of negation we say they are originally nonexistent.

Dzogchen Lineage

The Dzogchen teachings originated in the ultimate enlightened realm of Akanishta, where the primordial buddha Samantabhadra transmitted them to the awakened manifestations of buddhas and bodhisattvas through his great wisdom and compassion. Samantabhadra is known as the dharmakaya buddha. *Dharmakaya* means "truth body," or the genuine body of absolute truth. The dharmakaya buddha is depicted as being blue in color, which symbolizes expansive, unchanging space that is the ground for all manifestation, the basis for all appearances and the source of all Dharma. He is also depicted as naked, without robes or ornaments, symbolizing the primordial reality of phenomena, the ultimate truth beyond any conceptual or philosophical clothing—beyond any dualistic expression. The dharmakaya buddha symbolizes the heart of enlightenment that transcends form and physical existence.

The Dzogchen teachings are transmitted from the enlightened heart of the dharmakaya buddha to the more manifest form known as the sambhogakaya buddha, which in this case is the buddha Vajrasattva. *Sambhogakaya* means the "body of enjoyment." In this realm, there is a sense of complete joy and complete wealth: wealth of dharma, wealth of wisdom, and wealth of compassion, which manifests endlessly without any limitation. It is not just wealth for oneself; it is wealth that manifests for other sentient beings. Thus, enjoyment here points to both the experience of enlightened beings as well as the experience of those who come into contact with this aspect of reality, for they as well benefit from this wealth of dharma, joy, and wisdom. To show the richness of this realm, the sambhogakaya buddha

Vajrasattva is depicted wearing elaborate ornaments and silken garments. He appears white in color, symbolizing the qualities of luminosity and clarity. Whereas when we look into space, it seems deep blue, the sambhogakaya manifests as radiance, like the light of the moon or sun. Thus, within the space of dharmakaya, we see the sambhogakaya qualities of luminosity, richness, warmth, and clarity. It is taught that the buddha Vajrasattva continually transmits the Dzogchen teachings within the sambhogakaya realm to the five Buddha families.

From the sambhogakaya realm, the lineage descends from Vajrasattva to the *nirmanakaya* buddha, which means the "buddha of manifestation." A nirmanakaya buddha may manifest in the human realm as a human being like Buddha Shakyamuni. The first and most important Dzogchen master in this world was the great *vidyadhara*, or "master of awareness," Garap Dorjé, who was born in a place called Oddiyana in the northwest of India. At the great Blazing Mountain Charnel Ground, Garap Dorjé received the complete transmission and key instructions of Dzogchen from Vajrasattva.

Thus, the teachings of Dzogchen emanated from the ultimate sphere of reality, the enlightened nature of mind itself, and by means of great wisdom and compassion were transmitted to this world. The vidyadhara Garap Dorjé, along with wisdom dakinis, gathered and compiled all the Dzogchen tantras and divided them into 6,400,000 verses.

At the Cool Grove Charnel Ground, this vidyadhara met his principal disciple and future dharma heir, Manjushrimitra, with whom he spent many years. To him, he transmitted the full cycle of Dzogchen teachings. Before passing into parinirvana, Garap Dorjé entrusted to his lineage successor his final, extraordinary testament, "The Three Statements That Strike the Vital Point," which distills all the Dzogchen tantras into three concise principles.

After his guru's parinirvana, Manjushrimitra classified the 6,400,000 verses of the Dzogchen tantras into three categories:

- the outer category—*semdé*, "Mind Class"
- the inner category—*longdé*, "Space Class"
- the secret category—*mengakdé*, "Key Instruction Class"

At the Sosa Ling Charnel Ground, Manjushrimitra met his principal student, Shri Simha, and transmitted the entire range of Dzogchen teachings to his Dharma heir. When he departed from this world, Manjushrimitra left Shri Simha his own last testament, which came to be known as "The Six Experiences of Meditation."

Shri Simha then classified the third category, the Key Instruction Class, into four parts:

- the Outer Cycle, which is like the physical body
- the Inner Cycle, which is like the eyes
- the Secret Cycle, which is like the heart
- the Extremely Secret Unsurpassed Nyingtik, or "Heart Essence," which is like the whole body with everything complete

At the Siljin Charnel Ground, Shri Simha met his primary student, Jnanasutra, to whom he transmitted the Heart Essence of the Dzogchen teachings. Shri Simha also passed on the Heart Essence teachings to Padmasambhava at Sosa Ling Charnel Ground. Before passing away, he further entrusted to Jnanasutra his last testament, entitled "The Seven Nails." Jnanasutra then passed on the lineage to his disciple Vimalamitra. Jnanasutra, too, left his last testament, called "The Six Methods of Resting," to Vimalamitra.[1]

Padmasambhava, who is known as the Lotus Born, came to Tibet in the eighth century, bringing the Dzogchen teachings with him. Padmasambhava, Vimalamitra, and the Tibetan translator Vairochana (who had traveled to India to study) are the masters primarily responsible for bringing the Dzogchen teachings from India to the land of Tibet. From the time of Padmasambhava, there has been a continuous transmission of Dzogchen instruction and practice. These teachings have been passed on by great masters like Patrul Rinpoche, all the way down to our own time. There are many Dzogchen masters living today.

Nyingtik: the Heart Essence

The innermost, quintessential teachings of Dzogchen that were brought to Tibet by Vimalamitra and Padmasambhava were concealed as treasure, or *terma*, for future generations. They were later revealed by Dangma Lhungyal and Pema Ledrel Tsel, respectively. The Nyingtik or "Heart Essence" teachings of Vimalamitra became renowned as the Vima Nyingtik (Heart Essence of Vimalamitra), and those of Padmasambhava renowned as the Padma or Khandro Nyingtik (Heart Essence of the Dakinis).

These two root scriptural collections served as the basis for later developments of Nyingtik traditions, as well as for the subsequent composition of two sets of commentarial literature by the great Dzogchen master Longchen Rabjam. His commentaries on the Vima Nyingtik came to be known as the Lama Yangtik (Guru's Quintessence), while those that pertain to the Khandro Nyingtik are referred to as the Khandro Yangtik (Quintessence of the Dakinis). The two root and two clarifying collections are collectively known as the Fourfold Heart Essence.

There are three different traditions of classifying these four.[2] The primary way of classifying the Fourfold Heart Essence includes (1) the Vima Nyingtik; (2) the Khandro Nyingtik; (3) the Lama Yangtik; and (4) the Khandro Yangtik. A second classification includes (1) the Vima Nyingtik; (2) the Lama Yangtik; (3) the Khandro Nyingtik and Khandro Yangtik, counted as one; and (4) the Karma Nyingtik, which comes from the Third Karmapa, Rangjung Dorjé. A third way of classifying the four, according to the Dzogchen masters Kongpo Dzogchenpa and Rigdzin Tsewang Norbu, includes (1) the Vima Nyingtik; (2) the Lama Yangtik; (3) the Khandro Nyingtik and Khandro Yangtik, counted as one; and (4) the Dorsem Nyingtik. These scriptures comprise one of the most famous collections of Dzogchen treatises, entitled *Nyingtik Yabshi,* or the Fourfold Heart Essence.[3] Of these profound lineages of Dzogchen, the teachings presented here are from the cycle of the Khandro Nyingtik, the Heart Essence of the Dakinis.

Heart Essence of the Dakinis

The Khandro Nyingtik, or Heart Essence of the Dakinis, was transmitted by Padmasambhava to Princess Pemasel. It was later revealed by her reincarnation, Pema Ledrel Tsel, and then descended to the omniscient Longchen Rabjam. The details of this lineage are clearly presented in the translation that follows.

The Khandro Nyingtik cycle of teachings is regarded as one of the main practices of Dzogchen Monastery, one of the Nyingma tradition's "six mother monasteries." The first Dzogchen Rinpoche, Pema Rigdzin, and the first Dzogchen Ponlop Rinpoche, Namkha Ösel, held and propagated the lineage of Khandro Nyingtik teachings in eastern Tibet. I received the full transmission of these teachings directly from my own gurus: His Holiness Dilgo Khyentse Rinpoche, the incomparable Dzogchen vidyadhara, and the most venerable Alak Zenkar Rinpoche, the renowned scholar and treasured lineage master.

This book, Dzogchen Ngetön Tenzin Zangpo's *The Excellent Chariot*, issues from this unbroken lineage. As one of the most beautiful and lucid explanations of the Heart Essence of the Dakinis, it provides invaluable guidance for practitioners of the Dzogchen teachings. As all journeys go, this book goes through three stages: a beginning, middle, and end. It begins with the preliminary practices of the Dzogchen Khandro Nyingtik, which are crucial for the actual practice in the middle stage. The preliminary practices are like the story line of a joke. Without the set-up, the actual punch line will not make any sense; it won't cause you to burst into laughter. This is why we have a saying in Tibetan Buddhism that goes, "The preliminaries are more profound than the actual practice." Ngetön Tenzin Zangpo's presentation of the preliminary teachings is especially profound and deeply moving. The manner in which he writes is not duplicated elsewhere in teachings on the preliminaries.

This book contains a very important set of instructions from my lineage that will be of benefit to all practitioners of the Dzogchen tradition. Therefore, I would like to express my profound appreciation and gratitude to my student, Cortland Dahl (Karma Tsultrim Shönu), for his exemplary and dedicated efforts in translating this book into English. He not only worked diligently on the translation but also prepared himself well by receiving the transmissions and explanations of the text. Furthermore, he consulted both myself and others for clarifications throughout the project. This translation was also made possible through the great generosity of David Lunsford and the Bodhi Foundation, whose support I wholeheartedly appreciate.

I am happy to see the first part of this book, which contains all the profound and unique teachings on the preliminary practices of the Khandro Nyingtik, published here. The second half of this text, which includes the actual Dzogchen instructions of the Heart Essence of the Dakinis, is being published in a separate volume.

May the merit of this effort bring peace and harmony to the hearts of all beings in the world. May the seeds of the dakini's heart essence take root in the heart of this Western land and spread their fragrant blossoms of great wisdom and boundless compassion.

Dzogchen Ponlop Rinpoche
Nalanda West
Seattle, WA
USA

Translator's Introduction

ACCORDING TO THE NYINGMA School of Tibetan Buddhism, the Great Perfection is the supreme spiritual approach and the culmination of the Buddha's teachings. Stripped of the symbolic imagery and meditative ritual so common in other forms of Tibetan Buddhist practice, the Great Perfection deals directly with the nature and functioning of the mind. These profound instructions present a spiritual shortcut, a radically direct approach that cuts through confusion and lays bare the mind's true nature of luminous purity. Its teachings are said to be so powerful, in fact, that when given by a qualified teacher to a devoted student at the right moment, the shift from delusion to enlightenment can take place in a single instant.

Though the term "Great Perfection" can be used to refer to the fundamental nature of reality as well as the fruitional state of buddhahood, it most commonly refers to a continually evolving set of spiritual instructions and the lineage of enlightened beings who have mastered these teachings and passed them down through the ages. The Third Dzogchen Rinpoche's *Excellent Chariot*, the Tibetan text translated here, offers one of the clearest and most comprehensive presentations of these instructions in the Tibetan language. For centuries, this profound text has served countless meditators as a guidebook to rarefied states of consciousness. It is designed to lead spiritual aspirants through the entire Buddhist path, starting with basic Buddhist contemplations that work to dislodge deeply ingrained patterns of thinking and behaving, and continuing on to the most advanced and secret meditative practices of the Great Perfection.

As a meditative system, the Great Perfection is a complete path to liberation. Practitioners of this tradition utilize a series of increasingly subtle practices first to turn their minds away from mundane activities towards liberation and then to purify the factors that block realization from taking place. Once the mind has been thoroughly trained and refined via these preliminary steps, the advanced practices of breakthrough and direct leap are utilized to help the meditator initially identify and experience the pure, nondual awareness that underlies all experience and then hasten the process of realization by working directly with the active manifestations of reality itself.

Though different cycles of Great Perfection teachings each have their own unique approach to this progression, the general structure of practice is similar in most presentations. According to the *Structure of the Heart Essence of the Dakinis Practice*, the first step in Great Perfection meditation is to practice the outer preliminaries. Prior to formal meditation practice, however, it is essential to seek out a fully qualified Dzogchen master. More importantly, a student must carry out a thorough self-inventory to determine if he or she meets the requirements laid out in instruction manuals of the Great Perfection. These qualifications are covered in detail in the second and sixth chapters of the translation that follows.

Once these preparatory steps are complete and a link has been formed between a qualified teacher and sincere student, the cycle of teaching and practice may commence. The first step involves contemplating the rarity of the freedoms and endowments, karmic causality, the shortcomings of samsara, the benefits of liberation, and death and impermanence.[4] These contemplations comprise the outer, common preliminary practices. Their main function is to eliminate the tendency to become obsessed with mundane endeavors and to intensify one's motivation to pursue liberation wholeheartedly.

Next the meditator practices the five inner preliminaries: refuge, bodhichitta, the meditation and recitation of Vajrasattva, mandala offering, and guru yoga. Each of these five practices serves a different function. Taking refuge is the foundation for all Buddhist practice and is said to sow the seed of liberation in one's mind stream. As the altruistic motivation to attain buddhahood for the welfare of all beings, cultivating bodhichitta is the defining practice of the Great Vehicle. Vajrasattva practice purifies the negativity and obscurations that hinder the development of meditative experience and realization. In this practice, visualization and mantra recitation are linked with a sincere sense of remorse for the negative actions one has committed and a resolve to refrain from committing them again in the future. The mandala offering adds to this by creating favorable conditions for spiritual practice. Here one makes real and imagined offerings to a visualized assembly of enlightened beings. This is taught to be a particularly effective way to gather the two accumulations of merit and wisdom.

The fifth and final practice of the inner preliminaries is guru yoga. This profound practice opens the practitioner's being to the blessings of the guru. Though realization comes from within, working with a spiritual teacher is taught to be an indispensable way to activate one's innate wisdom. In the practice of guru yoga, the meditator infuses a series of visualizations with devotion. Viewing the animate and inanimate universe as a pure realm populated with buddhas, the meditator supplicates the guru, makes offerings, and then merges his or her mind with the wisdom mind of the guru. When the devotion of the student is sincere and heartfelt, this merging of minds can bring about an immediate and profound shift in consciousness.

These outer and inner preliminaries prepare the mind of the student for the more advanced meditations that follow. Once complete, the student receives guidance from his or her teacher concerning the most appropriate course of meditation to follow. This may include development stage meditation (visualization and mantra recitation), completion stage practice with symbolic attributes (working with the body's subtle energies), and/or formless completion stage practices (recognizing and familiarizing oneself with the nature of mind). In the Great Perfection tradition, the spiritual path culminates in the stages of breakthrough and direct leap. Respectively, these two practices relate to the principles of original purity and spontaneous presence.

Dzogchen Monastery and the Third Dzogchen Rinpoche

The book translated here is one of the primary practice manuals used at the retreat center of Dzogchen Monastery in Eastern Tibet, where it is said that twenty-eight Great Perfection yogis attained the rainbow body by relying solely upon this text.[5] Along with Mindroling, Dorjé Drak, Palyul, Shechen, and Katok monasteries, Dzogchen Monastery is one of six "mother" monasteries of the Nyingma lineage. Over the centuries, it has hosted some of the most notable siddhas and saints of the Great Perfection tradition, including the Dza Patrul Rinpoche, Khenpo Pema Vajra, Mipam, Khenpo Künpal, Khenpo Ngaga, Khenpo Shenga, Pöba Tulku, and more recently, Khenpo Petsé Rinpoche.

In accordance with a prophecy made by the great Fifth Dalai Lama, Dzogchen Monastery was founded in the late seventeenth century by Drupwang Pema Rigdzin, the First Dzogchen Rinpoche. He founded the monastery along with his three main students, the First Dzogchen Ponlop Rinpoche, the First Shechen Rabjam Rinpoche, and Rigdzin Nyima Drakpa. Soon after, it became one of the Nyingma school's primary centers for the study and practice of the Great Perfection teachings, and for the Heart Essence of the Dakinis in particular. The historical abbots of this monastery have been the successive incarnations of the Dzogchen and Dzogchen Ponlop Rinpoches, and later the reincarnations of Gyalsé Shenpen Tayé, who are known as the Dzogchen Gemang Tulkus.

The main retreat center of Dzogchen Monastery was constructed during the lifetime of the Third Dzogchen Rinpoche, author of *The Excellent Chariot*. The idyllic spot where the center was built was chosen by the great treasure revealer Jigmé Lingpa, who consecrated the spot from afar. It quickly became a primary center in the Nyingma world for the study and practice of the Heart Essence of the Dakinis, due largely to the efforts of the Third Dzogchen Rinpoche to preserve, practice, and transmit these profound teachings. Sadly, this center was destroyed during the Chinese invasion of Tibet and has yet to be rebuilt.

The Third Dzogchen Rinpoche, Ngetön Tenzin Zangpo, ordained as a novice monk at a young age and studied both sutra and tantra with the most respected teachers of Dzogchen Monastery. In particular, he received many teachings from Dzogchen Ponlop Rinpoche,[6] including experiential guidance[7] on the Heart Essence teachings of Vimalamitra and Padmasambhava. With other teachers he studied and received transmissions for the Collected Tantras of the Nyingma School, the works of Longchenpa, the treasure teachings of Pema Lingpa, teachings from the Northern Treasures, and the treasures of Mindroling Monastery, where he took full monastic ordination.

He also traveled extensively on pilgrimage to Tibet's most sacred monasteries and power spots, where he continually sought out the great masters of his time, such as Jigmé Lingpa and the Karmapa. He did not limit his travels to the sacred sites of the Nyingma sect, however, but traveled to sites linked with other traditions as well. He visited the main Geluk monasteries in Lhasa, Tashi Lhunpo (seat of the Panchen Lamas), Tsurpu (home of the Karmapas), and many others. As he traveled, he made lavish offerings to support the sanghas of Tibet's four main lineages.

Ngetön Tenzin Zangpo's great passion, however, was intensive spiritual practice. Even in the midst of his other activities, he would spend most of the night absorbed in deep meditation. He showed a particular fondness for remote, uninhabited locales, where he spent time cultivating his meditative practice. Though he was continually absorbed in the true nature of reality, he never lost sight of the importance of relative acts of virtue, such as prostrations and circumambulation. A spiritual prodigy from a young age, throughout his life he experienced visions of various deities and masters, including Padmasambhava, Yeshé Tsogyal, Vimalamitra, and the main Dharma protectors of the Great Perfection lineage.

The Excellent Chariot

The Excellent Chariot is one of the most accessible and comprehensive presentations of the Heart Essence teachings ever written. The Heart Essence of the Dakinis comprises sixty-five texts that span two volumes and more than a thousand pages.[8] Such a vast collection of instructions and practices can be daunting to all but the most learned and experienced practitioners. *The Excellent Chariot* organizes these instructions into a format that can be readily taught, studied, and practiced, distilling the teachings of the Heart Essence of the Dakinis into one three-hundred-page volume.

After a beautiful opening poem, the text offers instructions on the proper way to receive spiritual teachings, a presentation of the lineage history, and a short chapter on the importance of receiving empowerments. Following these introductory topics, the author launches into a presentation of the preliminary practices. Rather than presenting the outer and inner preliminary practices in a sequential manner, as is usually the case, the author pairs them together. The rarity of the freedoms and endowments is paired with refuge, impermanence with bodhichitta, karma with the three vows,[9] the faults of samsara with Vajrasattva practice, the benefits of liberation with the mandala offering, and faith and devotion with guru yoga. Interwoven with these teachings is the liturgy for *The Pure Path to Liberation*, the preliminary practices of Dzogchen Monastery. This liturgy has been set out in boldface type in the translation that follows. An extensive glossary of the key terms employed in the text is appended, composed almost entirely of extracts from the works of masters of the Great Perfection lineage. Original Tibetan and Sanskrit titles may be found in the Texts Cited list.

The preliminary practice section of *The Excellent Chariot* draws extensively from the writings of Great Perfection authors. In particular, most of the content related to the outer preliminaries (the first of each pair listed in the previous paragraph) is actually written by Longchenpa. The author uses two main sources: Longchenpa's *Precious Wish-fulfilling Treasury* and his autocommentary on *Resting in the Nature of Mind,* the *Great Chariot.*

Following the outer and inner preliminaries, which take up roughly one hundred and ninety of the three hundred and thirty pages of the Tibetan text, the author addresses the practices of the Heart Essence, including the unique Great Perfection preliminaries and the breakthrough stage. These profound instructions are meant as a supplement to, rather than replacement for, the oral teachings of a qualified Great Perfection master. To help maintain the integrity of the lineage, these sections are being published in a second restricted volume, which will be available to those who have received the appropriate transmissions to study and practice these teachings.

Traditionally, a text such as this would be studied in a retreat setting under the guidance of an experienced Great Perfection teacher. Such circumstances provide ample time to receive extended teachings and put them into practice. In particular, meditating on the Great Perfection teachings under the supervision of a qualified teacher helps the student avoid the numerous pitfalls and missteps that inevitably occur on the spiritual path. The teacher-student relationship also ensures that teachings are transmitted in an effective manner, with each set of instructions imparted at a time and place best suited to the disposition and aptitude of the student.

Acknowledgments

This translation project was carried out at the request of the seventh Dzogchen Ponlop Rinpoche, without whose guidance, blessings, and support the translation of this profound text would not have been possible. The very first Dzogchen Ponlop Rinpoche, Namkha Ösel, was a great master of the teachings contained in this book. He was also a clear source of inspiration for the author, as evidenced by the latter's extensive praises of Namkha Ösel in the lineage history chapter of this very work. Throughout their successive incarnations, the Dzogchen Ponlop Rinpoches continued to uphold the teachings of the Heart Essence of the Dakinis at Dzogchen Monastery in Eastern Tibet, working together with the Dzogchen Tulkus to ensure that this profound lineage of teachings and realization remained available to future generations in its purest form.

It is fitting, then, that the seventh incarnation of Namkha Ösel, the current Dzogchen Ponlop Rinpoche, is one of the driving forces in transmitting these teachings to the West. In 2006 and 2007, Rinpoche transmitted the teachings contained in this book in their entirety at the annual Nalandabodhi Sangha retreat. Rinpoche also took the time to meet with me on numerous occasions to clarify key points in the text and answer my many questions. For his encouragement to work on this project, for his boundless love and compassion, and for his example of what a true Dzogchen yogi should be, I am forever grateful.

Throughout this project, I have been blessed to have the support and guidance of many masters of the Dzogchen lineage, friends and family members, and fellow translators. In particular, I would like to thank the following Dzogchen masters for contributing to this project through their empowerments and transmissions, teachings, and blessings: Chatral Rinpoche Sangye Dorje, Trulshik Rinpoche, Shechen Rabjam Rinpoche, Tsoknyi Rinpoche, and Khen Rinpoche Sherab Sangpo. I would especially like to thank Yongey Mingyur Rinpoche, whose kindness and generosity to me as a student surpass anything I could ever say or write. If anything of the profundity and power of the original Tibetan manuscript has made its way into this book, it is due solely to the blessings of these masters and the enlightened lineage they represent.

I am also deeply grateful to the many fellow translators, friends, and family who contributed to this project. First and foremost, I must thank my friends Thomas Doctor and Heidi Köppl for taking the time to check my entire translation against the original Tibetan. I would also like to thank lotsawas Sarah Harding, Anne Helm, and Erik Pema Kunsang for their support and mentorship, and my friends Douglas Duckworth, Andreas Doctor, Tyler Dewar, Adam Pearcy, and Joe McClellan for the helpful comments and resources they provided.

The translation itself was edited by James Fox, a skilled poet and devoted student of the Dzogchen teachings. Thanks to his keen eye and skilled pen, some of the poetic flavor of the original text has made its way into the book you are now holding. Equal thanks goes to Belinda Griswold, who cleaned up the manuscript before publication and infused some much-needed dakini wisdom into the project. I would also like to thank Sidney Piburn at Snow Lion Publications for his support of this project and editorial advice, and Susan Kyser for her careful editing work.

I would especially like to thank David Lunsford of the Bodhi Foundation, who so generously sponsored this work and who continues to do so much to ensure the preservation of the Dzogchen teachings and aid in the transmission of these teachings to the West. I would also like to thank all those who have supported the Rimé Foundation over the past years. Without the contribution of these generous individuals, this translation project would never have seen the light of day. In particular, the Rimé Foundation owes a great debt to Beth Foss, Kit Dahl, Molly Brooks, Richard Perkins, Anna-brown Griswold, Sky Brooks, David Doth, Hans Schumacher, Jennifer Manion, Stephanie Chew-Grossman, Mary MacEachen, Dan Pennie, Rob McIlhargie, and all the other kind individuals who contributed to the foundation's activities in so many ways.

Last but not least, I would like to thank my wonderful family. My mother, father, and brother have supported me in every possible way throughout my life. Their love and guidance means the world to me and I can never hope to repay their kindness. I am especially grateful to my wife Tenzin Dekyi and little boy Sangye, both of whom have given me the love and companionship I so needed while working on this challenging project.

As someone who is still very much a beginner when it comes to the Great Perfection, what I have written here reflects my own limited understanding of this profound topic. I feel truly blessed to have been asked to translate this text, yet both the introduction and the translation that follows are sure to contain inaccuracies. It is my hope, however, that this translation will kindle interest in the teachings and encourage others to improve upon my efforts. Whatever merit has resulted from this endeavor I dedicate to the flourishing of the Great Perfection teachings in all times and places and to the long lives of the great masters who uphold this tradition. Through this, may all beings recognize mind's true nature!

Tsultrim Shönu [Cortland Dahl]
Namo Buddha, Nepal
September, 2007

The Excellent Chariot

A VEHICLE FOR THE PATH TO LIBERATION

An Instruction Manual for
The Great Perfection,
Heart Essence of the Dakinis

Tibetan:
*rDzogs pa chen po mkha' 'gro snying thig gi khrid yig
thar lam bgrod byed shing rta bzang po*

Sanskrit:
*Mokṣa panthaṁ gatiṣu ratho nāma mahāsaṁdhi
dākinī cittatilakasya kṣiptalekha viharatisma*

by the Third Dzogchen Rinpoche,
Ngetön Tenzin Zangpo

Ngetön Tenzin Zangpo, the Third Dzogchen Rinpoche.
DRAWING BY GUME GYATSO.

Homage and Pledge of the Composition

HOMAGE to my glorious sacred guru, inseparable from the glorious sovereign, the primordial protector Samantabhadra!

To the excellent teacher Samantabhadra, primordially present as the essence of the dharmakaya;
To the victorious blissful ones of the five buddha families and their heirs, the sambhogakaya endowed with the fivefold certainty;
To the lineage of the Great Perfection, the masters of awareness and those who keep the treasury of the secret oral lineage;
I supplicate you in every way, respectfully prostrating, making offerings, and praising you with my body, speech, and mind!

Self-arisen on the pollen bed of a lotus
On a radiant island in the pristine land of Oddiyana—
Embodiment of all the victorious ones' compassion,
Padmasambhava, watch over me on this very day!

The all-pervasive sphere of reality—pure and unborn;
The risen sun of wisdom—unobstructed knowledge and love;
Teacher of the essential meaning—unerring, profound, and clear;
I praise you, peerless lord of siddhas Pema Rigdzin.

You actualized the true realization of the teachers of the three forms
And showered down a rain of Dharma upon beings throughout the three times,
Sowing the seed of liberation within the three planes of existence—
I bow to you, my glorious guru, unrivalled throughout the three realms.

> Splendid as a saffron mountain lit by a hundred thousand rising suns,
> Wielding the sword of natural knowledge, you cut through the web of ignorance.
> You who hold the essential text of the 84,000 teachings,
> Protector Manjugosha, adorned as you are with the marks and signs,
> Please dwell in my mind and bestow upon me unobstructed eloquence.
>
> As the very heart of the Victorious One's 84,000 teachings,
> The Heart Essence of the Dakinis is more profound than profound.
> Here I will explain the instructions of this treasury
> Of the secret Great Perfection—the pinnacle of all vehicles.

Contained herein is the true realization of Samantabhadra, the progenitor of all the buddhas throughout the three times.[10] It is the way that has been traversed by the masters of awareness and siddhas, an excellent path that leads to the isle of liberation and omniscience. In order to teach this to those who are worthy, I will now map out its main points and set them down briefly in writing, just as the masters of the past practiced, transmitting the oral lineage in teaching sessions over a period of days.

How to Listen to the Teachings

BEGIN BY GIVING RISE to supreme bodhichitta. Think to yourself, "I will now attain the state of complete buddhahood so that I may benefit all the infinite number of sentient beings. To this end, I will study and practice the vast and profound path that matures and liberates!" With this attitude, listen attentively.

How one should behave when listening to the Dharma is taught in the *Jataka Tales*:

> Take the lowest seat
> And give rise to great discipline.
> Gaze with eyes full of joy and interest,
> And drink in the words as though they are nectar.
> Generate an immaculate, pristine respect,
> And one-pointedly bow.
> As patients listen to their doctors' advice,
> Reverently listen to the Dharma.

As shown here, when you listen to the Dharma you should be free from the three flaws of a vessel and the six stains. The first of the three flaws of a vessel involves failing to listen to the words and their meanings. This is likened to pouring liquid onto an overturned vessel. The second example is pouring liquid into a vessel that contains poison, in which case whatever you pour in will become contaminated with poison. Similarly, when your mind is stained with an affliction, even if you study the Dharma it won't be of much benefit. Pride, lack of faith, and other flaws will keep the Dharma from acting as a remedy against the afflictions. Instead, it will only serve to support them. Third, if a vessel has holes in it, it won't be able to retain anything, in the same way that not practicing carefully and in the right order will result in an unstable realization. You should reject all of these faults.

Listen to the Dharma as taught in the sutras: "Listen extremely well, keep the teachings in mind, and I will teach you." As indicated here, listening well will keep you free from the fault of a poisoned vessel, while listening extremely well will result in being free from the fault of an overturned vessel. Keeping the teachings in mind will eliminate having the fault of a vessel with holes.

The six stains are taught in the *Principles of Elucidation*:

> Pride, lack of faith,
> Disinterest, outer distraction,
> Inward withdrawal, and lack of motivation—
> These are the six stains of the listener.

When you listen, you should eliminate any feelings of pride you may have about things such as status and any positive qualities you may have. You should reject any lack of faith you may have towards the Dharma or guru. You should also not feel disinterested or dispassionate about the Dharma, nor should you be outwardly distracted or inwardly withdrawn, such as when your eyes, ears, or mind are distracted by objects or when your mind feels drowsy and dull. Finally, eliminate any lack of motivation or feeling of discouragement that you may feel about listening to the Buddha's teachings.

The Dharma you are listening to is the pinnacle of the nine vehicles, the natural Great Perfection. The Great Perfection contains many divisions and categories: Three Classes; The Ninefold Expanse; 6,400,000 Stanzas; 35,000 Chapters; 21,000 Volumes; 180 Spikes; 1,500 Condensations; 3,000 Essential Points; 400,000 Delineations of Errors and Obscurations; 20,000 Individually Named Tantras; and so on.[11] All of these, as well as the essential meaning of all the sutras and tantras, are distilled into key instructions and contained in the luminous vajra essence. Coming to a definitive understanding of the stages of these liberating instructions entails three factors: the lineage history, empowerments, and key instructions. The lineage history instills confidence, while the empowerments mature the practitioner and the key instructions are used to teach the practices.

The Lineage History

To BEGIN, I will explain a bit about the history of the lineage to instill confidence in its pure origins and instructions. The *Tantra of the Sun and Moon's Union* states:

> If one does not teach the significance
> Of the history of these definitive teachings,
> People will mistakenly distrust the great secret.

This sentiment is echoed in the *Treasury of Magic*, while the *Tantra of the Clear Expanse* says:

> To instill confidence in fortunate students,
> Clearly explain the lineage history.

And in the *Essence of the Oral Lineage*:

> When the victorious ones enter the world,
> They first stress the origins and history of the lineage,
> Because there are hostile outsiders
> Who will dispute their great transmission.

Explaining the origins of this particular lineage, the *Essence Tantra That Liberates Upon Wearing*[12] states:

> The teachers Samantabhadra and Bhadri
> Blessed their embodiment Vajrasattva,
> A recipient none other than themselves.
> Entrusting him with a single understanding that liberates all—
> Beyond the confines of bondage and liberation.

Namkha Ösel, the First Dzogchen Ponlop Rinpoche.
DRAWING BY GUME GYATSO.

Through the blessings of Vajrasattva,
This arose in the heart of self-arisen Garap,
Who entrusted the tantra to Simha.
This supreme, perfect fruition—
The *Tantra That Liberates Upon Wearing*—
Was then entrusted to Padma of Oddiyana.
Teach the fivefold to a fortunate child![13]

As taught in the preceding passage, the perfect place is the pure Richly Arrayed Realm, the palace of the sphere of reality. There, the perfect teachers, glorious Samantabhadra and Samantabhadri, spontaneously arose out of the dharmakaya, a state free of elaborations, and manifested perfectly as the five sambhogakaya families. The perfect teaching is the natural Great Perfection, the doctrine of the spontaneously present fivefold rainbow light. This was taught through natural blessings to the perfect retinue, the sambhogakaya buddha Vajrasattva, in the unchanging moment of fundamental perfection, the perfect time.

At the vast Blazing Mountain Charnel Ground, Vajrasattva put these teachings into a series of elegant verses and taught them to the incarnation Garap Dorjé. Through his own direct realization, Garap Dorjé then taught them to the great master Shri Simha at the Charnel Ground of the Wild Jungle. Shri Simha went on to teach Pema Tötreng Tsel of Oddiyana at the great Sosa Ling Charnel Ground, where, in a nonconceptual way, he showed him the true nature of reality. Padmasambhava then used what he had directly ascertained to teach Yeshé Tsogyal, a dakini inseparable from Vajravarahi, at the White Rock of Zhotong Tidrö. The blessings of the clear and profound realization of Master Padma and his spiritual partner—the true wisdom that was to be revealed—were then transmitted to the fortunate master of this teaching, Princess Pemasel, and then sealed with aspirations and empowerments. The lineage of coded verse was set down in writing as the vehicle for this realization, entrusted to the dakinis and treasure guardians, and hidden at Taklung Tramo Rock. Later on, once the five degenerations and fifty rendings had become rampant, past aspirations reawakened and this treasure, the primary cycle of the Heart Essence of the Dakinis, was removed by the incarnation Pema Ledrel Tsel. The lineage was then gradually transmitted and passed on to Gyalsé Lekpa, Rinchen Lingpa, and others.

In accordance with the treasure's prophecy, the actual form of the treasure revealer Pema Ledrel Tsel was to succumb to the influence of obstacles. Consequently, his work for the benefit of beings was left unfinished. His subsequent incarnation traveled throughout the sambhogakaya pure realms and eventually became Longchen Rabjam. This prophesied embodiment of wisdom was known as Drimé Özer [Longchenpa] and many other names. He was blessed directly by both Padmakara and his spiritual partner at Chimpu Rimochen, and then went on to clarify the key instructions they taught him concerning the profound points of the primary Heart Essence. These instructions were given to Guru Yeshé Rabjam[14] and the lineage was then passed down through the following masters:[15]

- the learned and accomplished Samtenpa
- the great saint Jinpa Zangpo
- the one known as Dzogchen Shakya
- Sonam Rinchen
- Chakyungwa Ngakwang Padma
- Dzogchen Sonam Wangpo
- Rigdzin Chökyi Gyatso
- the great saint Pema Rigdzin[16]

Pema Rigdzin gave these teachings to a master who was the sovereign of all classes and mandalas and who was inseparable from the all-pervasive, primordial protector. It is difficult to refer to such a supreme, sacred guide using words, but since it is necessary, I will refer to him as Namkha Ösel (Luminous Space). This sacred individual, protector of all beings including the gods, was given these teachings as if liquid were being poured from one vase into another. He then opened the door of this excellent treasure, the wealth of instructions that was the very essence of this sacred master's enlightened mind, and in so doing matured and liberated those who were fortunate.[17]

This lineage has been passed down from these masters to ourselves. Its stream of blessings and compassion has not been broken, nor have its instructions been corrupted. The lineage has also been well maintained; no lapses of the samaya vows have crept in. Though there are many different approaches and lineages, this one is the ultimate—the profound, true lineage. Therefore, you should have confidence and conviction in these teachings.

The underlying reasons concerning the necessity of explaining the lineage history are taught in the *Tantra of the Array of Lamps*, where it is written:

The validity of the Secret Mantra's meaning
Comes from the realization, symbolic, and oral lineages.
One recognizes this meaning by relying on examples.
In dependence upon signs, this turns into conviction.
By gaining certainty about the essential meaning,
The threefold knowledge will be ripened like a grain.
Present as it is in the basis, like a seed in the ground,
The knowledge that arises through conditions
Will then clear away the darkness of ignorance
And the cognitive obscurations will be self-purified.
With this, one will behold the fruition, even without practice.

Empowerment

IN THE CONTEXT of the maturing empowerments, two topics are taught: the actual empowerments and the samaya vows. There are a great many benefits of receiving empowerments and faults in not doing so, which are summarized in the following passage from the *Tantra of the Full Array*:

> How can one gain accomplishment without relying upon the Secret Mantra's empowerments? Like a ferryman with no oars, how will one cross to the other shore? If one receives empowerments well, however, all secret mantras will be attained, even without practice.

And in the *Tantra of Penetrating Sound*:

> There are four types of empowerment
> That mature the fortunate:
> The elaborate, unelaborate,
> Extremely unelaborate,
> And the utterly unelaborate.
> The approach of these four divisions
> Should be used to mature the mind streams of those with faith.[18]

And, in the *Tantra of the Secret Essence*:

> If one neither pleases the master,
> Nor receives empowerment,
> Those who engage in study and so forth
> Will achieve no result and be lost.

The *Two-Part Tantra* states:

> Receiving empowerment means to be empowered
> In the Dharma and to obtain the three vows.

The same text says:

> In this life, the intermediate state,
> Or within seven lifetimes,
> Accomplishment will be attained, even without meditating.

And in the *Tantra of the Assembly of Blissful Ones*:

> Empowerment cuts the root of the five poisons
> And purifies the habitual patterns of the five types of beings.

The *Tantra of Precious Empowerment* states:

> Once a guru who has abandoned desire
> Completes the ritual of empowerment
> And bestows the appropriate stages,
> One will become the great vajra holder
> In this very life, have no doubt.

As these passages point out, one should begin by using the stages of empowerment to mature that which is immature. The various empowerments from the texts of the Heart Essence will purify the disciple's mind stream. This includes the elaborate vase empowerment, as well as the unelaborate, extremely unelaborate, and utterly unelaborate empowerments. Have no doubt that these are of the utmost importance.[19]

There are many explanations concerning the vows one must maintain once empowerments have been received. These are summarized in the following passage from the *Tantra of Penetrating Sound*:

> There will never be enough time to explain all the details
> Of the samaya vows involved in receiving empowerment,
> But in brief, one should maintain enlightened form, speech,
>   and mind.

This quotation shows what needs to be maintained once one has received empowerment. Without losing sight of the purpose of maintaining the vows, one should keep a restrained mind, along with its seed.[20] This can be classified in terms of the various main and subsidiary samaya vows, as well as the particular injunction not to stray from the samaya vows of enlightened form, speech, and mind. In brief, however, the supreme samaya vow is when there is *no* restraint or vow, when the scores of things to be maintained and focused upon are understood to be unestablished and maintained from the very outset. On this point, it is said of this great, primordial lack of anything to maintain, that there is no dividing line to be sequentially established when it comes to keeping a vow, and also that to have conquered all such boundaries is the highest form of samaya.

The Common Preliminaries

IN THIS SECTION, the practical instructions that lead to liberation are taught. This contains two divisions:

- The common preliminaries that purify the mind
- The unique preliminaries that allow one to ascertain the true nature[21]

The first section contains two further divisions:

- An overview of the preliminaries
- A detailed presentation of the stages of contemplation and the way to meditate

Explaining the first of these two divisions, the *Last Testament* states:

> Train in impermanence, compassion, and bodhichitta.

Similarly, in the tantras, it is written:

> With impermanence, compassion, and bodhichitta,
> Train in the Dharma and follow the path of the Great Vehicle.

The purpose of highlighting this threefold meditation on impermanence, compassion, and bodhichitta is to show what is of primary importance. In addition, since a human existence with certain freedoms and endowments is the basis for meditating on impermanence, the difficulty of obtaining such an existence is also taught. Each of the following chapters contains two divisions. The first provides a general presentation of the main topics of the preliminaries, while the second gives a detailed description of the way to meditate on the stages of contemplation.

CHAPTER 1

The Precious Human Existence & Refuge

—— The Freedoms and Endowments ——

Resting in the Nature of Mind states:[22]

> What are the freedoms and endowments?
> Not born in hell or as a spirit,
> As an animal, a long-life god, or barbarian,
> With wrong views, in a time with no buddhas, or as an idiot—
> To have thus totally transcended these eight restricted states.
> Born human, in a central land, and with all the senses intact;
> Without a harmful vocation and with faith in the right place—
> With these, the five supreme personal endowments are complete.
> A buddha has come, taught the Dharma, and the teachings endure;
> Because they endure they are practiced, and there is love from others—
> These are the five circumstantial endowments, making eighteen.
> Now that you possess these in their entirety,
> Exert yourself from the heart and gain liberation!

These are also taught in the *Great Commentary on the 8,000 Verse Perfection of Knowledge*:

> Hell beings, spirits, animals,
> Barbarians, long-life gods, wrong views,
> Absence of a buddha, and idiots—
> These are the eight restricted states.

As shown in these passages, those born into the three lower realms experience agonizing suffering and have a terrible physical form. These factors keep them from practicing the Dharma. The gods of the desire realm, in contrast, are distracted by their attachment to sense pleasures and have little disenchantment with samsara, while most of those in the form and formless realms are perpetually intoxicated by the states of meditative concentration they have achieved. These factors restrict the gods from practicing the Dharma. One can also be born in a place where no buddha has come, a realm devoid of a buddha. Alternately, one could take birth in a world where a buddha has come, but as a barbarian in a borderland where the Dharma has not spread. One could be born in a place where the Dharma is present, yet still have wrong views that prompt one to distrust the existence of past and future lives, the principle of karmic causality, and the Three Jewels. Finally, those who are stupid do not know right from wrong; they lack any sense of what to do and what to give up. Together, these comprise the eight restricted states. Of these, those in three lower realms, along with the long-life gods, are non-human restricted states, while the remaining four are associated with humanity.

The eight restricted states can also be classified in terms of the three gates. Those born as hell beings, spirits, and animals are distracted by suffering, which is a physical restriction. Mutes lack the capacity to link words with their meanings—a verbal restriction. Most long-life gods do not give any thought to Dharma practice, while there are others who do but who are born in a dark age where there are no buddhas and the teachings have not appeared. For barbarians, the teachings may appear, but they are not inclined to practice them. There are still more who do wish to practice but whose wrong views propel them into the extremes of exaggeration and depreciation. These latter four are instances of mental restriction. The individuals in these eight states lack either the environment or the good fortune to practice the Dharma. Since they lack the karma, they are preoccupied with other things. The *Condensed Perfection of Knowledge* states: "Abandon the eight restricted states and you will always find the freedoms." Thus, not being born into the eight restricted states itself comprises the eight excellent freedoms.

There are ten qualities that make up the endowments. Of these, the following passage presents the five personal endowments:

> Being human, born in a central land, with the senses complete,
> Without a mistaken vocation and with faith in the right place ....

To elaborate, the general factor that needs to be obtained is a human body. In addition, there are four specific requisites that are needed as well: one must be born in a central land where the Dharma has spread; the five sense faculties must be intact to the extent that one can discern right from wrong; one must be free of having committed any of the five acts of immediate retribution or having made another do so; and one must have faith and interest in the objects that give rise to all wholesome qualities, the mundane as well as the transcendent. The latter refers to Buddhist scriptures, such as the Vinaya collection. These five are necessary conditions for accomplishing the Dharma. Since they relate to one's own mind, they are referred to as "the five personal endowments." These five endowments are essentially the same as the freedoms that result once one has turned away from the eight restricted states.

The following passage presents the five circumstantial endowments:

> A buddha has come and taught the Dharma,
> His or her teachings endure and have followers,
> And there are those with heartfelt love for others.

As stated here, the five circumstantial endowments are for a buddha to have come into the world and taught the sacred Dharma, for these teachings to remain and have many followers, and for there to be many others who have heartfelt love for Dharma practitioners, such that they provide requisites like food and clothing. Love of others is also explained to mean that there are spiritual teachers who will provide guidance out of their love for the Dharma. These five are also necessary conditions for accomplishing the Dharma. Since they relate to the mind streams of others, however, they are referred to as "the five circumstantial endowments." In the sutras, it is said: "The endowments are referred to as such because the mind becomes 'endowed' with, or joins, its own pure nature. In other words, one comes to know the nature of the mind."

The freedoms are the essence of a precious human existence, while the endowments are the specific qualities it possesses. Finding a form that possesses these eighteen freedoms and endowments in their entirety is very rare. For this reason, focus your mind one-pointedly and think to yourself: "Now I really need to put some effort into the Dharma!" As said in the *Way of the Bodhisattva*:

> Now that I've found such an opportunity,
> If I don't practice what is virtuous,
> There could be no greater deception,
> And nothing more stupid! [IV.23]

The rarity of finding such an existence is likened to the following example. In the depths of the ocean lives a turtle who surfaces only once every hundred years. On the surface of the ocean is a wooden yoke with one hole. Buffeted by the wind, the yoke doesn't stay still for a moment. In samsara, emerging from the lower realms and finding a human existence is said to be even less likely than this turtle coming to the surface of the ocean and sticking its neck through the hole of the yoke. The *Letter to a Friend* states:

> A turtle putting its head through the hole
> Of a wooden yoke floating in the deep blue sea
> Is more likely than an animal becoming human.
> So heed the Dharma, O King, and bring meaning to your life!

And again, in the *Way of the Bodhisattva*:

> For these very reasons, the Blessed One has said
> That obtaining a human existence is extremely difficult,
> Like a turtle sticking its neck through the hole of a yoke
> Tossed about on the surface of a vast ocean. [IV.20]

The source of this example is the following passage from *A Bunch of Flowers*:

> The arrival of the transcendent and victorious buddhas in this world is very rare, and obtaining a human existence and the freedoms in their entirety even more so. To illustrate this, the following example is given. Shariputra, imagine the earth to be a vast, windswept ocean, within which there is a wooden yoke with a single hole. In this ocean lives a blind turtle that comes to the surface only once every hundred years. One may say that it is possible for this turtle, who only comes up once every hundred years, to stick its neck through the hole of this swiftly moving yoke. One may not, however, say that someone who has fallen to

the lower realms will be able to attain a human existence again and again in the future, for it is exceedingly difficult for those who have fallen into such states to become human.

In the *Precious Wish-fulfilling Treasury* as well, it is written:

> While it may be just barely possible for a turtle to stick its neck
> Through the hole of a wooden yoke that floats in the middle of the ocean,
> It is even more difficult to free yourself from the lower realms and become human.
> Just so, while it may be possible to get a pea to stick to the face of a plastered wall,
> It is even more rare to be born in a central land, even once one has become human.

As shown here, to attain a human form while cycling throughout samsara is even more difficult than getting a pea to stick to the face of a smooth, plastered wall. The *Tent of the Moon's Essence* states: "To reverse course from the eight restricted states and become human is even less likely than getting a pea to stick to the face of a smooth surface." Similarly, finding a spiritual human existence that has these freedoms and endowments is even more difficult than getting a whole piece of cloth through the eye of a needle, more difficult than finding an udumbara flower in the world, and even more difficult than finding a precious, wish-fulfilling jewel.

Sentient beings in the lower realms are said to be great in number—as boundless as the grains of sand on a vast plain. In contrast, those in the higher realms are as few as the particles of dust on a single fingernail. Furthermore, within the three lower realms, animals are the fewest in number, yet the number of animals that live in the depths of the ocean is beyond reckoning, and those that are scattered throughout the rest of the world fill the earth, mountains, rivers, and atmosphere. From this perspective, one can see that becoming a god or human being is just barely possible.

Generally speaking, humans are few in number even when compared with the gods, and the human beings in Jambudvipa are especially scarce. Even more rare is a spiritual human existence, which again is just barely possible. Those who practice virtue are scarce as well, while the great number of sentient beings who engage in negative acts is boundless. In comparison, there are hardly any who practice virtue, and of these, those who maintain a discipline that contributes to the attainment of a human existence are even more rare. On this topic, the *Precious Wish-fulfilling Treasury* states:

> Thus, if you just look at the bodies of sentient beings,
> Attaining a human form is as unlikely as becoming the emperor of the universe.
> And among humans, those who are spiritual and have faith are rarer still,
> As rare as the attainment of buddhahood.
> Hence, you should always contemplate the freedoms and endowments!

When you think about it from a general point of view, the number of sentient beings is as vast as the expanse of space, whereas the sentient beings in Jambudvipa would occupy the space in the eye of a needle, comparatively speaking. Leaving aside all the other creatures on this continent, relative to the number of living creatures in a single forest, a single river, or in a single pond, obtaining a human form is as probable as becoming the emperor of the universe. Similarly, when you think about humans, there are many gathered in each region and each market, those in India, China, Lhojang, Mön, Lho, Nepal, Do, Mongolia, and so on. Yet consider how rare those who practice and faithfully follow the Buddhist teachings are. They are even rarer than the arrival of a buddha in the world. So rejoice in these freedoms and endowments you have and don't let them go to waste! The *Middle-length Perfection of Knowledge* states, "If just being human is difficult to achieve, then why even mention the excellent freedoms?"

In the *Liberation of the Brahmin Gyalwey Drökyi Kyechey*, it is written:

> It is difficult to turn back from the eight restricted states, and also to attain a human existence. Finding the totally pure freedoms in their entirety is a rare event, as is the arrival of a buddha. Having all of your senses intact is also rare, likewise the opportunity to listen to the Buddha's teachings. It is difficult to find a chance to befriend a holy being, and also to meet a genuine spiritual teacher.

At this point, you have managed to obtain the precious freedoms and endowments in their entirety. You've met with a qualified spiritual teacher and can practice these divine and sacred Buddhist teachings. Now that this has come to pass, your long-term goals depend upon this very moment. So set out on the path to liberation and progress towards the isle of peace. Don't let yourself get attached to the appearances of this present life, nor to your wealth, possessions, or relatives. Don't be attached to samsara, nirvana, or anything else. Instead, focus on applying yourself with the urgent resolve of a dancing girl whose hair has caught fire or a coward who's just had a snake slither into his lap. As written in the *Sutra of the White Lotus of Compassion*:

> Abandoning the eight restricted states and obtaining the freedoms in their entirety doesn't happen often, so be careful and apply yourself diligently. If you don't, you will live to regret it!

The *Sutra Requested by Rashtrapala* states:

> The great sages, the buddhas who protect the world, only come once every billion eons. Now that you've found these sacred freedoms, don't be careless if you desire liberation!

While in the *Sutra of Totally Pure Discipline*, it is written:

> Monks, since taking ordination in the Victorious One's teachings is an opportunity even more difficult to find than having attained these [freedoms and endowments], why wouldn't you practice and exert yourselves with stable discipline? Illness, disease, and death will come to you for sure, and the teachings of the Able One will wane. Once this happens, you will come to regret such laziness.

In the following passage, the *Meeting of Father and Son Sutra* addresses the freedoms and endowments and the rationale behind practicing the Dharma:

> Having totally abandoned the eight restricted states
> And obtained the freedoms in their entirety, so rare,
> The wise practice the yoga of reasoning
> With the faith they've found in the Tatagata's teachings.

Thus, now that you have all the conducive conditions for doing so, it makes sense to practice the Dharma assiduously. Just as when you have a ship, you should cross the ocean; when you have a great steed, you should set out on a long journey; when you have warmth, water, and manure, you should plant your seeds; when you've amassed a great force of warriors, you should subdue your enemies; when you've hit a vein of gold or silver, you should take as much as you can; when your crops are ready to harvest in the fall, you should do so; when you have a force of escorts, you should cross dangerous paths; and when you have borrowed goods, you should put them to use. Now that you have these freedoms and endowments, you should take advantage of them and exert yourself as best you can. The master Shantideva wrote:

> These freedoms and endowments are exceedingly difficult to find.
> If I don't take advantage of this chance
> To make my existence meaningful,
> How will such a perfect attainment be mine in the future? [I.4]

And in *Resting in the Nature of Mind,* Longchenpa wrote:

> If you don't use this precious vessel when you have it
> To cross over the boundless ocean of samsara,
> How could you hope to do it once you're being endlessly tossed about
> On the waves of suffering and affliction?
>
> So don the armor of diligence with haste!
> Set out on the path of immaculate, luminous wisdom,
> Get rid of obstacles on the path to enlightenment,
> And calm the troubled waters of your thoughts and mind.

As Longchenpa points out, the beginning and end of this vast ocean of samsara cannot be seen. Now that you have a human body—a vessel that will allow you to cross over this frightening and unbearable sea—you need to act! The *Way of the Bodhisattva* states:

> Use this vessel, your human existence,
> And liberate yourself from this great ocean of suffering.

> In the future such a vessel will be hard to come by.
> So there is no time, O ignorant one; do not fall asleep! [VII.14]

Therefore, now that you've obtained these rare freedoms and endowments, if you don't set out on the path to liberation, it will be even more idiotic than venturing to an island filled with jewels and returning empty-handed. Think this over well and practice diligently!

Taking Refuge

The next topic relates to the previous section and addresses the progressive stages of taking refuge. When you first begin to bring these practices onto the path, you should focus your efforts on the act of taking refuge in the Three Jewels. This section contains five divisions:

- Identifying the sources of refuge
- The act of taking refuge
- The benefits of taking refuge
- The refuge precepts that concern what to eliminate
- The refuge precepts that concern what to practice

When it comes to the sources of refuge, there are four different categories: the outer refuge, inner refuge, secret refuge, and the refuge of reality itself. The first of these refers to the Buddha, Dharma, and Sangha. The etymology of the term "buddha" is as follows. In essence, a buddha is innately empty and originally pure; one in whom all the incidental accumulations of delusion have been purified, in whom impartial compassion and wisdom have blossomed, and who is skilled in the methods that allow him or her to emanate in various ways to tame others.[23]

There are three kinds of Dharma: the Dharma of the teachings, the Dharma of accomplishment, and the Dharma of peace and nirvana. In brief, the Dharma is wholly positive in essence and characterized by its empty nature. It can be divided in various ways, into cause and result, for example, or into the three collections and nine vehicles.

The Sangha as well is said to comprise three categories: the Sangha of listeners, the Sangha of solitary buddhas, and the Sangha of bodhisattvas. The true Sangha, in short, is that which is devoid of vice, while the etymology of the word means "those who are oriented towards virtue." The Sangha can be divided into the symbolic Sangha that is an outer reflection, the Sangha that develops bodhichitta in order to benefit others, and the genuine, true Sangha. The Buddhist scriptures state:

> The Buddha is the teacher, and the Dharma, the path;
> The Sangha are one's companions—use this approach when
>   taking refuge.

The three inner sources of refuge are the guru, yidam deity, and dakini. Gurus are qualified spiritual teachers who have liberated their own minds and are capable when it comes to the skillful means that allow them to tame the minds of others. In particular, this refers to the root gurus we have right now, as well as the gurus of the lineage—the captains who guide us across the ocean of samsaric suffering to the isle of peace, happiness, and liberation. This can also refer to the second buddha Padmakara, the source of all blessings who is totally flawless and has perfected every positive quality.

The yidam deities are the vast array of peaceful and wrathful deities and those associated with the Eight Sadhana Teachings. This term can also refer to the entire range of deities associated with the six classes of tantra.[24] In particular, it refers to the crown ornament of all samsara and nirvana, the great and powerful wrathful deity Hayagriva—the sacred treasury of all spiritual attainment.

The dakinis are those associated with the three abodes. This term refers especially to Vajravarahi, the divine mother who gives birth to all buddhas and is the sole embodiment of enlightened activity.

There are three secret sources of refuge as well: the dharmakaya, the sambhogakaya, and the nirmanakaya. The dharmakaya is Samantabhadra, who is surrounded by the ocean-like host of wisdom. He is the father that begets all blissful ones. The sambhogakaya includes the male and female buddhas of the five families, who are surrounded by the assembly of bodhisattvas. These are the true deities, those with the five forms of wisdom. The nirmanakaya is Vajradhara, the very embodiment of compassionate love towards sentient beings. He is surrounded by the nirmanakaya assembly.

The fourth source of refuge is reality itself, inclusive of its essence, nature, and compassionate resonance. Its originally pure essence is free of all elaborations and entails four great liberations. Its spontaneously present nature possesses the entire range of positive qualities and radiates with self-illuminating fivefold rainbow light. Finally, its compassionate resonance is unobstructed and all-pervasive—manifold, self-liberated, and unconditioned.

Being under the protection of these supreme forms of refuge is similar to being protected by royal decree. When someone takes refuge in the presence of a king, no matter how unresourceful they may be, no one can do them harm. Just so, when you entrust yourself to the Three Jewels, you will be freed from the entire range of unpleasant problems and will eventually encounter all forms of happiness and goodness.

Furthermore, if a saintly being pursues liberation and goes for refuge in these nine sources with an understanding of the suffering that samsara entails, the compassion of these sources is such that they can protect such a being from all forms of suffering. In the *Ten Wheels of Kshitigarbha Sutra*, it is written:

> The happiness of all the three realms
> Arises from the Three Jewels.
> Thus, those who desire happiness
> Should always make offerings to the Jewels.

And in the *Sutra of Varahi's Realization*:

> Taking refuge in the Three Jewels
> Will make one fearless.
> One who has taken refuge in the Three Jewels
> Will wander no more in the lower realms.
> Abandoning human forms,
> The form of a god will be attained.
> And abandoning the form of a god,
> The enlightenment of buddhahood will be attained.

And further:

> As they protect one from the lower realms, incorrect methods,
> And the inferior view of the transitory collection,
> These are held to be the most sacred refuge.

In the *Sutra Requested by Ananda*, it is written:

> The Buddha, Dharma, and realized beings
> Are the refuge of the entire world.
> Whosoever desires realization
> Accepts refuge in these Three Jewels.

The *Seventy Stanzas on Refuge* states:

> One who goes for refuge in the Three Jewels
> Will soon attain buddhahood.

For these reasons, you should entrust yourself entirely to the Three Jewels, the sources of refuge. With firm conviction that they know best, focus one-pointedly and take refuge. Then proceed to the visualization, maintaining a genuine understanding of the rationale behind taking refuge in these sources.

The Practice of Taking Refuge

OM AH HUM

> Arrayed in the space before me,
> In a luminous and vast pure realm,
> Is the three-kaya guru of Oddiyana.
> Surrounded by every source of refuge,
> At one with Samantabhadra he sits,
> A jeweled throne and lotus beneath him,
> Upon which are discs of sun and moon.
> Humbled before these protectors,
> Together we take refuge, one and all,
> Refuge 'til enlightenment is attained!

Purified by chanting the three syllables OM, AH, HUM, imagine that the space before you transforms into a realm of natural purity—unconfined, unrestricted, and totally enchanting. Everything in this magnificent place is perfectly arranged, and the entire landscape blazes with light. In the midst of this vast and spacious land is a jeweled throne, held aloft by eight snow lions, elephants, steeds, peacocks, and shang-shang birds.[25] A lotus, sun, and moon-disc seat rests upon the throne, and on this seat sits your own kind root guru, appearing as the nirmanakaya buddha of Oddiyana. He has one face, two arms, and his skin is white with a tinge of red. With his right hand, he holds a gold five-pronged vajra at his heart; in his left, a white skull cup brimming with wisdom nectar, which rests in front of his navel. The crook of his arm cradles a trident. It has three skulls arranged one above the other at its top and is ornamented with a small ritual drum and a pair of cymbals. As he sits in the vajra posture, the lotus crown atop his head streams with five different sashes and a vulture's feather. He wears a blue silk gown, a red silk monastic robe embroidered with gold, and an undergarment. His presence is so majestic that the three levels of existence are overwhelmed and the three realms are in his thrall.[26]

Visualize the Buddha Shakyamuni sitting in front of him, surrounded by the buddhas of the three times—the supreme nirmanakaya. Beside him is the assembly of realized beings—on his right, Manjushri and the Sangha of Bodhisattvas, and on his left, Shariputra and the rest of the Sangha of Listeners. Behind him is the jewel of the Dharma in the form of Buddhist texts. All the space between these figures is filled with yidam deities, dakinis, dharma protectors and protectresses, as well as their retinues. Visualize all of these figures present before you.

Above the crown of the central figure sits the sambhogakaya buddha of Oddiyana, Amitayus. He is red in color and has one face. His two hands are in the posture of meditation and rest upon his crossed legs, and upon them is a nectar-filled vase. He is adorned with the attire of the sambhogakaya. His secret spiritual partner, who is inseparable from the wisdom dakini, embraces him, and he is surrounded by an ocean of sambhogakaya buddhas.

At their crown is the dharmakaya buddha of Oddiyana. This figure is dark blue in color, with one face, two hands, and in union with his spiritual partner, the white dakini. Upon their crowns sit the male and female buddhas Samantabhadra and Samantabhadri, the dharmakaya itself. They as well are surrounded by their retinue, which consists of an ocean of wisdom. Visualize that all the three kayas, along with their retinues, are delighted and gaze upon you in a loving manner.

Next, imagine that you yourself, along with the infinite number of sentient beings, bring to mind the excellent qualities and compassion of these sources of refuge. With intense devotion, supplicate them to provide refuge to all the sentient beings who have at one time or another been your very own mother, to protect them all from the frightening torments of samsara. With this in mind, recite the following:

Namo
I take refuge in the Buddha, Dharma, and Sangha.
I take refuge in the guru, yidam, and dakini.
I take refuge in the dharmakaya, sambhogakaya, and nirmanakaya.
I take refuge in the essence, nature, and compassionate resonance.
I take refuge in the dharmakaya buddha guru.
I take refuge in the sambhogakaya guru.
I take refuge in the compassionate nirmanakaya guru.
I take refuge in my own kind root guru.
I take refuge in the lineage gurus, the source of blessings.
I take refuge in the compassionate gurus who give me guidance.
I take refuge in the yidam and the divine assembly of its mandala.
I take refuge in the warriors, dakinis, and dharma protectors.

In a state of clarity and non-distraction, apply yourself diligently and recite these prayers as many times as you can, whether it be a hundred, a thousand, ten thousand, or a hundred thousand.

As a temporary benefit of taking refuge, you will accomplish whatever you put your mind to. You will also join the ranks of Buddhists and become a suitable basis for positive qualities to grow. You won't be affected by the harmful actions of any being, human or otherwise, and wherever you are born, you will always be in the presence of a guru and the Three Jewels.

The ultimate result of taking refuge is the attainment of buddhahood. The sutras state:

> One who takes refuge in the three
> Will swiftly attain buddhahood.

And in the scriptures, it is taught:

> The qualities of the Buddha are inconceivable.
> The Dharma is inconceivable as well,
> As is the Sangha of realized beings.
> If you have faith in the inconceivable,
> The ripening of this will be inconceivable too—
> You will be reborn in a pure realm.

It is said that even the Buddha's words fall short when it comes to enumerating the benefits of taking refuge.

At this point, you may wonder whether or not there are any other sources of refuge. Worldly gods, your parents and children, relatives and friends, local rulers, and so forth, cannot grant you refuge. They may be able to do so in a limited way, but when it comes to the compassion that enables one to provide refuge in the ultimate sense, this they do not possess. Since they are of the world, their ability is no different than a blind man's inability to guide others. For this reason, worldly gods, such as the four great gods of the Hindu tradition—Shakra, Brahma, Vishnu, and Ishvara—are not true sources of refuge. As it is said:

> If you take refuge in mountains and caves,
> Or in forests, secluded groves, trees, and stupas,
> Such places will not provide refuge in the supreme sense.
> For relying upon such sources of refuge
> Will not liberate you from samsara,
> Nor will your pain and suffering be pacified.
> Yet if you take refuge in the Three Jewels,
> You will attain a state of fearlessness
> And all good things will come to you.

And in the *Sutra Requested by the Girl Ratna*:

> Once the time of death has come,
> Nothing will be able to protect you—
> Not your youth, nor your strength.
> You will have to move on, come what may.

And in the scriptures:

> When the lord of death's henchmen arrive,
> Your parents cannot give you refuge,
> Nor can your relatives, whether near or far.
> They will leave you behind, one and all,
> And you will venture alone to your next life.

As these passages show, the Three Jewels are the only sure, constant, and undeceiving source of refuge. They alone can protect you from the frightening suffering of samsara and guide you to the isle of great bliss and liberation.

Once you've taken refuge in this way, the next thing you should do is train in the various precepts associated with taking refuge. There are nine different precepts, which are grouped into three sets of three:

1) the three precepts that concern what to eliminate
2) the three precepts that concern what to practice
3) the three conducive precepts

For the first set of three, once you've taken refuge in the Buddha, you are no longer to take refuge in worldly gods. Having taken refuge in the Dharma, you should not harm any sentient being. And once you've taken refuge in the Sangha, you should not rely upon non-Buddhists.[27] Concerning this latter point, no non-Buddhist has actually appeared in Tibet, but this can be taken to mean that you shouldn't associate with friends who have a negative influence on you, such as those who denigrate the principle of causality.

Next are the three things that should be practiced. Once you've taken refuge in the Buddha, you should regard even the tiniest representation of the Blissful One's form, even down to a broken piece of a tsa-tsa,[28] as the Buddha himself. With this in mind, you should act with respect, doing things like prostrating, making offerings, and acting with reverence. Having taken refuge in the Dharma, you should look upon any representation of the jewel of the Dharma, even a single letter from the Buddhist scriptures, as being the Jewel of Dharma itself, again, treating it with respect by bowing with deference, showing reverence, and so forth. Likewise, once you've taken refuge in the Sangha, you should treat anything that represents this Jewel, from ordained monks and nuns down to a shred of yellow cloth, as if it were the actual Sangha. Treat such objects with respect, bowing deferentially and acting with reverence.

The third topic concerns the three conducive precepts. Always exert yourself in making offerings to the Three Jewels. At the very least, offer the best part of whatever you eat or drink. You should take refuge at all times, and also train in faith, pure perception, and reverence in a consistent way by making prostrations and engaging in other such activities.

Mindful of these benefits and precepts, take refuge as many times as you can. Once you're ready to bring the session to a close, imagine that light streams out from the sources of refuge, leading all sentient beings to the pure realms. Conclude by visualizing the sources of refuge melting into light and dissolving into you. Then dedicate the virtue that you've accumulated to the welfare of sentient beings.

CHAPTER 2

Impermanence & Bodhichitta

Death and Impermanence

THE SECOND MAIN SECTION addresses death, impermanence, and how to bring these factors onto the path. As before, begin by developing bodhichitta. Think to yourself: "I must bring all of the infinite number of sentient beings to the state of buddhahood. To this end, I will listen to the various Dharma teachings of the Great Vehicle and put them into practice!" Then, with this pure mindset, listen well.

Qualifications of Teacher and Student

In general, those who wish to be liberated from the ocean of samsaric suffering and who practice the Dharma with this mindset need to rely upon a spiritual teacher. As stated in The *Precious Wish-fulfilling Treasury*:

> To cross over the ocean of samsara's suffering,
> Rely upon a captain, the glorious guru.

Furthermore, the guru with whom one studies must have certain qualifications. The *Flower Ornament Sutra* explains:

> "Spiritual teachers" are those who have abandoned vice and applied themselves to what is virtuous. They teach the Dharma as it really is and without mistakes, while keeping their behavior in line with what they teach. Possessing the seven riches of realized beings, they connect others as well with the quest for enlightenment.

And in the *Precious Wish-fulfilling Treasury*:

> A guru with the blessings of the lineage is one who holds the lineage
> Of accomplished masters who please their elders,
> Knows the mind treasury, and has the instructions of the oral lineage;
> One who is skilled in accomplishing the twofold benefit with an
>   understanding of the practices,
> Has attained clouds of accomplishment by being diligent in practice,
> And is able to transform the perceptions of others and lead them
>   along the path to liberation;
> One who has the transmissions of sutra and tantra and has kept his
>   or her samaya vows pure—
> Follow such a wise, accomplished, and glorious protector with the
>   utmost respect.

According to this passage, a qualified guru is someone who holds the lineage of accomplished masters who please their spiritual elders. He or she must know the mind treasury of the guru and thereby possess the instructions of the oral lineage. A guru should be skilled in accomplishing the twofold benefit, which, in turn, comes from seeing the practice tradition of the elders. Having always exerted him- or herself in practice, a guru must have gained the power of spiritual attainment. A guru is someone in whom the blessings of the lineage have entered, and who is, thereby, able to transform the perceptions of others. He or she should also be skilled in the various methods that allow others to be led to liberation. A guru is one who has merged his or her mind with the Dharma and, thus, someone in whom all Three Jewels are complete. He or she should have received the transmission of both sutra and tantra through the blessings of the victorious ones and, through his or her strong karmic link with the Secret Mantra, kept the sacred samaya vows of the transmission pure. To this, the *Magical Vajra* adds:

> The qualifications of a guru of the Secret Mantra are
> To have studied extensively and possess great knowledge,
> To have truly realized the intent of the scriptures,
> To be unconcerned with obtaining material things,
> To possess fortitude and little disenchantment,
> To have many key instructions and be liberated by the path,
> To be skilled with different types and to know the signs of progress,

To have bodhichitta and great compassion,
To hold a lineage and be skilled in accomplishing the transmitted teachings,
To possess a treasury and a complete stream,
To have liberated one's own mind and to be diligent in working for the welfare of others.

When giving teachings, teachers with this set of qualifications should start by seating themselves cross-legged on a throne and developing bodhichitta of aspiration and application. Next, they should think to themselves, "I will open the Dharma eye of all sentient beings! I will light the lamp of wisdom! I will make sure that the Buddha's teachings last for a long time!" Finally, they should proceed to explain the teachings, keeping the meaning of development and completion clearly in mind.[29]

On this latter point, the *Precious Wish-fulfilling Treasury* says:

> For the nirmanakaya Dharma, visualize the Shakya King.
> For the Secret Mantra of the sambhogakaya, envision the five families and Vajradhara.
> And for the space-like Dharma, that of the dharmakaya—
> Visualize Samantabhadra and the Mother, the perfection of knowledge.

In this context, the Dharma being taught is that of the dharmakaya, the natural Great Perfection. For this reason, teachings should be given while visualizing oneself as Samantabhadra and Samantabhadri in union or as the Great Mother.

In this context, it is possible for a master to complete both the accumulation of merit and that of wisdom. The *Precious Wish-fulfilling Treasury* explains:

> At this point, the teacher will be practicing the six perfections:
> Clearly explaining words and their meanings is the generosity of Dharma;
> Being free from afflictions, the perfection of discipline;
> Freedom from weariness is patience, and being enthusiastic, diligence;
> Non-distraction is meditative stability and discernment, knowledge.

As stated here, to unravel and clearly explain the words and meaning of the Dharma is generosity. To explain them without getting embroiled in the afflictions is discipline. Being able to tolerate fatigue, hunger, thirst, heat, cold, and other difficulties while you teach is patience. Having a sense of enthusiasm and not succumbing to fatigue while teaching is diligence, while being one-pointed and explaining the teachings without being distracted is meditative stability. To individually discern each point of the topic you are discussing and to realize their lack of nature is knowledge. In this way, practicing the six perfections in the context of giving a teaching condenses the various qualifications and conduct needed by a master who is actively teaching.

Concerning the disposition of the student, there are certain qualities that one needs to have when receiving teachings on the Dharma. On this topic, the *Precious Wish-fulfilling Treasury* says:

> Take the right approach when listening
> And study the Dharma with these thirty-six qualities:
> The six ways to have appreciation, including the thought of the Jewel,
> The six austerities, such as tolerating the afflictions,
> The six ways to remain unchanged by circumstances, like pursuing many teachings,
> The six objectives, such as generating compassion,
> The six necessities, including knowing the particulars,
> And the six things to seek, such as seeking the Dharma.

The six ways to have a sincere interest and appreciation are taught in the *Sutra Requested by Subahu*:

> Think of the guru who teaches you the Dharma as a treasury of jewels and the Dharma as a wish-fulfilling gem. Regard listening to the Dharma as an extremely rare opportunity. Hold memorizing and contemplating the Dharma in high regard and as something meaningful. Think of the precise realization of the Dharma as something very difficult to find and regard one who gives up the quest for the Dharma to be like somebody giving up divine nectar and drinking poison in its place. Think of those

who listen to and ponder the Dharma as individuals who are doing what is meaningful. This is the perspective you should cultivate.

Concerning the six austerities, the same text adds:

> Endure being afflicted by heat and cold for the sake of your spiritual teacher and the Dharma. Endure the afflictions of hunger and thirst, as well as those of ridicule and taunts. Endure being afflicted by fatigue and the work of sentient beings. Endure the afflictions of giving away certain things and seeking others. Value such endurance, even at the cost of your life.

And on the six armors that allow one to remain unchanged by circumstances, it is written:

> Do not let even a spear deter your exertion when it comes to teaching and earnestly pursuing the Dharma. Take hold of a great many teachings, comprehend the meaning of the Dharma, and put it into practice. Rely upon those who take this approach and show them great respect.

In the following passage, the same text explains the six special objectives:

> You should understand all the basic virtues, and with this understanding, put them into practice in the right way. Develop great compassion for sentient beings, and take hold of the entire range of sacred Buddhist teachings. Do not break the lineage of the Three Jewels, and bring sentient beings to a state of complete maturation—these are the objectives you should have.

The *Sutra Requested by Kashyapa* explains how to accomplish the six necessities:

> It is necessary to understand the details of the Buddha's teachings once you've heard them. With this knowledge, it is necessary to do nothing inappropriate. It is necessary to teach others in the same way, and having done so, it is necessary for both

you and others to attain liberation. It is necessary to refine your knowledge, and also that of others. It is also necessary to cut through the doubt of those who come from the four directions. Apply yourself to studying in these six ways.

Concerning the six things to seek, the *Buddha Avatamsaka Sutra* states:

> Seek the Dharma sincerely, without guile or deceit. Do not seek for your own benefit, but for the welfare of all. Seek with the wish to eliminate the afflictions of beings, not out of desire for wealth and fame. Seek with the practice of knowledge, not out of hypocrisy. Seek without any second thoughts, and in order to cut through the doubts of all. Seek to perfect the qualities of the buddhas, free from conceit and desire. You should seek earnestly in this way.

The tantras speak of a way that the six perfections can arise when a student who has these particular characteristics of the vessel listens to the Dharma. On this topic, the *Precious Wish-fulfilling Treasury* states:

> Offering flowers, a seat, and the like is generosity.
> Totally restraining the three gates is the perfection of discipline.
> Tolerating pain is patience, and enthusiasm is diligence.
> To listen undistractedly and retain what one hears is meditative stability,
> While cutting through doubts and elaborations is supreme knowledge.

As shown in this passage, when listening to the Dharma, you may practice generosity by arranging the guru's Dharma throne and cushions and ornamenting them with flowers and the like. Restraining your body, speech, and mind and eliminating any malice you may have towards the little creatures in the area, such as lice, is discipline. Patience involves tolerating factors such as heat and cold. Enthusiastically supplicating your guru and listening is diligence, while listening one-pointedly, without a distracted mind, is meditative stability. Being intelligent involves cutting through elaborations and doubts about the meaning of what you hear, and being able to discern the various flaws and merits of virtue and vice in a definitive way;

keeping in mind the fact that the listener, Dharma, and guru all appear, but lack inherent existence, is the perfection of knowledge. These skillful methods are also mentioned in the *Key Instructions on All Dharma Activities, the Tantra of the Manifest Realization*:

> Offer flowers, a seat, and the like.
> Maintain the area, restrain your behavior,
> And do not harm any sentient being.
> Supplicate the guru, listen one-pointedly to the instructions,
> And ask questions about problematic points to clear away doubt—
> Possess these six branches of Tara.[30]

Tara is mentioned in this passage to show that the listeners should meditate that they themselves are Tara or Manjushri, while possessing the six branches relates to the practice of the six perfections.

The following quote from the *Precious Wish-fulfilling Treasury* explains how concentration can be practiced while listening to a teaching:

> Imagine that you are Manjushri
> And that the light of the Dharma penetrates your heart.

As stated here, you should train in the following manner. If those who are listening to the Dharma are male, they should visualize themselves as Manjushri, orange in color and holding a sword and text, each of which rests on an utpala flower. Women should visualize themselves as the goddess Green Tara holding an utpala flower. Imagine that the teacher emits the light of Dharma from his or her mouth and that this penetrates the core of your heart, purifying the darkness of ignorance and causing the lotus of knowledge to bloom. Then listen one-pointedly. These are the qualifications and requisites of the listener.

There are also additional benefits that hold for both the instructing teacher and the students who listen. The sutras state:

> If enlightenment can be attained by hearing
> The sound of the drums and wooden blocks
> That mark the time the sacred Dharma is being taught,
> Then why even mention coming to hear [the teachings].

Thus, since innumerable other benefits in doing so can be found, you should listen carefully, free from the three flaws and the six stains.

Contemplating Impermanence

As mentioned in the various teachings that have been taught thus far, this precious human existence, adorned as it is with the eighteen freedoms and endowments, is difficult to come by. This difficulty can be demonstrated using various examples, such as that of the rare occurrence of the udumbara flower, the likelihood of a turtle sticking its neck through the hole of yoke floating in the middle of a great ocean, and the difficulty of throwing a pea at a plastered wall and getting it to stick.

This difficulty can also be demonstrated by showing the relative improbability of obtaining such a birth. The three lower realms are like the base of a giant mound of grain. They are vast in number and entail a great deal of suffering. The three worlds of the three higher realms, in contrast, are like the very peak of this mound. Within these three worlds, spiritual human beings are even rarer. One could also say that the beings of the lower realms are as numerous as the particles of dust on the earth, whereas the sentient beings of the higher realms number no more than the particles that would fit on the tip of one's finger. And again, that even within the higher realms, spiritual beings are exceedingly rare.

One can also show how difficult it is to obtain a precious human existence by showing its cause. The principle of karmic causality is infallible. For this reason, if you use your human existence to exert yourself in virtuous activities that are in harmony with the Dharma, while at the same time rejecting negativity and vice, you will attain a human birth with the freedoms and endowments as a result. Negativity, vice, and the desirous attachments of samsara, on the other hand, will bring you a sure rebirth in the lower realms.

These freedoms and endowments, the rarity of which was just shown using its examples, probability, and cause, are easily destroyed and impermanent by their very nature. The omniscient Longchen Rabjam writes:

> Though you may have obtained these rare freedoms,
> They are momentary, impermanent, and subject to decay.
> When thoroughly examined, you will see that they have no essence at all,

> And are as unstable as a water bubble about to burst.
> Hence, you should contemplate the certainty of death day and
>   night!

The attainment of the freedoms and endowments cannot remain permanent for even an instant. Examine their nature. Like a plantain tree, they have no essence and cannot withstand the mind's analysis. They appear for a single moment like a water bubble and then each of their main and subsidiary parts decays and falls apart. As stated in the *Collection of Purposeful Sayings*:

> Alas, conditioned things are impermanent!
> They arise and then decay.
> Because they arise and decay,
> How pleasant it would be if peace were to come quickly,
> For conditioned phenomena are like shooting stars,
> Like visual distortions, butter lamps,
> Illusions, dew, and bubbles of water;
> Like dreams, the lightning, and clouds.

Impermanent and transitory in this way, these bodies of ours have no essence. They fall apart and are unstable. For this reason, you should cast aside the attachment you have towards your body and apply yourself continually, night and day, to the contemplation of impermanence.

Right now, we perpetually cling to our body as "me" and "I." We offer it food and clothing and perform rituals to keep it healthy. Even the slightest insult from another pains us; we respond in kind and retaliate for the harm done to us. Yet when the Lord of Death unexpectedly separates our body and mind, this body will be left behind and won't come with us. Instead, it will become food for birds of death, wild dogs, foxes, vultures, and other wild animals.

Consider how pointless our clinging to this treasured body is and how pointless all the negative things we do for its benefit are. Instead, we should put it to work in virtuous endeavors like a servant. The appropriate thing to do is to give it just the right amount of food and clothing as its wage, and then apply ourselves night and day to the Dharma. The *Sutra of Advice to the King* states:

Great king, imagine that in each of the four directions there are four massive mountains, firm and solid; mountains that cannot be damaged or split; that reach up to the sky and penetrate deep into the earth. Now, if it came to pass that these four mountains came crashing together and pulverized into dust all of the grass, trees, tree trunks, branches, leaves, and living, elemental creatures, then for you to quickly flee, turn them back by force, seduce them with wealth, or reverse their course with substances, mantras, and medicines would be no easy task.

Great king, the four great terrors will come in just the same way. Once they are upon you, it won't be easy to flee quickly from them, to turn them back by force, to seduce them with wealth, or reverse their course with substances, mantras, and medicines. What are these four great terrors? They are aging, sickness, death, and decay.

Great king, aging will come and overpower you in the prime of life. Illness will come and overpower your good health. Decay will come and overpower all your abundance. Death will come and overpower your life-force. It will be no easy task to quickly flee from these, to seduce them with wealth, or to reverse their course with substances, mantras, and medicines.

Great king, a lion, king of the beasts, can move amongst other wild animals and catch them. He has the power to do exactly as he pleases. Any animal that he has in his powerful and terrible jaws is powerless.

Great king, in the same way, once you are caught on the stake of the Lord of Death, you will lose your pride; you will have no one to go to for refuge and no one to protect you. You will have neither friends nor guards to defend you. Your joints will be dislocated and come apart. Your flesh and blood will dry up. Illness will torment your body. You will be thirsty, your countenance will transform, and your limbs will convulse. Unable to do anything, you will have no strength. Saliva, snot, urine, and disgusting vomit will cover your body. Your sense of sight, hearing, smell, taste, and touch will cease, as will your power to think. You will hiccup and wheeze. The doctors will give up on you and all of your medicine, food, and drink will be tossed aside.

Setting out towards another existence, you will lie down on

your deathbed, only to fade into samsara's beginningless stream of birth, aging, illness, and death. With hardly any life-force left, you will be terrorized by the Lord of Death's henchmen. You will fall prey to misfortune, the movement of your breath stopped, your mouth gaping and nostrils flared. With teeth clenched, you will supplicate, saying, "Oh, please be generous!" You will then pass from one karmic existence to another, all by yourself and without any companions. This world will be left behind and you will move on to the next. The great shift will take place and you will enter a great darkness, fall into a great abyss, enter into a thick jungle, go to a vast and desolate place, and be carried away by a huge ocean. You will be driven by the winds of karma, going in a direction with nowhere to stop, entering into a great battle, caught by a great malevolent force, and wandering through space.

Your mother, father, elder siblings, sons, and daughters will gather around you. Your breath will cease and they will start talking about divvying up your wealth. "Oh, my poor father!" "Oh, my poor mother!" "Oh, my poor son!" they will say, letting their hair down [in mourning]. At that time, your only companions will be the generosity and austerities you have undertaken in the past and the Dharma. You will have no protection except the Dharma, no other protector or forces to defend you.

At that time, great king, at that moment, the Dharma will be a sanctuary, a dwelling, a protector, and a teacher. At such a time, great king, you will experience the appearances of your future [life] as you lie in bed. If you are going to the lower realms, the frightening appearances that occur in those places will arise. At such a time, there will not be a single thing that will protect you other than the Dharma.

Great king, though you may protect the body in this way and guard it carefully, the time will come for it to die. It may have every positive quality and you may develop it for years, contenting it with food, drink, and many other pure things. Yet when you lie on your deathbed and your doctors have given up hope, once everything has been given up as useless, the painful moment of death will arrive.

Great king, though your body will be bathed, anointed, and

scented with perfumes and the sweet smell of flowers, it will inevitably come to emit a foul stench.

Great king, though it may now be wrapped in the finest Benares cottons and silks, when you are lying on your deathbed, it will be as though you were clothed in reeking filth. The time of death will come and you will venture forth, naked and alone.

Great king, though you may have enjoyed various desirable things, you will have to abandon them all. Your desires left unsatisfied, the time of death will arrive.

Great king, though you may have various riches in your home—incense, flowers, silk brocades, and cushions—and though you may lie in bed, with pillows to your left and right, your body will inevitably be thrown into a charnel ground filled with crows, foxes, and revolting human corpses. Motionless, it will be left lying in the dirt.

Great king, though you may ride on the backs of elephants, horses, and the like, enjoying all sorts of melodious and pleasing instruments as victory banners, parasols, and other such things are being raised above your head; though kings, ministers, relatives, and friends may praise you with pleasantries and do your bidding, before long you will be lying on your deathbed. Four pallbearers will hold you aloft, as your parents, elder siblings, and others carry you by hand, beating their chests and overcome with grief. You will be brought through the south gate of the city. In an isolated, desolate place, you will be buried underground or eaten by crows, vultures, foxes, and other animals. Your bones will burned, thrown into water, or buried under the earth... whatever the case may be. The wind, sun, and rain will turn them to dust that will be scattered in all directions and decay.

In this way, great king, all conditioned things are impermanent. In this way, they are nothing you can rely on.

From the bottom of your heart, remind yourself of what this passage has taught in such detail. Understand that every appearance in this life has no significance, and exert yourself continually, day and night, for the sole purpose of accomplishing the sacred Dharma.

The merit of gods like Brahma, Maheshvara, Vishnu, Shakra, and the four great kings who guard the universe is so famous that it pervades all of heaven and earth. They are masters of the three realms—the subterranean realm, the terrestrial realm, and the celestial realm—and are adorned with the most superior wealth. Nevertheless, they too will die. The scriptures state:

> Even Brahma, Shakra, the wrathful Thousand-Eyed One,
> And Narayana are impermanent and will die.
> The sun and moon play for just a moment.
> Look how the universe and its four continents disappear!

The gods of the four absorptions, as well as the other gods, demi-gods, ascetics, and those accomplished in awareness mantra are no different. It is in their very nature to die. The Vinaya scriptures state:

> If even gods accomplished in states of absorption,
> If even the centaurs, demi-gods, sages, and ascetics, blazing in glory,
> Live for a long time, eons in fact, yet are still impermanent,
> Then why even mention that this human body
> Will decay and fall apart, unstable as it is, like a bubble of water?

The rulers of the four continents, the emperors of the universe, along with all the kings, ministers, monks, priests, householders, and every other ordinary person are not beyond death either. The *Collection of Purposeful Sayings* states:

> Kings with their seven treasures,
> Lords, ministers, and monks,
> Priests, householders, and every other being—
> They are all impermanent,
> Just like the beings in a dream!

This meaningful body you now have, with its freedoms and endowments, is impermanent too. Nothing can be added to your life span; it only dwindles away. Like a flash of lightning in the midst of a thick bank of monsoon clouds or water tumbling off a steep cliff, it doesn't remain unchanged for a single moment, night or day, not even for a fraction of a second. One day passes, then another, as death grows closer and closer. There is no doubt that you will soon die. In the *Sutra of the Vast Display*, it is written:

> The three realms are impermanent, like an autumn cloud,
> And the birth and death of beings, like watching a dance.
> The lives of beings flash by like lightning in the sky.
> Swift and quickly they go, like water cascading off a cliff.

The same holds for the universe's external environment. A single solar system is made up of four continents, eight subcontinents, a central mountain, seven golden mountains, seven lakes of play, a sun, moon, and a surrounding ring of iron mountains. The perimeter of one thousand such solar systems is encircled by iron mountains whose height is the same as the Heavenly Realm of Thirty-three. Together, these comprise a first-order thousandfold universe. The perimeter of one thousand of these systems is encircled by another ring of iron mountains, this time equaling the height of the Heaven of Mastery over Others' Creations. This is an intermediate, second-order thousandfold universe. The perimeter of one thousand of these systems is encircled by iron mountains that are as high as the first state of absorption. This is the great, third-order thousandfold universe. If you count each set of four continents and iron mountains, a third-order thousandfold universe is made up of one billion solar systems.

This universe first comes into being, then abides for an intermediate period, and is finally burned to ash by seven fires. These ashes are then washed away by water and dispersed by wind. In the end, the universe merges with space—empty, just as it was in the period before it came into existence. The *King of Samadhi Sutra* states:

> The entire universe arises at one point in time,
> And then later becomes space;
> Just as it was before, so it is after.
> All phenomena should be understood to be just the same.

Just as the external environment and those who inhabit it are subject to destruction, as the passage above shows, the inner body as well can be understood to be prone to decay. Initially at one with the space of the mind's reality, the subtle energy of ignorance and imagination function as a basis, and the body then comes into existence. It then abides in an intermediate period, before finally entering into a process of decay. Because it is made up of parts that have come together, it falls apart. Because it is born, it dies. And because it is conditioned, it decays. Once the time of death has arrived, the four outer elements dissolve into the four inner elements. This results in an eight-stage process of dissolution. The first seven of these stages see the incineration of the elements, while the final stage is one of liquefaction. The inner elements then dissolve into luminosity, once again entering into a state of unification with space.

You can also think about the multitude of teachers who have come to these inconceivable world systems, the victorious and transcendent buddhas. Though these buddhas achieved a vajra-like form, they too, along with their retinues, passed into nirvana, and their teachings into a state of decline. As this is the case, what, then, of the permanence and stability of our own body, which is as unstable as a bubble of water? In the *Collection on Impermanence,* it is written:

> The form of the Blissful One's essence blazes with a thousand signs
> And is established from a hundredfold merit. Yet if it is impermanent,
> Then why would it not be certain that my own body will be destroyed,
> Since it is as unreliable as a water bubble that is about to burst.
> Just look at the victorious ones, as they carry out the welfare of beings,
> And the treasure of sacred Dharma... both set like the sun and the moon.
> All of your riches, acquaintances, and enjoyments—
> All of these are impermanent as well.

There are many analogies and examples that show how the universe and its external environment are impermanent, as are all the sentient beings who inhabit it—high and low, good and bad, and so on. In short, we can be sure that all the beings who presently live upon this earth, whether great, small, or something in between, will be gone in a hundred years. The omniscient Longchenpa himself said:

> All the beings who live on this earth right now
> Will surely be gone in a hundred years' time!

So think carefully about the fact that you will definitely die, and that there is no way to tell when this will happen. You can't even be sure that it won't happen in this very place or because of some present circumstance! Ponder the fact that your life cannot be lengthened, and that it is perpetually ebbing away. Think about the multitude of conditions that could cause your death, how few there are that sustain it, and so on. Since there isn't any time to spare in life, it makes sense to rein in your mind and devote yourself to the Dharma.

To elaborate on these themes, because things arise, they will also surely perish. In the *White Lotus of the Sacred Dharma*, it is written:

> If there is birth, there is death.
> If things come together, they fall apart.

Since there is nothing certain about time itself either, we cannot know when we will die. The *Sutra of the Good Night* states:

> Who knows whether or not they will die tomorrow?
> Today is the day to act accordingly.
> The Lord of Death and his great legions
> Are not your friends, are they?

The location of your death is also unpredictable, so whenever you happen to be going somewhere, sitting, or doing anything else, think to yourself: "I wonder if I will die in this very spot!" The *Sutra of Subahu* states:

> A mountain, ravine, narrow pass, or precipice;
> At home, in a street, or on the bank of a river;
> Where, on this earth, your final place will be
> There is no way to know.
> So put an end to worldly delights!

It is also uncertain whether or not some present circumstance will be the cause of your death. The scriptures state:

> Some die choking on food,
> And some taking their medicine,
> Not to mention those whose death
> Is due to harmful circumstances.
> So there is nothing you can be sure about!

Death is also certain because we cannot lengthen our lives—they only dwindle away. In *Advice on Impermanence*, it is written:

> Like a pond whose source has run out,
> Our lives do not grow longer, but only diminish.
> Since we all set out on the path of death,
> Who can trust this fleeting life?

And in the *Way of the Bodhisattva*:

> Without staying put, day and night,
> My life is constantly slipping away.
> Since it does not get any longer,
> How would I myself not die? [II.39]

The multitude of conditions that can bring death, and the scarcity of those that sustain it, also ensure the certainty of death. The *Jewel Garland* states:

> There are many conditions that bring death,
> Yet only a few that sustain life.
> And these, as well, can bring death.
> Therefore, always practice the Dharma!

Furthermore, you will eventually have to let go of the people around you, as well as your wealth, friends, relatives, and this illusory body that you hold in such esteem. In the end, you will venture forth alone. The *Sutra of Advice to the King* states:

> Once the time has come, O king, and you have passed away,
> Your enjoyments, friends, and relatives will not come with you.
> Yet wherever beings are, and wherever they go,
> Their karma follows behind them like a shadow.

Not only will your parents, siblings, children, spouse, servants, wealth, and close relatives not accompany you, the virtue and vice that you've engaged in, your positive and negative karma, will follow you like a body and its shadow. This is what will happen when you die. The *Sutra Requested by Shri Datta* states:

> A combination of karma causes you to seek out enjoyments
> And to nurture your children and spouse.
> Yet when you suffer the pains of death,
> Your spouse and children will afford you no protection.
> As you encounter all that you've done in the past,
> Your spouse and children will be left behind
> And the experience of suffering will come to you alone,
> For they cannot take your lot once this has come to pass.
> The multitude of parents, siblings, children, spouses,
> Servants, wealth, close family, friends, and relatives
> That you have will not go with you when you die.
> You will be followed by your karma, childish one,
> When the time has come to die.

As this passage implies, when the time of death is upon you, there is no protection other than the sacred Dharma, so you should apply yourself to the Dharma with intense diligence. In *Resting in the Nature of Mind*, Longchenpa writes:

> Retinue, enjoyments, and close friends,
> Form, youth, power, wealth, and position—
> All will be left behind and you will die alone.
> Your positive and negative karma, in contrast,
> Will not disappear, but will follow after you.
> When it does, nothing will protect you aside from the Dharma.
> Since this is the case, then why, today,
> Would you not spend your time with diligence.

And in the *Precious Wish-fulfilling Treasury*, he writes:

> Look at the jeweled palace that adorns the four continents,
> The beautifully arrayed appearances of this enchanting land.
> Even it will end up in ruins, until not even a fraction of an atom
> Is left behind, and it naturally disappears altogether.
> This body that you cling to so dearly,
> The enjoyments and appearances of this life, one and all,
> Have an impermanent, illusory nature and will deceive you.
> Whatever you can think of has no essence,

And whatever you may think about them, they will do you no good.
So develop disenchantment, renunciation, and focus your mind.
Practice the sacred Dharma from this very day!

In *Resting in the Nature of Mind*, Longchenpa also explains how to gauge whether or not you have familiarized yourself with impermanence as outlined above:

> This will prompt you to practice the Dharma, bringing benefit and
>   happiness here and hereafter,
> And to apply yourself to practice with intensity and diligence.
> This life will be cast aside and the delusion of self-fixation destroyed.
> In short, the accomplishment of all good qualities, the eradication
>   of all negativity,
> And sacred liberation itself are caused by focusing the mind
> On the fundamental teaching of impermanence.

And in the *Precious Wish-fulfilling Treasury*, he writes:

> You can gauge your familiarization by whether or not you see
>   conditioned things as transitory;
> By whether or not you are diligent, fearful, and have cast aside the
>   activities of this life;
> By whether or not you can keep from slipping into an ordinary
>   state, even for an instant,
> And by whether or not you have renunciation, disenchantment, and
>   a focused mind.

To think about impermanence day and night, and see whatever appears as transitory, will cause an attitude of detachment towards external objects to arise from the depths of your heart. It will elicit a burning desire, prompting you to devote yourself to virtue. A deep-rooted panic and fear of the sufferings of samsara will set in, unlike anything else you may have experienced. Knowing that nothing will be able to help you at the moment of death, you will cast aside the activities of this life. You won't remain in an ordinary state of indolence for even a moment. Instead, you will practice the Dharma via the three gates. Seeing the ripening of cause and effect will bring forth a sense of disenchantment and renunciation, while understanding that the time of death is uncertain will keep you from putting your trust in anything worldly—these are the signs that you have taken impermanence to heart.

The benefits of this kind of habituation are innumerable. The Vinaya scriptures state:

> Thinking about the impermanence of conditioned things for a single moment is superior to making offerings of mid-day food and alms to one hundred fully ordained monks.

And in the *Parinirvana Sutra:*

> Of all harvests, getting the fall harvest is the greatest. Of all footprints, that of the elephant is greatest. Of all ideas, those of impermanence and death are the greatest, for these will reverse all thoughts associated with the three realms.

The omniscient Longchenpa taught:

> Its benefits are completely boundless—
> Samsara's problems will be abandoned and positive qualities will naturally assemble;
> One will be freed from fixating on permanence, and the attachment and aversion to friend and foe, pacified;
> One will have great diligence when practicing virtue and understand that this life is delusion;
> The two accumulations will be totally completed and one will be looked after by the famed gods;
> One will have a peaceful death, go to the higher realms,
> And quickly attain the nectar of deathlessness.

To sum up, no matter how complete and perfect the attainments you may have in this life, they are just like the pleasures you might dream of when taking a nap, which disappear once you wake up. Think this over and keep firmly in mind the benefits of thinking about the impermanence of life that were just mentioned. Once you've done so, prepare yourself well so that you have no regret when it comes time to die.

Compassion and Bodhichitta

The next section teaches how to meditate on compassion and bodhichitta. The *Fortunate Eon Sutra* states:

> When someone develops the mindset of supreme enlightenment
> The merit involved surpasses any example that can be given,
> And is superior even to that of someone who makes defiled offerings
> To sentient beings for an entire ten billion eons.

From a general point of view, developing bodhichitta is an important part of practicing the path of the Great Vehicle. As stated in the tantras:

> Love and compassion are the general path of the Dharma,
> For they provide access to the Great Vehicle.

This section has four divisions:

1) Aspiration bodhichitta
2) Application bodhichitta
3) Bodhichitta in practice
4) The benefits of bodhichitta

Aspiration Bodhichitta

Space extends infinitely in each of the ten directions. No matter how precisely you may try to measure it, you will never find its edge. The universe is infinite in just the same way. It is completely filled with the sentient beings of the six classes of existence, to the point where no empty space remains at all. Of all these sentient beings, there is not a single one who has not been your mother or father at one time or another. There are not any whose womb you have not slept in and whose breast milk you have not drunk. Just as your own births are beyond reckoning, the number of times these beings have been your mother is also infinite and incalculable. As stated in the *Stainless Confession Tantra*:

> Gathered together, my flesh and bones would equal the extent of the earth,

And my pus and blood could fill a giant ocean.
My residual karma is inconceivable, beyond words.
I have cycled throughout the three realms, through a succession of births and deaths.

The mothers and fathers we've had each of these times have looked after us in just the same way that our mother and father in this present life have. They protected us from all harms and nurtured us with a loving heart. Having reared us with such love, they are no different than our own benevolent mothers, who have helped us in ways too innumerable, too immeasurable, to count. What sense is there in making distinctions between our present mother and those of our previous births? What sense is there in choosing between them and making arbitrary divisions?

Though all of these mothers of ours desire happiness, they cast away virtue, the cause of happiness, as though it were poison. And while they do not want to suffer, they take up the causes of suffering, negativity and vice, as if they are medicine. Vice is precisely what they put into practice, and in so doing they circle around and around in samsara.

How could you not feel compassion for their wretched plight? Bring the four immeasurables to mind, thinking to yourself: "I will bring them happiness and deliver them from suffering. I will bring them a happiness free of suffering and bring them to the level of the ultimate—the precious state of buddhahood!" This is the bodhichitta of aspiration. The *Tent of the Lotus Heart* states:

> Aspiring for the welfare of sentient beings
> Is the shortcut to perfect buddhahood.

You can also bring to mind the fact that, from time immemorial, these mothers who have reared you so kindly have been dazed, lost in the darkness of ignorance, and intoxicated by the afflictions that disturb their minds. Blind and unable to tell right from wrong, they have no spiritual teacher to guide them. They engage in nothing but negative behavior and do nothing but negative deeds, all of which has plunged them into the abyss of samsara and its lower realms.

Keep this in mind until you feel unbearable compassion for them, until tears flow from your eyes. Then think to yourself: "I will free them from the suffering of samsara and establish them in a state of happiness!" Use this attitude, in which you consider others more important than yourself, to practice the profound contemplation of sending and taking for all the sentient beings in the six classes of existence. Breathing in, take the suffering, negativity, and downfalls of the six classes of existence into your own being. Breathing out, allow all of your own potential happiness, pleasure, and positive qualities to ripen in the hearts and minds of all sentient beings. Bring forth unsurpassed bodhichitta with the wish that all their suffering be purified and that each gets exactly what he or she wishes for. In the *Sutra Requested by Akshayamati* it is written:

> With love and compassion, work for the welfare of beings.
> Joyfully link others with the Dharma
> And be free from malice, the supreme dharma of impartiality.
> This is the mind training of the Omniscient One.

And in the *Way of the Bodhisattva*:

> In brief, you should understand
> That there are two types of bodhichitta:
> The mindset that aspires to enlightenment
> And the mindset that actually engages it. [I.15]

Developing aspiration bodhichitta entails an immeasurable amount of merit. As stated in the *Sutra of Maitreya's Way*:

> When compared with one who fills
> The three thousandfold universe with jewels
> And offers them to those with the ten powers,
> Aspiring to be enlightened will lead
> To a much greater increase in merit.
> Even if you were to fill the buddha fields
> With as many jewels as there are grains of sand in the Ganges,
> And then generously give them away,
> Aspiring towards supreme enlightenment
> Will lead to a much greater increase in merit.

Application Bodhichitta

In the *Tent of the Lotus Heart*, it is written:

> Others work to free themselves from existence,
> While Bodhisattvas work for the welfare of beings.
> So practice the six perfections.

You should apply yourself continually to the four ways of attracting students and the four types of generosity. The four ways of attracting students are being generous, speaking in a pleasing way, being consistent, and acting meaningfully.

Dharmic generosity refers to any act of giving that serves to foster the conducive conditions and requisites for practicing the Dharma. In particular, this refers to the use of maturing empowerments and liberating instructions to teach the genuine nature of reality. In short, giving reading transmissions, transmitting precepts, or giving any other teaching of the Great or Lesser Vehicles that matches the capacity of the student is Dharmic generosity, the supreme form of generosity.

Material generosity refers to giving away any of one's possessions and enjoyable things. This can include horses, oxen, other species of four-legged animals, fields, houses, even one's children or spouse. In short, this means giving away whatever someone happens to need. Alternately, this can refer to acts such as the generosity of one's own body, one's own flesh and blood, in which case the head, limbs, five sense faculties, and so forth are given away. It can also mean being generous in an internal way, with the mind. This can refer to making aspirations, such as meditating on boundless compassion.

The generosity of fearlessness involves protecting others from illness, malicious forces, fire, floods, weapons, the fear of rulers, the pain of famine, and so on. In short, this means to use whatever strength and abilities you may possess to protect others from any kind of fear.

Bodhichitta in Practice

Concerning the training that developing bodhichitta entails, the *Sutra Requested by Akshayamati* explains:

> Casting aversion far away is pure generosity,
> Developing a loving mind, pure discipline.
> Developing the strength of patience is pure patience,
> And the wisdom of the buddha is pure diligence.
> Total peace of mind is pure meditative stability,
> And absence of sounds and words, knowledge.

As stated here, you should train by gathering students through practicing the Dharma in a genuine way, through renown and material goods, and through the appropriate level of conducive factors; you should also engage in the conduct—the six perfections and the perfect and complete practice.

The Benefits of Bodhichitta

The benefits and merit that come about from developing bodhichitta are immeasurable. In the *Sutra of the Inconceivable Secret*, it is written:

> If the merit associated with bodhichitta
> Were to take physical form,
> It would fill all of space,
> And even then could not be contained.

As this passage implies, you will always be protected by bodhisattvas and masters of awareness and will hear teachings directly from the buddhas. Once you die, you will go on to pleasurable states, riding the steed of bodhichitta. This will culminate in the attainment of enlightenment. In this way, its benefits are immeasurable.

[Developing Bodhichitta]

All of your elderly mothers are wandering in an ocean of samsaric suffering. Though you may wish to establish them in the state of liberation and omniscience, right now you don't have the power to do so. As this is the case, think to yourself: "I must swiftly attain the state of buddhahood, which will allow me to liberate all beings! To this end, I will practice the profound path." With your mind fixed one-pointedly on this supreme mindset, recite the following as much as you can:

> From now until enlightenment is attained,
> I will think of all those in the six realms
> As my very own mother, and I their child.
> Delivering those undelivered and freeing those unfree,
> I will bring them relief and to the state of nirvana—
> Giving rise to bodhichitta, both aspiring and applied.

The meaning of the prayer is as follows: From this point forward, until each and every being throughout the six realms has attained liberation and enlightenment, you need to meditate on the four immeasurables. Immeasurable compassion is likened to the feeling a mother would have if her child were killed right before her eyes. Immeasurable love is similar to a mother hen rearing her eggs into chicks. Immeasurable joy is like the feeling of a mother who has found her lost child. Immeasurable equanimity is likened to a Bodhisattva's act of generosity, or a feast given by a sage. Meditate on these four immeasurables from the depths of your heart, without letting them become hollow words.

You need to have a courageous attitude! Think to yourself: "I myself will deliver all the sentient beings that were not delivered from samsara's ocean of suffering by the victorious ones of the past! I myself will free all the sentient beings who have not been freed and are bound by the afflictions! I myself will relieve those who are tormented by the afflictions and have no relief! I will bring them to a state that is totally beyond suffering!"

There are boundless benefits associated with developing bodhichitta. As written in the *Way of the Bodhisattva*:

> Once bodhichitta has been aroused, in that very instant,
> Even wretched creatures, bound in the prison of samsara,
> Are called "children of the blissful ones"
> And are worthy of reverence in the world of gods and men. [I.9]

This is how aspiration and application bodhichitta are developed. These two form the basis and support for all the vehicles that lead to the higher realms and true goodness. Their purpose is to actualize the fruition associated with the qualities, merit, and wisdom that are conducive to liberation.

CHAPTER 3

Karma & the Three Vows

THE PRINCIPLE OF KARMIC CAUSALITY

ONCE AGAIN, those of you gathered here should remain undistracted and focus all your attention on the teachings you are about to receive. With the attitude that you are spontaneously accomplishing both your own and others' welfare, listen attentively. The *Sutra Requested by King Chandra* states:

> Speech, ears, faith, knowledge,
> And freedom from hindrances—
> These five are hard to come by,
> So always listen to the Teacher's speech.

As taught here, you should listen one-pointedly and with great respect, and then practice by bringing what you've heard into your own experience.

The buddhas have many skillful methods. Their wisdom and compassion is free from prejudice and their enlightened activities are wondrous. The teachers of the three kayas who possess these qualities have given an inconceivable number of teachings to establish us in the state of liberation. In other words, their teachings are intended to bring all sentient beings throughout the three realms to the state of unsurpassed enlightenment.

All of these teachings can be condensed into two categories: the Vehicle of Perfections and the Secret Mantra Vajra Vehicle. In the former, the path functions as the cause, whereas in the latter, the fruition is taken as the path. In the present context, the step-by-step instructions you are receiving are being taught from the perspective of the Secret Mantra Vajra Vehicle.

As explained above, the freedoms and endowments are difficult to obtain in their entirety. By nature, they are impermanent, unstable, and easily destroyed. Our environment is in a constant state of flux as well; the four seasons—summer, fall, winter, and spring—come and go. Hence, the universe we live in is also impermanent. The beings that inhabit the world are no different. There is no telling if they will experience happiness or suffering in their early years or in old age, or whether their life will be long or short. They are impermanent by their very nature, changing with each passing day. In general, things that gather together will eventually disperse, that which has been accumulated will run out, and whatever is built will end up in ruins, for conditioned things have no essence of their own.

This is particularly relevant in terms of the aggregates, elements, and sense fields, which gradually transform under the influence of birth, aging, sickness, and death. There is no way to know for sure how long you have to live. Like the flame of a butter lamp flickering in the wind, people gathered together on market day, the drop of dew on a blade of grass, or a bubble of water about to burst, any one of a great number of harmful conditions could be your end. You could be beset by the four hundred and four illnesses, for example, or attacked by malicious and evil forces.

When this comes to pass, the wealth you have accumulated will be left behind. Your beloved companions, the place where you live, and this illusory body that you treasure so dearly will be cast away and you will have to venture forth to an unknown place, with no knowledge of where you are going. As for your body, it might be cremated or cast into a river. It could end up being brought to some terrifying place, a remote charnel ground, forest, island, or the bank of a river, and cast before birds and wild animals. Your given name will disappear and, as if carried by the wind, your consciousness will wander aimlessly away.

Your death will not result in a state of vacant nothingness, however. In contrast, the consequences of your past actions will accompany you when you die, like a body and its shadow. The excellent fruition of the virtuous acts you have undertaken in the past will be a rebirth in the higher realms, where you will experience happiness, joy, and prosperity. Negativity, on the other hand, will result in the horrible and unbearable suffering of the lower realms. And when a mixture of virtue and vice has been acted out, it will ripen in various forms that involve both happiness and suffering.

Just as karma can be accumulated in a variety of ways, its ripening too can take place in a variety of different forms. It can ripen as the result of individual effort, for example, or as a fully ripened result, a result that resembles its cause, or a dominant result. Negativity results in suffering, while virtue results in either a rebirth in the higher realms or liberation. Because virtue and vice are infallible, you should analyze the principle of causality in great detail and give it due consideration. Put great effort into rejecting negativity and putting virtue into practice.

The *Jewel Garland* states:

> All suffering comes from vice,
> And the lower realms as well.
> While from virtue comes all happiness,
> Pleasure in all its forms.

As this passage points out, there is a definite correspondence between virtue and happiness on the one hand, and negativity and suffering on the other. In both cases, the former is the cause and the latter, the result. For this reason, you should abandon the ten forms of vice and every other form that vice can take no matter how insignificant they may seem, even if it means risking your own life. You should also undertake virtuous endeavors to the best of your ability, including the ten virtuous acts and other types of virtue, trifling though they may be. All neutral activities can be incorporated into the path of virtue as well; you should do all this as best you can.

Those who are presently experiencing happiness and pleasure in the higher realms, or suffering in the lower realms, are doing so as a result of the karma they accumulated in the past. In *Resting in the Nature of Mind*, Longchenpa writes:

> The Able One taught that the pleasure and pain of existence,
> The high and the low, arise from karma accumulated in the past.

When the various karmic predispositions that beings possess meet with particular conditions, the results associated with these actions ripen as the places they live in, the sense pleasures they enjoy, and all their joys and sorrows. The *Hundred Actions* states:

> How wondrous, the universe arises from karma!
> Pleasure and pain are drawn by karma.
> Conditions gather and karma arises—
> Karma creates pleasure and pain.

And:

> Karma never goes to waste, not even in a hundred eons.
> When the conditions come together
> And the right time is found,
> Its result ripens in those with bodies.

The *White Lotus [of the Sacred Dharma] Sutra* states:

> Like a painter, karma creates everything,
> Making patterns like a choreographed dance.

And *Gathering the Accumulations of Enlightenment* reads:

> Three forms of affliction and their absence, respectively,
> Lead to meritorious karma and that of liberation.
> Due to the mind and karma, beings are linked with a cause,
> Hence, the workings of karma are great and seminal.

The *Jewel Garland* states:

> To not take life, to abandon stealing,
> And to leave the spouses of others alone;
> To totally refrain from telling lies,
> And saying divisive, harsh, or senseless things,
>
> To be detached and free from malice,
> And to totally give up nihilistic views—
> These are the ten wholesome ways to act,
> While their opposites are unwholesome.

Hence, vice produces suffering and leads to a birth in the lower realms, while virtue allows one to attain the pleasurable states of the higher realms. In the *Application of Mindfulness,* it is written:

> Vice results in the lower realms and suffering,
> While virtue brings happiness and the higher realms.

And in the *Sutra on Individual Liberation*:

> Engage in no negativity whatsoever,
> Practice virtue, perfect and complete,
> And thoroughly tame your own mind—
> These are the teachings of the Buddha.

The *Delineation of Karma* states:

> The Brahmin boy Neytso, son of the householder Touta, asked: "O Gautama, what are the causes and conducive factors that result in sentient beings having short lives and long ones, good health and poor, being attractive and ugly, powerful and powerless, of noble class and low, rich and poor, with great knowledge and little?"
>
> The Buddha replied: "O Brahmin boy, sentient beings are created by karma. Their karmic allotment is what they experience and their births and lives are karmic too. They depend upon karma, which can be classified in different ways. It can be lowly, noble, or average, high or low, good or bad. Sentient beings have different types of karma, different views and different ways of acting. Their negative actions will bring them a birth in hell, as a spirit, or as an animal. Their positive actions, on the other hand, will bring them a birth as a god or a human."

To boil this down to a single point, virtue is the sole cause of pleasurable states, while the sole cause of states of suffering is vice.

Virtue can take two forms. When consistent with merit, virtue produces the pleasurable results associated with existence. These factors, which disappear as soon as they produce their respective results, include the ten virtues, the four absorptions, and the four formless absorptions. These factors are not associated with liberation. When conducive to liberation, virtue acts as a cause that leads to the transcendence of suffering, nirvana.

The Ten Virtues

Explaining the first topic, the ten virtues that are consistent with merit, the *Precious Wish-fulfilling Treasury* states:

> The three physical, four verbal, and three mental virtues—
> When these ten are not linked with the formless absorptions,
> They produce a pleasurable result, a birth as a desire realm god or human.

To give up three factors—the taking of life, taking what has not been given, and desirous sexual misconduct—and to put three more into practice—ransoming lives, being generous, and maintaining one's vows—constitutes the three physical virtues.[31] The four verbal virtues are to give up dishonest, divisive, harsh, and pointless speech, on the one hand, and to speak honestly, create harmony, praise others, and speak with decorum, on the other. The three mental virtues are to abandon covetousness, malice, and wrong views, while at the same time having a good heart, an altruistic mind, and devotion towards the Dharma.

Provided they are not naturally linked with the cultivation of states of absorption and the formless realms, engaging in these ten virtues will result in the enjoyment of the pleasures associated with the higher realms of gods and humans. In other words, the ripened result of these acts is a birth as a human being in one of the four continents or eight subcontinents, or as one of the six types of desire realm god.

However, as the *Precious Wish-fulfilling Treasury* states:

> Linked with the absorptions and formless states, the two higher realms,
> Virtue produces pleasurable states and all forms of happiness.

Thus, if your training involves linking the ten virtues with the four absorptions, you will be reborn in the form realms, whereas when they are linked with the four formless states and this is brought to a state of culmination, one of the four spheres of perception will be attained.[32] To elaborate, the ten virtues create karmic momentum and perform the function of completing certain pleasurable factors, whereas the presence of the coarse mental states associated with the absorptions and formless states comes about by meditating on them. As this is the case, virtue leads to the actual attainment of the status and body associated with a birth in the higher realms.[33]

The ripened result of the ten virtues is a birth in the higher realms as a god or human. The dominant result is that aspect which will ripen as your environment; in other words, being born in a place filled with flowers and plentiful harvests, a safe place where one can travel freely and with other positive features. There are two types of results that resemble their cause, one behavioral and one experiential. Concerning the former, acting virtuously will result in your taking delight in performing the ten virtues, while in terms of the latter, practicing virtue will bring you good health, wealth, and other such experiences.

The *Precious Wish-fulfilling Treasury* goes into more detail on this topic:

> Giving up the taking of life
> Brings longevity and good health.
> Giving up theft leads to great prosperity,
> And giving up sexual misconduct,
> To intimate relationships free from strife.

By giving up the three physical forms of vice and practicing virtue in this way, you will have a long life, material prosperity, and a household free from negative influences.

The same text continues:

> Give up lying and others will praise you;
> Give up harsh speech and their kind words will bring peace of mind;
> Give up divisive speech and you will not appear antagonistic;
> Give up pointless speech and your words will be taken to heart.

As shown here, in giving up the four verbal forms of vice, you will be universally praised and acclaimed. You will be pleasing to the eye, have a harmonious atmosphere, and your words will be considered worthy of trust.

The same scripture then reads:

> Give up covetousness and your hopes will be accomplished.
> Give up malice and you will be attractive, your mere sight bringing peace.
> Give up wrong views and you will attain the excellent view.
> These ten virtues are a chariot to the higher realms.
> You who desire the happiness of the exalted states, put them into practice!

Hence, by giving up the three acts of mental vice, your goals will be accomplished just as you wish and you will appear pleasing and peaceful to others. In all your existences and births, you will believe and have confidence in the principle of causality as soon as you are born. This is also mentioned in the *Jewel Garland*:

> Whatever worldly being
> Has the great, authentic view
> Will not go to the lower realms
> For a thousand lifetimes.

Anyone who desires pleasurable states and experiences should put these ten into practice.

The Ten Forms of Vice

As for the factors that conflict with virtue, the *Precious Wish-fulfilling Treasury* states:

> The ten forms of vice are the cause of the lower realms' suffering.
> Great, average, and minor acts will plunge you into the hell, spirit,
> Or animal realms, along with the various forms of suffering they entail.

The ten forms of vice mentioned here are (1) the taking of life, (2) taking what has not been given, (3) sexual misconduct, (4) telling lies, (5) divisiveness, (6) pointless speech, (7) harsh speech, (8) covetousness, (9) malice, and (10) wrong views. On this topic, the *Treasury of Higher Dharma* states:

> The taking of life means to kill another,
> Intentionally and not by accident.
> Taking what has not been given is to take
> Another's belongings as one's own, by force or stealth.
> There are four types of sexual misconduct,
> Including desiring intercourse in an inappropriate way.
> Lying means to deceive another,
> With the meaning of one's words accurately understood.

> Divisiveness is speech that creates schisms between others,
> And harsh speech is saying unpleasant things.
> All talk that involves the afflictions is pointless speech.
> Having negative ideas and a covetous mind
> Mean to be wrongly attached to another's belongings.
> Malice is aversion directed towards a sentient being,
> While wrong views concern the belief
> That virtue and vice do not exist.

There are three results associated with the forms of vice outlined above—the ripened result, the result that resembles its cause, and the dominant result. The ripened result is as follows. The motivations that underlie vice can vary in intensity. These differences result in there being major, average, and minor acts. Major acts lead to a rebirth in hell, average to a rebirth as a spirit, and minor to a rebirth as an animal. Consequently, each of these three leads to an experience of the specific suffering associated with one of the three lower realms.

Second is the result that resembles its cause, which has both an experiential and behavioral aspect. Concerning the former, taking life will lead to a short life, theft to poverty, and sexual misconduct to having many enemies. In telling lies, you will be slandered by many others. By being divisive, you will have no friends and will not get along with anyone else. Instead, you will make enemies. Say harsh things and what you hear will always be negative; speak pointlessly and your speech will be ignoble. Covetousness will cause your hopes to go unfulfilled, and malice will bring you a perpetual state of fear and anxiety. As a result of wrong views, you will be foolish and ignorant. The result that resembles its cause also has an impact on behavioral patterns. This refers to the fact that in the future you will continue to enjoy doing the same things you did in the past.

Third is the dominant result, which ripens externally. By taking life, the fruits of your effort, such as medicines and so forth, will have little potency. Stealing will result in poor harvests. Sexual misconduct will result in your surroundings being filled with dust, mist, and rain. Lying will lead to foul-smelling surroundings filled with filth. Divisiveness will bring you to uneven places with cliffs and ravines. Harsh speech will result in your surroundings having desolate plains, thorns, and salt. Pointless speech will bring erratic seasons. Covetousness will lead to poor or bad harvests. Malice makes things that initially taste good taste bad, while wrong views result in one's grain stores going from little to none at all. There are other results as well. Dominant results and those that accord with their cause can arise in one's present life or in a future life; there is no way to tell.

For all these reasons, intelligent individuals should cast aside the ten forms of vice as though they are poison. The *Precious Wish-fulfilling Treasury* states:

> These ten forms of vice are like poison,
> So learned people should reject them outright.

Whoever engages in vice will experience an unpleasant result once it ripens. Therefore, vice should be rejected in all circumstances, whether anyone else notices or not. As it is said:

> Those who commit negativity while unobserved
> Will feel no ease, as if they had swallowed poison,
> For it is impossible that the gods, yogis,
> And those with pure perception will not see what they have done.

Virtue and Liberation

In this section, we will discuss virtue that is conducive to liberation. On this topic, the *Precious Wish-fulfilling Treasury* states:

> The path to liberation brings the peace of enlightenment—
> The transcendence of existence and elimination of suffering.

As these lines point out, virtue that functions as the cause of liberation allows one to transcend samsara and eliminate suffering. This refers to any deed or activity of the three gates that is linked with bodhichitta. As it states in the *Four Hundred Stanzas:*

> Because of their intention,
> For Bodhisattvas everything is virtue—
> Both virtue and vice alike. Why?
> Because they are in control of their minds.

And in the *Way of the Bodhisattva*:

> From that moment on,
> The force of merit is uninterrupted
> And equal to the extent of space,
> Even when one is careless or asleep. [I.19]

The *Precious Wish-fulfilling Treasury* states:

> Those who enter the path of the three vehicles
> Practice in the following way:
> They develop the appropriate mindset,
> Meditate on the four immeasurables, engage in the six perfections,
> And practice the factors of enlightenment.
> Practicing these day and night brings virtue.

Individuals of lesser capacity develop a mindset that involves seeking out the path of listeners. With this mindset, they meditate on the applications of mindfulness until perfected. This constitutes the first path. Those who enter the path of the solitary buddhas are of average capacity, while those of superior capacity develop the mindset of the Great Vehicle.

The individuals associated with each of these three classes develop their respective mindsets and then subsequently apply themselves to virtuous endeavors night and day. These virtuous practices are subsumed under the practice of the thirty-seven factors of enlightenment, the four immeasurables, and the six perfections, all of which should be linked with the dedication of the merit that has been gathered. This is referred to as "virtue conducive to liberation."

The Four Immeasurables

The four immeasurables are love, compassion, joy, and equanimity: the loving wish that sentient beings who are unhappy meet with happiness, the compassionate desire that those plagued by suffering be freed from it, the joyful wish that those who are happy do not lose their happiness, and the intention that those who are biased and have attachment and aversion reach a state of equanimity.

The Six Perfections

To give your possessions to another without hoping for anything in return is generosity. Discipline involves eliminating vice. To not get angry when another harms you is patience. Taking delight in virtuous endeavors is diligence, while states of absorption entail the mind's resting one-pointedly. Understanding the words and meaning of all the Buddha's teachings is knowledge. These six are brought to perfection by practicing with the understanding that all things appear but lack inherent existence.

The *Sutra Requested by Kashyapa* states:

> Though your ability to tolerate selflessness allows you to rest in equanimity,
> You still need to develop great compassion for all sentient beings.
> Though you may give generously to bring about their maturation,
> You shouldn't entertain hopes about the ripening of karma.
> Though your mind may be in a state perpetually beyond suffering,
> It should still remain engaged with samsara.
> And though you may realize the emptiness of all phenomena,
> You should still have conviction in the ripening of karma.

To elaborate, your virtuous acts will become conducive to liberation if you set the stage by developing bodhichitta, realize their lack of inherent existence as the main part of your practice, and conclude by dedicating the merit and making aspirations.

Compassion is the mental factor that keeps bodhichitta from degenerating once it has been attained, whereas emptiness refers to the lack of any observable essence. These two are essentially the same mental factor, though one can isolate two different aspects, those of skillful means and knowledge. The unity of these two aspects, the fact that there are no such reference points, is itself emptiness. This non-referential compassion, in which emptiness and compassion are essentially of one taste and undifferentiable, is what is meant by the term "union."

The *Precious Wish-fulfilling Treasury* concludes:

> All of your endeavors should be directed solely to the welfare of others.
> Your view—the eighteen emptinesses—should be like space,
> Your meditation on the thirty-seven factors, luminous,

Your practice of the six perfections, faultless,
And the fruition—the attainment of enlightenment—unsurpassed.

Next, there are two sections that conclude the discussion of karma, the first of which presents a definitive condensation of the way to reverse the causes and results associated with samsara.

Karma and Samsara

The various places we encounter and the feelings of pleasure and pain we experience, each of which appears in its own individual way, can be subsumed under the three realms and six classes of existence. All of these forms appear due to the deluded habitual patterns that have lodged themselves in the universal ground consciousness. The type of virtue that is consistent with merit produces rebirths as gods and humans. Vice, on the other hand, creates various types of suffering and causes one to be reborn in the lower realms. Thus, while the number of different experiences is infinite, they can all be grouped into the six classes of existence, which are collectively referred to as "deluded experience." Until these habitual tendencies have run out, it is not possible for these experiences to come to an end. As stated in the *Application of Mindfulness*:

> All that is experienced in the universe, whatever it may be,
> Arises wholly from one's own karma.

For this reason, you need to give up negative activities. The *King of Samadhi Sutra* states:

> Because it has been gathered, karma never disappears;
> It will ripen as a positive or negative result within samsara.

Hence, you should work to give up negative activities in the proper way. Never say that it will simply suffice to recognize the nature of mind and that causality is unimportant! In the *Jewel Garland*, Nagarjuna addresses this point:

> Saying that karma has no result
> Is, in brief, the view of nihilism.
> It is unmeritorious and [leads to] the lower realms.

Karma and Nirvana

The sure way to apply oneself diligently to the causes and result of nirvana is to take up and refine one's practice of virtuous endeavors, the full import of which can be condensed as follows: All the happiness associated with the higher realms results from virtue. In addition, all the oceanic qualities, generosity, and psychic powers that the bodhisattvas possess, as well as every conceivable quality of the buddhas, are caused by, and result from, virtue. For this very reason, you should make a concerted effort to gather the two accumulations.

The master Nagarjuna wrote:

> Pleasurable states come from virtue
> And the lower realms from vice,
> Whereas liberation is beyond both.

Those who wish to attain buddhahood quickly should familiarize themselves with its causes, the twofold perfection of skillful means and knowledge. The former, which entails appearance, refers to the accumulation of merit and the first five perfections, such as generosity. The latter does not entail appearance and refers to the accumulation of wisdom, i.e., reality, or emptiness. The *Jewel Garland* states:

> Hence, the two accumulations are the cause
> Of the attainment of buddhahood itself,
> So always rely on them!

Therefore, you shouldn't separate the skillful means of great compassion from the empty essence, pristine wisdom. On this point, the master Saraha wrote:

> One who practices emptiness but not compassion
> Has not found the supreme path.
> Just as one who meditates on compassion alone
> Will stay in samsara and not attain liberation.
> Yet those who are able to unite these two
> Will abide in neither samsara nor nirvana.

There are innumerable such references throughout the sutras and tantras, so have conviction in them and never let yourself become complacent when it comes to gathering the two pristine accumulations. Don the great armor of enthusiasm and gather them continually, throughout the ocean of time!

⸺ The Three Vows ⸺

The next section, which is linked with the previous section on the principle of karmic causality, is based on the preliminary practices titled "The Pure Path to Liberation."[34] Here we find three sets of precepts to be practiced:

1) the outer pratimoksha vows of individual liberation
2) the inner precepts of the bodhisattvas
3) the Secret Mantra's samaya vows of the masters of awareness

The Vows of Individual Liberation

The vows of individual liberation contain eight categories, the vows associated with (1) laymen, (2) laywomen, (3) novice monks, (4) novice nuns, (5) fully ordained monks, and (6) fully ordained nuns, as well as (7) temporary vows and (8) limited vows.

Lay vows are divided into three categories: (1) those that involve abstinence, (2) the complete set of vows, and (3) partial observance. Of these, observances involving abstinence include the four fundamental precepts and a fifth involving intoxicants. The observance of the complete set of vows involves restraining from taking of life, taking what has not been given, engaging in acts of sexual perversion, lying, and partaking of intoxicants. Partial observance involves a pledge to observe whichever of these five one feels inclined towards.

The observances of novice monks and nuns include the ten renunciations. Fully ordained nuns must observe three hundred and sixty regulations and fully ordained monks, two hundred and fifty-three. Temporary vows involve eight branches, while the limited observances are twenty-two in number. In brief, whatever vows one happens to have taken should be maintained as though one were guarding the eyes in one's head or the heart in one's chest.

The *King of Samadhi Sutra* states:

> If you are puffed up with learning but do not observe discipline,
> Your degenerate discipline will lead you to the lower realms,
> Where your education will afford you no protection.
> On the other hand, if you get the idea that study is unnecessary,
> And that having discipline alone will suffice, you are wrong.

The same text adds:

> If, however, you are enthralled with your discipline,
> Yet do not study extensively,
> The result of your discipline will disappear without a trace
> And in the future you will suffer in the lower realms.

As this is the case, you should practice the outer vows of individual liberation exactly as they are taught in the *Fundamental Vinaya*, the *Supreme Scripture* and *Vinaya Minutia*. These vows are summarized in a sutra:

> Engage in no negativity whatsoever,
> Practice virtue, perfect and complete,
> And thoroughly tame your own mind—
> These are the teachings of the Buddha.
> The physical vows are excellent,
> And so are the vows of speech.
> Mental vows are excellent too.
> Hence, the vows are excellent in all ways.
> Ordained individuals who observe them
> Will be liberated from all forms of suffering.

And in the *Ten Wheels of Kshitigarbha Sutra*:

> Guarding against the four fundamental and naturally negative deeds constitutes the supreme and ultimate cause of all virtuous endeavors, both the defiling and nondefiling. Therefore, guarding against these four factors is referred to as "the root of all virtuous endeavors." Similarly, with this great earth as their support, all sorts of fruit trees, flowers, trees, and forests can grow.

Just so, with the maintenance of these four fundamental disciplines as their basis, all virtuous endeavors arise and develop.

From this perspective, one can see that if maintaining just these four fundamental precepts has such beneficial qualities, then maintaining two hundred and fifty-three must entail infinite benefits. The sole basis and support for attaining the state of liberation and omniscience is this training in discipline, so it makes perfect sense to apply yourself to this practice.

The Bodhisattva Precepts

The inner precepts of the bodhisattva were explained above in the section on bodhichitta and will be mentioned just briefly here. The *Sutra of Maitreya's Way* states:

> When compared with one who fills
> The three thousandfold universe with jewels
> And offers them to those with the ten powers,
> If you aspire to attain supreme enlightenment
> Your merit will develop even more.
>
> Even if you fill the buddha fields with as many jewels
> As there are grains of sand in the Ganges
> And then generously give them away,
> Your merit will develop much more
> If you aspire to attain supreme enlightenment.

As you become aware of the benefits aspiring to enlightenment entails, you should also begin practicing the conduct of the Great Vehicle's teachings. Further, you should do so with the pure and superior mindset of considering others more important than yourself; you should develop the vast attitude of desiring to free all sentient beings, each of whom has been your very own mother, from the ocean of samsara's suffering. With this mindset, readily take up difficulties, apply yourself intensely, and never give up! The *Tantra of the Boundless Ocean of Great Power* states:

> Save lives and give generously.
> Maintain abstinence and teach the Dharma.

Have continuous and stable conscientiousness
And, if it benefits others, even conceptual thought.

Furthermore, becoming a child of the victorious ones and attaining perfect and complete buddhahood is caused specifically by, and depends on, developing supreme bodhichitta. On this important point, the sutras state:

> Those who wish to attain perfect and complete buddhahood do not need to practice many teachings but only one. This one teaching is bodhichitta.

In the *Way of the Bodhisattva*, it is written:

> Once bodhichitta has been aroused, in that very instant,
> Even wretched creatures, bound in the prison of samsara,
> Are called "children of the blissful ones"
> And are worthy of reverence in the world of gods and men. [I.9]

When it comes to the sacred Dharma, bodhichitta is the primary cause that enables one to free both oneself and others from suffering. It also causes the attainment of sacred happiness, in both its temporary and ultimate forms. The *Compendium of Instructions* states:

> Those who wish to bring suffering to an end
> And happiness to perfection
> Should stabilize their foundation, faith,
> And fix their minds on enlightenment.

And in the *Way of the Bodhisattva*:

> Never, even at the cost of your life,
> Should you forsake your spiritual teacher,
> Learned in the meaning of the Great Vehicle,
> And in the Bodhisattva's conduct, supreme. [V.102]

The sentient beings of samsara have shown you great kindness. They have been your mother and father over and over since time immemorial.

These same beings are now tormented by innumerable types of suffering here in samsara. For this reason, you should clear away their suffering until there isn't a trace left, bringing them to a state of unsurpassed happiness. To do so, you need to sacrifice whatever may be helpful to them without reservation: your own body, the things you enjoy, and all of your basic virtues. You should enjoy and take delight in every form of austerity and suffering and take them up readily. The *Letter to a Student* states:

> Those close to you have slipped into the ocean of samsara.
> As if swept up in a wave, they move from birth to death.
> Not to recognize them and to leave them behind,
> Only liberating yourself, what could be more shameful?

As stated here, you should focus on eliminating any self-centered mindset, never casting aside the welfare of others or working only towards your own peace and happiness.

Aspiration Bodhichitta in Practice

The actual practice of developing bodhichitta has two parts: aspiration bodhichitta and application bodhichitta. What follows concerns the first of these. Though all phenomena are unreal, just like an illusion, sentient beings do not understand this. Instead, beings see phenomena as real and solid, which brings them the perpetual torment and intolerable sufferings of samsara. These same beings have been your own mother and father over and over again, since time immemorial. They have shown you nothing but kindness, bringing you all kinds of benefit and happiness and protecting you from anything that could cause harm or injury. With nothing but you in mind, they have even given up their own life countless times, all this just for your benefit!

Though these beings just want to be happy, they are not; and though they do not wish to suffer, they do. They don't know a thing about creating happiness or eliminating suffering. These are the ignorant creatures that need to be liberated from samsara and all the suffering it entails. "Right now I don't have the power to do this," you should think to yourself, "so I must attain buddhahood. Then I will have this power!" This is aspiration bodhichitta.

Application Bodhichitta in Practice

To put this into practice, think to yourself: "The victorious ones of the past and their heirs trained themselves thoroughly in the bodhisattva precepts. They practiced the discipline of restraining from committing negative actions, the discipline of gathering virtuous qualities and the discipline of working for the benefit of sentient beings. I will now do the same. I will bring all sentient beings happiness and its causes, the two accumulations, and free them from suffering and its causes, the two obscurations. Having done so, I will establish them in the state of perfect and complete buddhahood!" With this thought, make the following pledge:[35]

> Just as the blissful ones of the past
> Developed bodhichitta
> And trained step-by-step
> In the bodhisattva precepts,
> I, too, for the benefit of beings
> Will develop bodhichitta
> And train just as they did,
> One step at a time.

With this vow, you have developed bodhichitta just as the victorious ones of the past did. You have put it into practice. The next section addresses how this vow can be safeguarded from degeneration.

General Precepts of Bodhichitta

The general precepts related to aspiration and application bodhichitta include the following: You should take an interest in, and follow, a spiritual teacher. You should not break the lineal transmission of the Three Jewels, nor should you forsake sentient beings. Having developed bodhichitta, you should safeguard it from degeneration, reading writings found in the collected teachings of the bodhisattvas and maintaining a continual sense of conscientiousness. Though there are, in fact, an inconceivable number of precepts to be practiced, they can be condensed into three categories: (1) perfectly actualizing the qualities of a buddha, (2) completely maturing sentient beings, and (3) training in the totally pure buddha realms.

Precepts of Aspiration Bodhichitta

There are three groups of precepts associated specifically with aspiration bodhichitta: the three aspirations, giving up the four negative acts, and putting the four wholesome endeavors into practice. The first of the three aspirations is an aspiration involving the fruition, in which one thinks, "I will attain complete enlightenment so that I can benefit others!" The next aspiration concerns skillful means, where one thinks, "I will train on the levels and paths." The third aspiration relates to enlightened activity, in which case one thinks, "I will fulfill the wishes of every sentient being!"

You should also apply yourself assiduously to giving up the four negative acts, which are (1) deceiving your guru or someone who deserves your generosity, (2) slandering those who practice the Great Vehicle, (3) acting hypocritically towards any sentient being, and (4) regretting something that is not cause for regret.

The four wholesome endeavors are also to be practiced with great care. These are (1) to never tell a lie, even at the cost of your life; (2) to praise the bodhisattvas and regard them as your teachers; (3) to give up hypocrisy and keep an altruistic attitude; and (4) to help set those sentient beings who are in need of guidance on the virtuous path of the Great Vehicle.

Precepts of Application Bodhichitta

When it comes to the precepts of application bodhichitta, there are certain things that should be given up and others that should be put into practice. Of these, the first five are things that can easily happen to a king: (1) taking things that have been offered to the Three Jewels; (2) rejecting the sacred Dharma; (3) doing things that bring harm to fully ordained monks and nuns, such as depriving them of their monastic articles; (4) engaging in any one of the five acts of immediate retribution; and (5) engaging in vice, or encouraging another to do so, out of wrong view.

There are also five downfalls that can easily occur to ministers, the first four of which are similar to the first four of the preceding group, but with conquering towns and cities in place of wrong view. There are then, progressively, eight things that can easily befall the beginner and other such categories.[36] All of these should be given up. The elimination of these factors is what needs to be put into practice.

In terms of the degeneration of one's attempts to eliminate and practice these, and to safeguard the precepts, the most negative downfall is mentioned in the *Condensed Perfection of Knowledge*:

> If, for instance, one were to practice the ten virtuous activities for many eons
> And then develop the wish to become a solitary buddha or foe destroyer,
> It would be mistaken discipline, distorted discipline.
> Developing such a mindset is extremely negative, even more so than a fundamental downfall.

As shown above, the discipline of refraining from committing negative actions involves applying oneself with care to the mindset of giving up the main and subsidiary downfalls. Practicing to accumulate virtue, on the other hand, can be condensed into the six perfections and refers to the discipline of gathering virtuous qualities. The discipline of working for the benefit of sentient beings entails working for both their temporary and ultimate benefit and happiness. Apply yourself assiduously to these three forms of discipline.

The benefits associated with safeguarding these precepts are taught in the *Sutra Requested by Shri Datta*:

> If the merit associated with bodhichitta
> Were to take physical form,
> It would fill all of space,
> And even then could not be contained.

These are the bodhisattva precepts.

Samaya Vows

The Secret Mantra's samaya vows of the masters of awareness are twofold: those associated with maturing empowerments and those associated with liberating instructions. Generally speaking, there are a hundred thousand different categories of samaya, out of which there are twenty-five essential samaya vows. These, however, can be condensed even further into the three samayas of enlightened form, speech, and mind. As stated in the *Tantra of the Clear Expanse*:

All samayas are explained to be contained
In those of enlightened form, speech and mind.

Concerning the samaya of enlightened form, you should not act disrespectfully towards the vajra master, the buddhas, bodhisattvas, yidam deities, dakinis, your brothers and sisters, vajra siblings, nor towards any sentient being, the five elements, or your own body. You should also refrain from taking their lives, stealing from them, abusing them physically or verbally, and so on. You shouldn't have a distorted sense of pure view or do anything that involves vice or negativity. In fact, the environment and its inhabitants, both inside and out, as well as your own body, are all divine; they are all the yidam deity. For this reason, you should have unbiased pure view towards anything associated with enlightened form, as well as make prostrations and offerings, sing their praises, and do other such things.

Concerning the samaya of enlightened speech, you should not deviate from anything that the vajra master says, nor should you belittle the Buddhist scriptures, from those of the Buddha himself down to those written by ordinary people. You should also avoid being angry or harboring malice towards any word or sound, whether it comes from the elements or a living being. Instead, act with respect and devotion, thinking of every sound as the enlightened speech of all the buddhas.

When it comes to the samaya of the enlightened mind, you should eliminate every unvirtuous thought, to the point where such thoughts do not even arise for a moment. Without breaking the continuity of virtue and bodhichitta, benefit others to the best of your ability.

As part of the samaya of enlightened form, you should meditate on the development stage of the divine yidam deity; as part of the samaya of enlightened speech, never part from the recitation of mantras; and as part of the samaya of the enlightened mind, never stray from the cycle of the completion stage.

The temporary benefits of maintaining the samaya of enlightened form in this way are that your body will be free from illness and of benefit to sentient beings. You will be pleasing to the eye, and all who touch or see you will be set on the path of virtue. Ultimately, you will arrive at the vajra seat and benefit others wherever you happen to be. Once you die, you will work for the welfare of sentient beings with an infinite number of manifestations. Your form blazing with the marks and signs, you will gain mastery over the great, enlightened activities of the buddhas and work for the welfare of others.

If the samaya of enlightened form degenerates, the temporary results will be a short life and ill-health. All sorts of undesirable things will take place and those who see or touch you will be reborn in the lower realms. Ultimately, you will experience the inescapable physical sufferings of Vajra Hell.

The temporary benefits of maintaining the samaya of enlightened speech are that your speech will be pleasing and everyone will regard what you say as the truth. As a result, gods, spirits, and humans will do your bidding. You will understand the tantras, scriptures, and key instructions[37] and will be able to compose all manner of poetry and treatises, a multitude of dharma words having burst forth from your mind. All the malice and ill-will of those who listen to your speech will be pacified, all of your aims will be accomplished, and you will be liberated in one life. Ultimately, the emanations of your speech will carry out the welfare of beings and turn the wheel of the Dharma in a faultless manner.

If the samaya of enlightened speech degenerates, the temporary effects will be such that you will be in danger of contracting diseases of the tongue. Your slanderous remarks and harmful comments will harm both yourself and others, and all those who hear your words will have bad luck and be reborn in the lower realms. Ultimately, you will suffer from having five hundred ploughs run through your tongue.

The temporary benefit of maintaining the samaya of enlightened mind is that your mental emanations will tame beings. The concentration born in your own mind will naturally bring about a state of meditation in the minds of other beings. Wherever you happen to be, concentration will arise and the sentient beings in the area will be reborn in the Realm of Bliss. Ultimately, all sentient beings will be established in buddhahood and, inseparable from the vajra mind, they will transcend suffering.

If the samaya of enlightened mind degenerates, the temporary results will be that vice will cause harm to everyone, to both yourself and others. None of your aims will be accomplished. Instead, they will be ill-fated and illness, malicious forces, and depression will beset you. Ultimately, you will have no chance to escape the lower realms.

In short, when the vows associated with the maturing empowerments are present in one's state of being, the samaya vows need to be maintained. You should, therefore, turn away from all forms of vice and practice only virtue. In all the tantras of the Ancient Translation School, such as the *Array of Samayas Tantra*, the Secret Mantra's samaya vows of the masters of awareness are taught to be of primary importance.

There are, in fact, boundless classifications of these vows, including the hundred thousand classes of samaya. The presentation here has followed that found in the texts of Heart Essence of the Dakinis, where these classifications are presented in a condensed form.

The following liturgy contains a brief presentation of the three vows that need to be maintained:

> HO
> Just as the victors of the past kept their vows,
> I, too, will give up all violence,
> Practicing virtue in body, speech, and mind.

With these verses, which address the three vows in general, you are pledging to use your own three gates to keep your vows in the same way that the victorious ones of the past kept theirs.

> I will always keep and safeguard the vows
> Of the layman, novice, and fully ordained—
> All the vows of individual liberation.

These are the outer vows of individual liberation, which were explained briefly above. An extensive presentation of the vows that are to be maintained in this context can be found in the Vinaya scriptures.

The next passage concerns the inner precepts of the bodhisattva:

> Nor will I turn my back on
> The disciplines of restraint,
> Of gathering virtuous qualities
> And working for the benefit of others.

With this stanza, you vow never to abandon the three forms of discipline that were taught in detail above: the discipline of restraining from committing negative actions, the discipline of gathering virtuous qualities, and the discipline of working for the benefit of sentient beings.

The following passage covers the secret samaya vows of the masters of awareness, both general and specific.

> I accept, will not give up, and will practice each of the Three Jewels,
> And will not let go of my guru or my yidam deity.
> As the samaya of the Buddha, first among the Three Jewels,
> I will apply myself to the true, essential reality.
> As the samaya of sacred Dharma, second among the Three Jewels,
> I will distill the very essence of all the vehicles' teachings.
> As the samaya of the Sangha, the third and final Jewel,
> I will look upon reality; I will behold pure awareness.
> And as the samaya of the guru and the yidam deity,
> I will take my very own mind, my pure mind, as a witness.

Generally speaking, the Three Jewels should be regarded as the ultimate place to take refuge. As was taught in the section on taking refuge, your mind should be focused one-pointedly, with all your hopes and trust placed in their care. The gurus are a lamp that dispels the darkness of ignorance. As the guides who lead you along the path to liberation, they are your sole source of refuge and protection, from now until you attain enlightenment. For these reasons, you should act with unwavering faith, pure view and devotion, and engage in the approach and accomplishment of the divine yidam deity.

More specifically, as the samaya of the jewel of the Buddha, you should apply yourself to the true, essential reality. In other words, you should apply yourself to the ultimate ground, path, and fruition, rather than applying yourself to those of the Lesser Vehicle—those of the listeners and solitary buddhas—or to the inferior belief in the transitory collection and mistaken paths. As the samaya of the jewel of sacred Dharma, you should distill the essence of all the teachings of the various vehicles, including the Causal and Fruitional Vehicles, this essence being your very own mind. The scriptures state:

> The eighty-four-thousand approaches of the Dharma
> Are all included in bodhichitta.

The samaya of the jewel of the Sangha is to behold awareness in its natural state. Self-illuminating and naked, awareness is totally unfettered; it does not fall into any extreme whatsoever. It is also clear and nonconceptual, as it doesn't involve any fixation on nothingness or slipping into a nihilistic void. In this great realization, one settles naturally into a timeless state, free from the impurities of conceptual imputation. This is the reality that is beheld.

When it comes to the samaya of the guru and yidam deity, you should have sincere pure perception, bringing the approach and accomplishment of the yidam deity to a state of culmination. These are the most important of the three ways to not be ashamed of oneself. Hence, you should practice by taking your own pure mind as a witness.

Next are the samaya vows associated with the five buddha families:

> As the samaya of the vajra family,
> I will not abandon bodhichitta
> Or the mudras of vajra and bell.
> As the samaya of the jewel family,
> I will always be generous in the four ways.
> As the samaya of the lotus family,
> I will explain the teachings of the three yanas.
> As the samaya of the karma family,
> I will work for the welfare of beings.
> As the samaya of the buddha family,
> I will not lose sight of the three mandalas.
> As the Great Glorious One of the supreme family,
> I will keep the vajra samaya and will not waver!
> For the benefit of all sentient beings,
> May all my vows be totally pure!

The mudras of the vajra and bell symbolize the empty essence and compassion, the natural unity of skillful means and wisdom. As the samaya of Akshobya, you should never abandon holding the mudras of appearance and emptiness, nor should you give up the vast activities of the bodhisattvas. For the samaya of Ratnasambhava, you should continually engage in the four types of generosity: Dharmic generosity, the generosity of fearlessness, material generosity, and the generosity of love. As the samaya of Amitabha, you should explain the teachings of the three vehicles.

The *Sutra of the Condensed Realization* states:

> The vehicles of classes that lead away from the source [of suffering],
> The ascetics and those with transformative methods....

As implied in this passage, the vehicles that lead away from the source [of suffering] are those of the listeners, solitary buddhas, and bodhisattvas. The Ritualistic Vehicle of the Ascetics refers to the three outer traditions of the Mantra Vehicle—Kriya, Upa, and Yoga—while the Vehicle of Transformative Methods refers to the three inner traditions of Maha, Anu, and Ati. These should be explained to disciples in such a way that the teachings match the individual character of the student.

For the samaya of Amoghasiddhi, you should start by working for your own welfare until your practice has reached a state of fruition. From then on, you can work tirelessly for the welfare of beings with a positive and altruistic attitude. To this end, you may offer transmissions, empowerments, instructions, one-day vows, transference transmission, and so on—all the way down to refuge vows. You should do all this with a sense of indifference to material things, in other words, without being greedy or seeking profit. As the samaya of Vairochana, you should never lose sight of the three mandalas: the physical mandala of the deity, the verbal mandala of mantra, and the mental mandala of concentration.

To uphold and not to transgress any of the samayas associated with these five families is itself the supreme of all the families. By upholding the vajra samaya in which the vows are maintained from the very outset, the great maintaining of vows where there is nothing to maintain, your vows will become totally pure, just like the aspiration that was made for the welfare of sentient beings.

CHAPTER 4

The Suffering of Samsara & the Practice of Vajrasattva

—— The Suffering of Samsara ——

How to Listen to the Teachings

AGAIN, BEGIN by giving rise to supreme bodhichitta. Think to yourself, "For the welfare of all the infinite number of sentient beings, I must attain the precious state of perfect and complete buddhahood, the unsurpassed state of liberation and omniscience. To this end, I will listen to the various stages of these profound, clear, and unsurpassed teachings; I will do so in the right way and put them into practice!" With this motivation, listen well.

The *Precious Wish-fulfilling Treasury* states:

> When receiving teachings, the student should
> Eliminate any flaws and listen respectfully.

As shown here, when listening to the Dharma, you should eliminate the three flaws of the vessel, the six stains, and the thirty-six faults. Not listening to the Dharma is like pouring liquid on an overturned vessel—nothing will go in. On the other hand, if you listen to the Dharma but don't maintain a sense of mindfulness and familiarize yourself with what you've heard, it will be forgotten, just like pouring liquid into a vessel with holes and having it leak out the bottom. And finally, in the same way that ingesting poisoned liquid will make you sick, if you fall under the sway of the afflictions, your studies will just make you arrogant. Hence, you should eliminate any such flaws.

As written in the *Middle-length Perfection of Knowledge*, "Listen extremely well, keep the teachings in mind and I will teach you." This passage advises us to listen well, meaning we should be free from the afflictions. We are also to listen closely, unlike a vessel turned upside down, and also to keep the teachings in mind, like a vessel with no holes. The six stains are pride, lack of faith, disinterest, outer distraction, sleepiness and other forms of inward withdrawal, and not being motivated to study the teachings.

The thirty-six faults comprise six sets of six. The first set includes the six works of mara: (1) laziness, (2) indolence, (3) lack of faith in the Dharma and the guru, (4) not showing respect and reverence to the guru, (5) not keeping the teachings in mind, and (6) showing contempt for the ripening of karma.

The six acts that obscure are (1) great pride, (2) rejecting the Dharma, (3) listening to the teachings of non-Buddhists, (4) not studying the collected teachings of the bodhisattvas, (5) having misguided views about one's spiritual teacher, and (6) having misguided beliefs about the Dharma.

The six causes of abandoning the Dharma are (1) being hypocritical in thought or deed, (2) pridefully acting disrespectfully to the guru, (3) being disrespectful towards the Dharma out of doubt, (4) being hypocritical and having a misguided livelihood, (5) being disrespectful towards one's parents, scholars, or preceptors, and (6) being coarse, both mentally and physically, and consequently perpetually combative and argumentative.

The six faults that distract one from the Dharma are (1) engaging in many worldly activities, (2) having a great many material possessions, (3) having many pointless conversations, (4) surrounding oneself with friends and companions that are negative influences, (5) having many misguided ideas, and (6) being sickly and obstacle-ridden due to the influence of negative karma.

The six faults of the crooked are (1) not repaying the kindness of others and deceiving them, (2) practicing the Dharma out of attachment to gain and renown, (3) being envious or covetous towards the wealth of others, (4) not keeping the positive qualities of those who teach the Dharma in mind and seeking out those who are confused, (5) having faith in and serving a corrupt master, and (6) not seeking to develop the qualities of the Dharma but approaching the teachings in a merely intellectual manner.

The six factors that steer one away from the Great Vehicle are (1) not pursuing the collected teachings of the bodhisattvas but seeking out the miraculous powers of the non-Buddhists instead, (2) giving worldly counsel, (3) not pursuing an extensive education, (4) pursuing a merely theoretical education rather than total liberation, (5) desiring expertise in the sciences, and (6) not seeking out a spiritual teacher. You should eliminate these three flaws, six stains, and thirty-six faults and practice listening with positive qualities.

Contemplating the Suffering of Samsara

The teaching you are presently listening to concerns the necessity of understanding that samsara, by its very nature, involves suffering. As explained above, a human existence that possesses the freedoms and endowments is both rare and easily destroyed. In other words, we are mortal. Yet we do not just die; whatever positive and negative acts we happen to be engaging in right now will ripen later on, resulting in either pleasurable states or the lower realms. As written in the Vinaya teachings:

> Karma never goes to waste, not in a hundred eons.
> When conditions come together
> And the right time is found,
> Its result ripens in those with bodies.

Let's take an example. If you plant a grain of wheat, it will not ripen into barley, nor will you get wheat from a barley seed. In the same way, virtue and vice each have their particular result. The former leads to a birth in a pleasurable state, while the latter brings a birth in the lower realms. Cycling around and around like a water wheel, we do all sorts of things and then experience the consequences of our actions. By its very nature, suffering is boundless.

The omniscient lord of Dharma Longchenpa wrote:

> The impermanent phenomena of samsara's three realms
> Are utterly transitory and bring terrible suffering.
> Suffering, change and conditioning itself
> Plague all beings in the six cities.

The *Sutra of Advice to the King* states:

> Great king, this existence is transitory. This existence is impermanent. This existence is one of suffering.

As these passages point out, there are three types of suffering that torment the six classes of existence, drowning them in an ocean of suffering. These three are overt suffering, the suffering of change, and the suffering of conditioning. Even before our previous sufferings are over with, we are oppressed by even more—our sufferings are unbearable and endless. The *Jewel Garland* states:

> In every single direction, space, earth,
> Water, fire, and wind are boundless.
> The suffering of sentient beings
> Is held to be boundless in just the same way.

And:

> Suffering for just a moment is difficult to bear.
> Why even mention suffering for a long time?

The *Delineation of Karma* explains:

> Like a pit of fire, the sufferings of existence provide no respite.
> They are fearsome and terrible, like ferocious beasts, and filled with danger like a savage land.
> Like a dank royal dungeon, they are difficult to escape,
> And like waves in the ocean, they come over and over again.
> Like poisonous wolfsbane, they destroy the very life-force of the pleasurable states.

Falling under the sway of ignorance, we do not practice what is right, nor do we give up what is wrong. Though we just want to be happy, we don't practice the virtue that causes happiness, and though we don't want to suffer, we engage in vice with great urgency, despite the suffering it brings.

The causes of suffering are the three- or fivefold thoroughly afflictive poisons. Since these are what we are primarily caught up in, it is as though we rush straight towards and engage what characterizes the very source of our suffering. Consequently, we experience various forms of suffering, which characterize the result of our actions.

Still, even this does not alarm us. Eagerly we take up vice again and again, just like a criminal who, having already been punished by having had his hands cut off, steals again, only to be punished by being beheaded. As written in the *Way of the Bodhisattva*:

> Though we think we want to be rid of suffering,
> Suffering is exactly what we rush straight towards.
> And though we want to be happy, in our ignorance
> We destroy our own happiness like an enemy. [I.28]

How does this happen? It starts with our falling under the sway of attachment and clinging to the five desirable sense objects. This causes the afflictions to grow in strength and we end up suffering as a consequence. This can be likened to a moth attracted to the light of a butter lamp and then scorched in its flames; a deer killed as it listens to the sound of a flute; bees sucked into a flower and smothered when the flower closes up; a fish killed by a fisherman, seduced by the taste of the bait on his hook; and elephants who desire the cool sensation of a lake's waters and end up drowning. This is sung about in the *Treasury of Songs of Realization*:

> Everyone is seduced by the symbol of existence!

And:

> Alas, the Archer said,
> See the ignorant as you would
> A fish or butterfly,
> An elephant, bee, or deer.[38]

The afflictions arise from the five sense objects. Once under their power, we wander endlessly throughout samsara. This is said to be even more frightening than poison. The *Letter to a Student* states:

> Sense objects and poison alike are pleasant when first experienced,
> And sense objects and poison alike are unbearably harsh once their effects are felt.
> Sense objects and poison alike are taken in a dark state of ignorance
> And sense objects and poison alike are potent and difficult to reverse.

But when sense objects and poison are truly examined by the mind,
The effects of poison are seen to be relatively mild,
While objects are unbearable by their very nature.
Poison only lasts for a single life,
Whereas objects continue to poison us in other lives as well.
Poison can be pacified when mixed with another poison;
It can be neutralized with supreme secret mantra and antidotes.
When used skillfully, poison can even be of benefit to mankind.
Yet this is never the case with the great poison of sense objects.

In *Resting in the Nature of Mind,* Longchenpa explains the various existences through which we cycle and the suffering they entail:

Gods and demi-gods, hell beings, spirits, humans, and beasts—
We cycle throughout the six classes like buckets on a water wheel,
Experiencing an infinite number of sufferings along the way.

The *Jewel Garland* states:

Three paths—no beginning, middle, or end;
These causes and conditions,
In mutual succession, spin the wheel of life,
Like the ring of a firebrand.[39]

When we meet up with certain conditions as we cycle throughout samsara, we end up as loved ones, enemies, and those who are indifferent towards one another. In the process, we bring each other innumerable forms of happiness, pain, benefit, and harm. The number of times our friends have been our enemies, and our enemies our friends, is also beyond reckoning. Drimé Özer once wrote:

When you tally up your lives, you'll see that each and every being
Has shouldered the burden of being a loved one, an enemy, and
    someone in between.
They've brought you happiness and suffering countless times,
    benefit and harm as well;
Fathers can become mothers, mothers sisters,
And sisters sons... there's no way to tell,

Just as there's no way to know when a loved one will become your enemy.

And in the *Letter to a Friend*, it is written:

> Grow weary with samsara, the source of so many sufferings,
> For there you are sure to be bereft of all that you desire;
> You are sure to experience death, sickness, aging, and more.
> So please listen to its flaws, kind sir, as I explain a few.
>
> Fathers become sons, and mothers, wives.
> Enemies change to friends,
> And the reverse occurs as well—
> For nothing is ever certain in samsara!

Further, in *Resting in the Nature of Mind*, Longchenpa writes:

> As you ponder the karma of the worlds, past and present,
> You will become more and more saddened.
> All of the bodies you had while an insect, if gathered together,
> Would be even bigger than Mount Meru, made of four precious gems.
> The tears you've cried could not be contained even by the four oceans.
> The molten copper, pus, blood, and other foul liquids you've had to drink
> When your mind was in the form of a hell being and spirit
> Would not even be matched by the rivers flowing to the ends of the earth.
> The same goes for the others as well; they're incalculable like space.
> Even all the motes of dust on the earth wouldn't equal a fraction
> Of the number of times our desire has gotten our heads and limbs chopped off!

And in the *Application of Mindfulness*:

> O monks, you should be saddened by the nature of existence. Why, you ask? From time immemorial, you've been born as

insects over and over again, only to cast these bodies aside. If you were to gather all of these bodies together, the pile would be higher than Mount Meru, the king of mountains, and even more massive. The tears you've cried would exceed the water found in the four oceans. As a hell being and spirit, you've had to drink molten copper, blood, lymph, pus, and mucus an untold number of times, even more than the waters of the four massive rivers flowing from the four continents into the ocean. And the number of times your head, eyes, and limbs have been chopped off or ripped out because of your desires would be greater in number than the subtle particles of earth, water, fire, and air found in as many worlds as there are grains of sand in the river Ganges.

The *Letter to a Friend* states:

> Every one of us has drunk more milk
> Than all the four oceans could contain.
> And if we continue to follow the ways of ordinary beings,
> We samsaric creatures will have to drink yet more.
>
> The heap of bones each one of us has had
> Would be greater than even Mount Meru.
> And if you were to make small pellets, each the size of a berry,
> For each of your mothers, there would not be enough earth in all the world.

As we wander through dreamlike samsara, our dualistic fixation plunges us into the stream of suffering. The various forms suffering can take are explained by the omniscient Tsultrim Lodrö[40]:

> Alas, from the bounds of samsara, so difficult to measure,
> Those worn out on the path of existence suffer.
> No matter where they are born, there is no happiness.
> The results born of vice are intolerable.
> Like the mistaken perceptions experienced in a dream,
> By nature, the experiences of the six beings don't exist, yet appear.
> Their confused sufferings are too numerous to count.
> Listen, now, as I give a brief explanation according to the scriptures.

In *Untangling the Vinaya*, it is written:

> There are no pleasant smells in a sewer,
> Just as the six classes of existence are never content.
> There is no cool sensation in a pit of fire,
> And no joy to be had in any existence.

The Suffering of the Lower Realms
The suffering of hell

Out of all of samsara's six classes of existence, those in hell have the greatest suffering; they experience the full ripening of the predominantly negative actions they carried out in the past. Within hell, the suffering of those in the hot hells is explained first. The *Precious Wish-fulfilling Treasury* states:

> The suffering of the hell realms is incalculable.
> Those in the Reviving Hell stab each other with weapons.
> Experiencing unbearable suffering, they die and are reborn again
>   and again.

The realm mentioned here is the first of the Eight Hot Hells, the Reviving Hell. Those in this hell see one another as enemies. As their anger wells up, all sorts of weapons appear spontaneously in their hands and they stab each other and die. A voice then bellows from the sky, "Revive!" and they are immediately restored to their previous state, again doing nothing but killing each other and being reborn over and over again. The *Letter to a Friend* states:

> Even if you were stabbed violently
> With three hundred spears for an entire day,
> The suffering still would be nothing
> Compared to the sufferings in hell.

In the next group of hells, the suffering becomes progressively more intense by a factor of seven. The *Precious Wish-fulfilling Treasury* explains:

> Marked with black lines and cut with iron saws,
> Gathered together and crushed by mountains, in mortars and valleys,

Wailing and burned alive in a blazing iron vault,
Wailing intensely, burning alive in a two-tiered iron vault.

In the Black Line Hell, the body is marked with black lines and then cut into pieces with a blazing iron saw, only to be rejoined and dismembered again. In the Crushing Hell, blazing iron pestles descend from the sky, grinding beings to a pulp between mountains, as well as in mortars and valleys. Those in the Wailing Hell are burned alive in a blazing inferno inside a doorless iron building, while those in the Howling Hell are burned alive in a two-tiered iron building.

In the following passage, the omniscient lord of Dharma, Longchenpa, explains the next group of Hot Hells. Again, the suffering in each of these hells is seven times more intense than the last:

In the Inferno, the ground is a blazing pit of fire.
One's skin is flayed and the body crucified with stakes.
Those in the Great Inferno are tortured with flames, inside and out,
Their bodies reduced to ash by boiling molten copper.

First we have the Inferno, where the ground is iron and blazes with fire. The bodies of the beings in this hell are skinned, crucified with stakes, and beaten with hammers. In the Great Inferno, fire comes from every direction. From without, fire comes from the four directions and the eight intermediate points, as well as from above and below. From within, a mass of flames incinerates the hearts and lungs of the beings who live there. Not only that, these beings are also beaten with blazing iron hammers and have molten copper poured into their mouths, which they are powerless to stop. All this burns their bodies until there is nothing left but ash.

In the Hell of Incessant Torment, the suffering is seven times greater than all of the lower hells. The *Precious Wish-fulfilling Treasury* states:

Incessant torment in an intolerable, blazing iron building,
Beaten and thrashed, dismembered and ground to dust,
Boiled, stabbed, and bound with burning iron restraints...

With suffering even more intense than before, nothing can be done about the agonies experienced in the Hell of Incessant Torment. Those in this hell are trapped inside a blazing iron building, where, at the hands of the Lord of Death, they are beaten with clubs, chopped with axes, cut with saws, ground in mortars, boiled in massive copper cauldrons and pierced with spears, tridents, and other weapons; they are tied up and bound from head to toe with red-hot iron straps—the suffering there cannot be measured.

On the outskirts of this realm are Sixteen Neighboring Hells, four in each direction. The *Precious Wish-fulfilling Treasury* explains:

> Encircled in all directions by swamps of festering corpses,
> Unfordable rivers, razor-filled plains,
> Jungles where the leaves are swords and Shalma trees—
> The hell beings there experience all manner of suffering!

On the periphery of the Hell of Incessant Torment is a swamp of rotting corpses, filled with decomposing bodies. This is where those in the previous hells end up once the gates open and they manage to get out. There, a multitude of tiny insects with iron and copper beaks bore into them, devouring their flesh and bones.

On the off chance that they get the idea to escape and are able to get out, they end up in an unfordable river of burning embers where, as the *Way of the Bodhisattva* points out, their flesh and bones are incinerated:

> Those engulfed in the unfordable river, as though in a pit of fire,
> Have their flesh destroyed, their bones bleached the color of
>   jasmine flowers. [X.10]

Since the Lord of Death's henchmen appear and guard each bank of the river, there is no escape.

On the rare occasion that someone does manage to get out, they end up on a razor-filled plain. On this plain, their feet are sliced open when they step down and healed when lifted back up. In the jungle of swords, all the leaves and branches of the trees turn to swords and cut up the bodies of those who enter. On Shalmali Hill there are iron thorns that face downwards when one climbs up and upwards when going down. The beings there are eaten by dogs, birds of prey, and other creatures.

There are four such hells in each of the four directions. Together, they comprise the Sixteen Additional Neighboring Hells. In the *Application of Mindfulness*, it is said that the beings in these places suffer there for half an intermediate eon.

There are no definite locations or forms associated with the Ephemeral Hells. They can occur on mountains, in oceans, the atmosphere, houses, rocky peaks, and many other environments. In such places, beings experience suffering by being mistreated in the form of insects, or as rocks, wood, brooms, pots, tools, woven tents, and other things.

The life span of the various hell beings is explained in the *Precious Wish-fulfilling Treasury*:

> For those in the Reviving Hell and the rest of the first six hells,
> One day is the same as the entire life of a desire realm god,
> And they are said to live for so many of their own years.
> Those in the Blazing Hell live for half an intermediate eon,
> And those in the Hell of Incessant Torment, an entire intermediate eon.

Each of the levels discussed above has a life span related to those of the six classes of desire realm gods. In order, one day in the Reviving Hell and the next five hells equals an entire life in a corresponding heaven. These beings then live for a certain number of their own years. For example, five hundred years in the Heaven of the Four Great Kings equals one day in the Reviving Hell. The beings in that hell live for five hundred of their own years. Progressively, those in the next five hells live for periods of time that correspond to 1,000 years in the Heaven of Thirty-three; 2,000 years in the Heaven of Gemini[41]; 4,000 years in the Joyous Heaven; 8,000 years in the Heaven of Enjoyable Manifestations; and 16,000 years in the Heaven of Mastery over Others' Creations. In the Inferno, the life span is half an intermediate eon, while the life span of those in the Hell of Incessant Torment lasts an entire intermediate eon. The *Treasury of Higher Dharma* states:

> In the Reviving and rest of the six hells, progressively,
> One day equals an entire lifetime of the desire realm gods.

The Cold Hells are said to be in the same vicinity as the Hot Hells. The *Precious Wish-fulfilling Treasury* states:

> There are eight types of creatures that experience intense cold
> Due to a multitude of ice storms and blizzards:
> Those with blisters and burst blisters,

> Those who wail and groan, with teeth clenched shut,
> Cracked open like a lotus, an utpala, and a great lotus—
> Beset by cold, their suffering is boundless.

As shown in the passage above, there are eight types of beings who dwell in extremely frigid places, where they are frozen by ice storms and blizzards. In the Blistering Hell, the cold causes blisters the size of one's thumb to break out on the body, while in the Hell of Burst Blisters, those blisters break open and become wounds. In the Wailing Hell, beings wail, and in the Groaning Hell, nothing escapes their lips but groans. In the Hell of Clenched Teeth, no sound comes out at all. The body just stiffens up and the teeth clench shut. The Hell of Lotus-like Cracks sees the body crack into four pieces, while in the Hell of Utpala-like Cracks, these wounds come apart, turn inside out and are held together by thin ligaments. In the Hell of the Great Lotus-like Cracks, these cracks multiply, becoming sixteen, then thirty-two, and then even a hundred or a thousand.

Concerning the life span of these realms, it is said, "If there were a container filled with a hundred measures of sesame seeds and one seed were taken out every hundred years, the time it would take these seeds to run out would equal the life span of someone in the Blistering Hell. The life span of the rest of these hells increases by a factor of twenty." Thus, if you were to take a container that holds a hundred Kosala measures, fill it with sesame seeds, and then remove a single seed every hundred years, one lifetime in the Blistering Hell would elapse in the amount of time it takes the sesame seeds to run out. It is also believed that the life span in the rest of these hells becomes longer by a factor of twenty. As written in the *Treasury of Higher Dharma*:

> When one seed has been removed from a container
> Of mustard seeds every hundred years, and they run out,
> One lifetime in the Blistering Hell will have elapsed.
> The life spans of the rest are multiplied by twenty.

The suffering of spirits

The second lower realm is that of the spirits. The suffering of these beings is as follows. Most spirits live deep beneath the earth at a depth of more than five hundred leagues. Those that are scattered elsewhere pervade every land, mountain, and river. According to the *Application of Mindfulness*, there are six different types of spirits, which can be condensed into three categories: (1) spirits with external obscurations, (2) spirits with internal obscurations, and (3) spirits with obscurations related to food and drink.

First are those with external obscurations. The hunger and thirst that pains these beings causes their mouths to dry out and their bodies to become emaciated. Their necks and limbs are frail, and their hair matted. Though they race all around in their quest for food and drink, they don't find a thing. They may, for instance, see a pile of food, a river, or an orchard filled with fruit far off in the distance, but once they get there, the food disappears without a trace, rivers dry up or turn to pus and blood, and fruit trees end up being dried out, hollow stumps with no fruit at all. Even if this doesn't happen, these places can be guarded by hordes of weapon-wielding creatures. There are all sorts of sufferings they must endure.

Of those with internal obscurations, it is said:

> There are some who are plagued by hunger,
> With mouths no bigger than the eye of a needle
> And bellies as big as a mountain.
> They don't even have the strength
> To look for a bit of cast away, ordinary rubbish.

Those with internal obscurations can't get any food or drink into their mouths, even if they manage to find some. On the off chance that they do get some food in, it just falls into their mouths and stays there. Liquids are evaporated by the poison in their mouths; not even a little bit makes it down their throats. When it does, their stomachs are never filled. These are just some of the sufferings they experience while being unable to eat or drink.

There are others with obscurations related to food and drink. Whatever these spirits eat or drink turns into a blazing fire and incinerates their innards. Other spirits, so-called "filth eaters," subsist solely on excrement, pus, blood, saliva, mucus, and all sorts of other foul, stinking things. The poison, pits of fire, and other negative things they experience bring nothing but suffering.

Generally speaking, all of these spirits perpetually undergo the intolerable sufferings of hunger and thirst. Bereft of clothing, they are scorched by heat and frozen by the cold; the summer moon burns them, while they are chilled by the winter sun. In the summertime, rains of fire pour down from the clouds. They are constantly fatigued and worn out from their search for sustenance. Due to their weakened state, their bones and joints get dislocated. Blazing fires torment them and their mutual hostility drives them to bind and beat one another. They also fear for their lives and experience tremendous, unshakable fear due to their hunger. These are just some of the intense sufferings they experience, all of which continues for ages.

Concerning their individual life span, the *Treasury of Higher Dharma* states: "One month, a day—five hundred of these...." What this means is that for these beings, one day equals a human month, and they live for five hundred of their own years. According to the *Letter to a Friend*, "They do not die for five thousand years, some ten thousand." Hence, it is explained that some spirits have a life span of five thousand years, while others live to be ten thousand.

Greed is the cause of this variety of suffering, as is hindering others from being generous, and other such factors, so you should be focused and conscientious when it comes to such things.

The suffering of animals

This section discusses how to contemplate the suffering of the third of the three lower realms, that of animals. There are two sub-classifications of animals: those that live in the depths and those scattered elsewhere. Animals that dwell in the depths live in the great oceans. Without any place or abode they can go to for protection, these creatures are driven about by waves and wander aimlessly. They eat one another, too: the big ones swallow up the little ones, while the little ones bore into the big ones and eat their flesh.

The nagas also experience unbearable suffering. These serpent beings are scorched by a rain of burning sand each and every day and are eaten by garudas. In fact, they live in a constant state of fear, never knowing when an enemy might appear.

Those scattered elsewhere live in the human realm. Undomesticated animals live in a continual state of anxiety concerning the arrival of predators. As they are eaten by wild animals and birds of prey, and powerlessly killed by humans, they have no peace of mind. Domesticated animals, on the other hand, have their hair plucked out and their noses pierced through. They are beaten, goaded, and burdened with heavy loads. They are also killed for their flesh, blood, skin, and bones. Stupid and ignorant, they have no understanding of right and wrong. All of this brings them suffering.

They also suffer as those in hell and the spirit realms do—from factors like hunger, thirst, heat, cold, and fatigue. In the *Letter to a Friend,* Nagarjuna writes:

> Those born as animals are killed, bound, and beaten;
> They experience all manner of suffering.
> Those who abandon the virtue that brings peace
> Will end up eating one another, an intolerable state.
>
> Some will be killed for pearls or wool,
> For their flesh and blood, or for their skin and bones.
> Others will be enslaved against their will,
> Punched, kicked, and beaten with prods and hooks.

The life spans of animals vary. It is said that some animals live for an extremely long time, even an entire eon. Those with short lives, on the other hand, have no fixed life span.

When you contemplate the suffering of these negative states, imagine what it would be like to stick your finger in a fire for a whole day, to live naked inside an icy cave in the middle of winter, to be without food or drink for a few days, or just be bitten by a bee, louse, or flea. If these seem unbearable to you, how could you possibly tolerate the sufferings of hell, the spirit realm, or those of animals?

With this in mind, use your own present experience as a guide while you contemplate these sufferings. As fear develops, let this bring forth an intense feeling of disenchantment and renunciation. Then put your freedoms and endowments to good use!

The Suffering of the Higher Realms

Now we will discuss the beings in the three higher realms. When linked with merit, virtuous karma can be minor, moderate, or great. Respectively, these three result in births as humans, desire realm gods, and gods of the higher realms, as well as in the temporary pleasures these beings enjoy.

At this point, you might consider doing some practice that will bring a birth in the higher realms, since there is no happiness to be had in the lower realms. This, however, would be pointless. By its very nature, all of samsara involves suffering. Not only do those in the lower realms suffer, the nature of the higher realms involves suffering as well. There are three types of suffering in the higher realms: the suffering of humans, the suffering of demigods, and the suffering of gods.

The suffering of humans

Generally speaking, the birth process involves staying in the mother's womb for a set number of months, a dark and confined space where the foul smells and shifting temperatures are difficult to bear. The body then flips upside down and moves through the birth canal, as if being drawn through a narrow iron slit. The sensation feels like being whipped with a thorned switch. Once delivered, you suffer like a small bird being carried away by a hawk.

Later you will grow old. When you do, the color of the body will fade, as it takes on an unattractive greyish-blue hue. Your hair will turn white and the vividness of your senses will disappear. Your appearance will wane as well: your teeth will fall out, the body will hunch over, and your limbs will become crooked. The flesh will dry out and the skin will sag. Your face will fill up with wrinkles, too. As the body's strength will be in decline, it will be difficult just to stand up. You will move about unsteadily and be unable to sit up straight. Your speech will become unclear and the degeneration of your faculties will make your sight foggy and your ears deaf. Your capacity to enjoy anything will decay as well. If you eat too little, you'll go hungry; too much, and you won't be able to digest it. You won't enjoy anything, in fact. Everything will become unpalatable.

Sickness brings an infinite amount of suffering as well. Once the temporary circumstances brought about by your past karma have disturbed the elements,[42] you will be stricken with illness. Your body will be in pain and start to decay, and you will be powerless to eat or drink the things you used to enjoy, sleep when you want to, and so on. You will have to take unpalatable medicines and treatments, all the while suffering at the thought of your own death.

Once it comes time to die, no medicine, treatment, or ritual will do you any good. All the wealth, power, acquaintances, and friends you worked so hard to get will be left behind, and so will your beloved body. The time to die will arrive, with all the intense suffering death entails.

These four types of suffering are experienced by human beings in general. This isn't the whole story, though. There are also certain kinds of suffering that occur when these four are not so intense. Sometimes we throw away our lives just to get a bit of wealth, power, or some other form of pleasure and riches, for example. We put ourselves through all sorts of hardship. In the end, though, we don't always get what we want and this brings us suffering. We also suffer when we meet with unpleasant circumstances, such as heat and cold, hunger and thirst, illness, hostile forces, enemies, and robbers. Likewise do we suffer when we lose the wonderful things that bring us joy and happiness: our relatives, friends, acquaintances, and material possessions.

In brief, those with many possessions suffer from having to maintain all that they have, their suffering equal to the size of their retinue and their level of wealth. Poor folk, on the other hand, suffer from what they don't have. Even when they search for food, clothing, and the other necessities they desire, they don't find any. In the *Jataka Tales*, it is written:

> One is afflicted by taking care of things,
> A second, worn out by seeking them.
> Whether rich or poor,
> Happiness eventually disappears.

And in the *Four Hundred Stanzas*:

> Those in high positions suffer mentally,
> While for ordinary folk it comes from the body.
> Every day, our world is overwhelmed
> With these two kinds of suffering. [v. 33]

We need look no further than our own experience for examples of this kind of suffering.

The suffering of demi-gods

Once they see the glory and wealth of the gods, the demi-gods are overcome with jealousy. This brings them intense and unbearable agony. Occasionally they wage war with the gods, but because their merit and strength are inferior, the demi-gods are killed, beaten, dismembered, and torn to pieces, which again brings them intense suffering. At such times, the gods do not die unless they are decapitated or cut in half at the waist. They can recover even from a direct hit. The demi-gods, in contrast, are like humans; they die when a vital organ is struck. It is also said that the reflection of their deaths can be seen in the Ever-Radiant Lake, which is on the golden earth below their battlefields. The loved ones of those who die know what has happened even before they return from war, and this brings them great grief.

For the most part, the demi-gods are of a nonvirtuous bent and are not interested in the Dharma. The few who do take an interest, moreover, lack the karmic link for any particular realization due to the ripening of their obscurations.

The suffering of gods

There are two forms of suffering associated with the gods, that of the desire realm gods and that of the beings in the form and formless realms. Seduced by the sense pleasures they so heedlessly enjoy, the gods of the desire realm do not sense the onset of death. Once the time has come for them to die, their bodies take on an unattractive pallor, they no longer find their thrones enjoyable, their flower garlands rot, their clothes start to smell, and, unlike before, they sweat. These five omens occur over the course of seven days in the heavens. During this time, they experience an intense and extended form of suffering.[43] Their spouses and retinues abandon them as well. When they are in the presence of other gods, their suffering and depression grow even greater. In particular, they know that they have no choice but to let go of the glories and pleasures of the gods, to which they have grown so attached.

Once they die, the chances are almost nil that they will be reborn as a god again. Not many end up as humans, either. Most, in fact, are reborn in the lower realms, where they must undergo intolerable sufferings for ages. Knowing this, these gods also encounter the unbearable suffering of falling to lower states. In the *Application of Mindfulness*, it is written:

> Enormous suffering arises
> When they fall from the heavens.
> The sentient beings in hell
> Don't suffer even one sixteenth of this.

And in the *Letter to a Friend*:

> Even Indra, once praised by the world,
> Will fall to earth under the sway of karma.
> Even one who has ruled the universe as king
> Will become a slave among slaves in samsara.

There is further suffering when those with less merit behold the glorious sense pleasures of those whose merit is superior, which overwhelms them with grief, and also when the powerful drive the weak from their homes. In particular, those in the class of the Heaven of the Four Great Kings and those in the Heaven of the Thirty-three fight and quarrel with the demigods. They experience intense suffering as their bodies are cut and dismembered with weapons, bringing death and so on.

The second type of suffering concerns the form and formless realms, the two highest heavens. Overt suffering does not manifest in these realms. It is the nature of the suffering of conditioning alone that these beings have not transcended. As the beings there are intoxicated by states of meditative concentration, the positive qualities of ordinary beings do not develop in these realms. Once they've had a taste of a particular concentration, they become addicted to states that give them the same experience. Once these states of concentration deteriorate, they die. Beings who live in these realms are reborn in the desire realm once the karma that propelled them to the two higher realms runs out. There, their past karma prompts them to engage in worldly meditations. At the time, they may have some bliss-like experiences associated with concentrations of the formless realms, but since they have no mental stability, the karmic momentum of their defiled virtue will eventually run its course and they will once again plummet to the lower realms, just as an arrow shot up into the sky plummets back to earth. The *Letter to a Friend* states:

> Once the sheer joy of the desire realm's heavens
> And the dispassionate joy of Brahma have been yours,
> Once again you will be kindling for the fires of hell,
> Experiencing the continuous suffering of Incessant Torment.

Fire is always hot; it doesn't matter if it's big or small. Just so, samsara's three realms involve suffering by their very nature. This holds regardless of where you are born, whether high or low. Wherever you live will be a place of suffering, whoever you befriend, a friend in suffering, and whatever you enjoy, nothing more than the enjoyment of suffering. This can be understood from the following passage in the *Sublime Continuum*:

> Excrement does not have a pleasant smell,
> Nor do the five types of beings have pleasure.

Their suffering is continuous, like the sensation
Of fire, weapons, salt on a wound, and so on.

The Three Forms of Suffering

The next section concerns the nature of the three forms of suffering. From a general point of view, there are two forms of suffering in samsara, causal and resultant. The first of these involves negative activity, meaning engagements linked with a nonvirtuous intent. These may occur even when the surroundings and enjoyments of the gods and humans are present. The second refers to those in the lower realms and higher realms who are destitute, physically ill, mentally pained, and so on.

These sufferings can be condensed into three categories: overt suffering, the suffering of change, and the universal suffering of conditioning. The first of these includes all painful sensations, such as heat, cold, hunger, and thirst. An example would be the experience of having poison put on an open wound. The second relates primarily to humans and the gods of the desire realm. This involves all pleasurable sensations, from life and enjoyments up to the bliss experienced in states of absorption. An example of this form of suffering is sitting next to a fire when cold. The third is exemplified by someone with a sickness that makes them thirsty drinking saltwater. The basis for the first two forms of suffering is the aggregate of formative factors that perpetuate samsaric existence. This is the basis from which the entire range of suffering is produced, from which birth, aging, and all the other forms of suffering successively arise. The suffering of conditioning pertains primarily to the four absorptions and strikes only once one experiences nothing but a feeling of neutrality. This can be understood in relation to the following quote from the sutras: "It could be any kind of sensation—all are suffering." One should also know that so long as one isn't free from this form of suffering, neither will one be free of the other two, just as a tree won't fall down until its trunk is cut.

These three types of suffering—overt suffering, the suffering of change, and the suffering of conditioning—afflict us constantly. No matter where we are born, whether high or low, we experience nothing but suffering in samsara; this is its very nature. The *Application of Mindfulness* states:

Sentient beings in hell are laid to waste by fire,
And spirits laid to waste by hunger and thirst.

Animals are laid to waste by preying on one another,
While humans are laid to waste by the scarcity of basic necessities,
And gods are laid to waste by their own carelessness—
There is not even the slightest shred of happiness
To be had throughout the reaches of samsara.

For all these reasons, you should run away from samsara and all its suffering like a criminal escaping from prison. But to free yourself, you need a skillful method—you need to take up certain actions and consequences and reject others in the correct way. So confess the wrongdoing you've done in the past with an intense sense of regret, and vow to refrain from doing such things from now on!

The Meditation and Recitation of Vajrasattva

The unique experiences and realizations of this profound path can be obstructed by adverse circumstances, negativity, and obscurations. These factors must be purified if such experiences and realizations are to arise. The ritual that enacts this purification is a yogic practice involving the meditation and recitation of Vajrasattva, concerning which the *King of Tantras: the Supreme Empowerment of the Hundred Syllables of Vajrasattva* states:

> And Vajrasattva spoke:
>
> What I have uttered is the realization
> Of the oceans of pure realms and victors,
> The quintessence of the enlightened minds
> Of all the buddhas throughout the three times;
> It contains the blessings of them all.
>
> Behold, this quintessence of the teachers,
> The enlightened victors of the three times,
> Purges the ripening of the most heinous crimes,
> Not to mention ordinary forms of vice,
> And restores the vows of Secret Mantra.

Even those wracked by illness
Will surely be liberated from their suffering.
When contagious epidemics occur,
Visualize me clearly as the yidam deity,
Recite this essence, and you will remain unharmed.

When attacked with black magic and weapons,
Recite this essence and their course will be reversed.
When in pursuit of something and setting off on a path,
Recite this and you will surely be freed from the enemies you fear.

When terrorized by demons and harmed by evil spirits,
Recite this awareness and the demons will be expelled.
If some sentient being were to desire a son,
From this awareness he or she will surely get one.

Those disturbed, destitute, and impoverished,
In reciting this essence will find riches.
One who gathers a retinue, in reciting this,
Will gather the three realms around him.
The four activities will be accomplished for sure.

I have uttered one hundred syllables
That purify all degeneration and obscuration
And restore all kinds of violation.

And in the *Stainless Confession Tantra*:

> The so-called hundred-syllable mantra is the quintessence of all the blissful ones. It clears away all violations, cognitive obscurations, and other such factors.

At the conclusion of which, it is said:

> When this is recited one hundred and eight times in a single session, all violations will be repaired and one will be liberated from the lower realms. If a yogi takes it as his or her main practice and does this recitation, in that very life this yogi will be

looked upon as the supreme heir of all the buddhas throughout the three times and protected and nurtured as such. When that yogi dies as well, he or she will undoubtedly become the supreme heir of the blissful ones.

And in the *Tantra of the Hundred Syllables of Vajrasattva*:

> The hundred syllables
> Of the supreme enlightened mind
> Are like the sun in the midst of darkness—
> They manifest, and enlightenment is attained.
> They are open and boundless,
> Like the sky;
> And like a precious jewel,
> There is nothing that does not come from them;
> They are the perfection of all good qualities.
> Like the finest gold,
> They become whatever you make them.
> They are like a torch to darkness,
> And constellations reflected in the ocean.

As these passages show, the practice of Vajrasattva purifies obscurations through its unique blessings, power, and compassion. The actual method for this practice is as follows:

> **On the crown of my head a white lotus, upon it a moon disc seat**
> **With the syllable HUM at its center, from which Vajrasattva appears.**
> **He has one face and sits with crossed legs, white and brilliantly clear.**
> **He smiles, holding vajra and bell; his hair rests in a topknot.**
> **His body is adorned with jewels, and in three places, three syllables.**
> **Surrounded by the hundred-syllable mantra, and resting within his heart,**
> **Is a white HUM syllable, from which divine nectar descends.**
> **This nectar purifies all illness, and all negativity and obscurations.**

Visualize yourself in your ordinary form, a white lotus with a thousand petals on the crown of your head. On top of this lotus is a full moon disc, in the center of which is a white HUM syllable. Light radiates out from this syllable, makes offerings to realized beings, and brings benefit to sentient beings. Gathering back in, the light transforms into Vajrasattva, who is white in color, with one face, two hands and a smiling expression. Seated in the vajra posture, his right hand holds the vajra of empty awareness in front of his heart center; with his left, he holds the bell of empty appearance at his hip. His hair is in a topknot, adorned with jewel ornaments. Visualize him in the garb of a sambhogakaya buddha—wearing earrings, a necklace, armlets, bracelets, anklets, a long necklace, a silk shawl and lower garment, a silk scarf, and so on. At his crown, there should be a white sphere marked with the syllable OM; at his throat, the syllable AH on a red lotus; and in his heart center a vajra, at its center a white HUM syllable standing upright on a moon disc, encircled by the chain of one hundred syllables.

The power of support is to have taken the Three Jewels as your refuge and to have developed bodhichitta. The power of remorse is to generate a sense of regret concerning all the negativity and vice you've engaged in. The power of turning away from wrongdoing is to restrain your mind, thinking, "I will not do such things from now on, even if it costs me my life!" And the power of applying the antidote involves practicing the meditation and recitation of Vajrasattva as a remedy for what you've done in the past.

With these four powers present in their entirety, in both thought and deed, focus on the mantra chain at Vajrasattva's heart center, thinking to yourself, "O blessed one, glorious Vajrasattva, think of me!" Generate a sense of devotion so strong that tears well up in your eyes, and recite the following:

OM VAJRASATTVA SAMAYAM ANUPALAYA VAJRASATTVA TVENO PATISHTA DRIDHO ME BHAVA SUTOSHYO ME BHAVA SUPOSHYO ME BHAVA ANURAKTO ME BHAVA SARVA-SIDDHIM ME PRAYACCHA SARVA-KARMASU CHA ME CHITTAM SHREYAH KURU HUM HA HA HA HA HO BHAGAVAN SARVA-TATAGATA VAJRA MA ME MUNCHA VAJRI BHAVA MAHASAMAYASATTVA AH

OM VAJRASATTVA HUM

As you recite, visualize the mantra chain circling clockwise around the HUM syllable at Vajrasattva's heart center, white and swaying gently in the form of a string of light rays. Like a stream of milk, wisdom nectar descends from the HUM syllable and its mantra chain, filling Vajrasattva's entire body. It then flows downwards, entering the aperture of Brahma. This causes the entire range of impurities you've accumulated in all your lifetimes, from time immemorial up to the present day, to be expelled from your body. Visualize all of your negativity, obscurations, wrongdoings, and downfalls, in the form of sooty liquid, pus, blood, and so forth, being expelled from your sense doors and each of the pores of your skin, like hay carried away in a stream. As you imagine all this, recite the hundred-syllable mantra as many times as you can, whether that be a hundred, a thousand, or more.

Next, visualize the stream of nectar that rains down from Vajrasattva's body filling your own body to the brim, like a crystal vase filled with curd. Meditate that the light radiating out from the mantra chain and seed syllable at Vajrasattva's heart cleanses and purifies the negativity, obscurations, afflictions, and habitual patterns of the beings of the six classes of existence, as well as all their suffering. This brings all sentient beings to a state of happiness.

At the end of all this, Vajrasattva is pleased and smiles. "Fortunate child," he says, "all of your negativity, obscurations, misdeeds, and downfalls are now purified." With this, he grants you absolution, melts into light and dissolves into you. Finally, visualize yourself as Vajrasattva, empty yet visible like the reflection in a mirror, and keep your mind fixed on the visualization. When you're done, settle evenly into a state of inexpressible bliss-emptiness.

Confession

In conjunction with the preceding section, perform this confession from the *Stainless Confession Tantra*, which concerns entering the path of the various vehicles.

> **OM**
> **I and every being throughout the three realms**
> **Are produced from our attachment to objects, is it not?**
> **In dependence upon mother and father, we appear in form,**
> **And without control, we come to see this world.**

Young, immature, and ignorant, under the sway of stupidity
    we fall,
Not realizing the full import of engaging in virtue and vice.
Under the sway of desire, we wander through samsara,
And under the sway of anger, we engage in negative acts.
All this will cause us to fall down to the lower realms.
Now that I've thought this through, I take refuge in the
    Dharma!

Faithfully entering the gate of six times, the full and new moon,[44]
I accept temporal vows on the full moon, the new moon, and the
    eighth lunar day.
Though unaware of any faults that would cause these vows to
    be damaged,
As one who maintains the lay vows of the full and new moon,
I confess if my vows have been damaged and my precepts broken!

When my outlook evolves and I enter the gate
In which the twelve ascetic virtues are practiced,
I receive the vows of the listeners in the proper way,
Including the four roots and the six branches[45]
And the two hundred and fifty precepts.[46]
Though unaware of any faults that would damage these vows,
As a novice who maintains the rules of the listeners,
I confess if my vows have been damaged and my precepts broken!

When my outlook evolves further and I enter the gate
Where the twelve links of interdependent origination are
    practiced,
And I receive the vows of the solitary buddha in the proper way,
I must directly realize that samsara has no nature of its own
And know apparent existence to be like an illusion.
Though unaware of any faults that would damage these vows,
As one who maintains the vows of the solitary buddha,
I confess if my vows have been damaged and my precepts broken!

When my outlook evolves further and I enter the gate
Of the Great Vehicle, taking on the bodhisattva vows,

Those of aspiration and application, relative and ultimate bodhichitta,
Though I may not have done wrong in terms of the twenty vows,
And though unaware of any faults that would damage them,
As a fully ordained monastic keeping these vows, applying myself as I should,
I confess if my vows have been damaged and my precepts broken!

When my outlook evolves further,
I enter the gate of the threefold purity,[47]
Taking up the Kriya vows in the proper way—
Those concerning the Three Jewels and the vajra master,
My vajra relations and vajra siblings,
And the practice of mantra and mudra.
Though unaware of any faults that would damage these vows,
As a yogi who maintains the Kriya vows,
I confess if my vows have been damaged and my precepts broken!

When my outlook evolves further and I enter the gate
Of the view and conduct of Upaya, and receive its vows,
With mudra, mantra, and key instructions as the ends of practice,
Though unaware of any faults that would damage these vows,
As a yogi who maintains the Upa view and conduct,
I confess if my vows have been damaged and my precepts broken!

When my outlook evolves further and I enter the gate
Of the four mudras, taking up the Yoga vows in the proper way,
The Three Jewels and attendant bodhichitta,
The vajra master, vajra siblings, and relatives,
As well as any yogi who has obtained empowerment, are not to be shown disrespect,
And one's own symbolic mudra is always to be maintained.
Though unaware of any faults that would damage these vows,
As a yogi who maintains the vows of the Yoga tradition,
I confess if my vows have been damaged and my precepts broken!

When my outlook evolves further and I enter the gate
Of means and knowledge, taking up the Mahayoga vows,

All phenomena in samsara and nirvana
Are linked with the five male and five female buddhas.
This has been said by the victors to be the supreme vow.
Though unaware of any faults that would damage these vows,
As a yogi who upholds the Mahayoga tradition,
I confess if my vows have been damaged and my precepts broken!

When my outlook evolves further,
I enter the gate of the expanse and wisdom,
And take up the Anuyoga vows.
Here, all that appears and exists, inner and outer, and all the three times,
Are none other than the self-aware wisdom-expanse,
And one holds the mudras of the vajra and bell.
Though unaware of any faults that would damage these vows,
As a yogi who upholds the Anuyoga tradition,
I confess if my vows have been damaged and my precepts broken!

When my outlook evolves further and I enter the gate
Of the vehicle of the great universal presence,
I receive the four vows of Atiyoga:
The vows of nonexistence, openness,
Oneness, and spontaneous perfection.[48]
These vows, beyond number and limit,
Are supreme, as the victors have said;
Nonexistent, since there is no border between being kept and damaged;
Open, as they are free from grasper and grasped;
One, because everything is included in the mind;
Spontaneously perfect, since they are complete with nothing left out.
Though unaware of any faults that would damage these vows,
As a yogi who upholds the Atiyoga tradition,
I confess if my vows have been damaged and my precepts broken!

The points to be maintained of the three collections
Are to keep pure discipline—the culmination of the Vinaya,
Manifest freedom—the culmination of the Abhidharma,

And pure knowledge—the culmination of the sutras.
Towards the eight classes of gods and demons, and the protectors,[49]
I confess if my vows have been corrupted!

The three factors to be maintained in Kriya and the other two outer yogas
Are the three purities, the culmination of Kriya;
View and conduct, the culmination of Upa;[50]
And the visualization of the forms of the thirty deities, the culmination of Yoga.
To the Glorious Protector and the other oath-bound protectresses
I confess if I have corrupted my vows!

The factors to be maintained in each of the three yogas
Are, in Mahayoga, to maintain the main and subsidiary vows.
The goal of Anuyoga concerns accomplishment and the individual vows,
While in the Great Perfection there are four superior vows.
To the eight classes of inner and secret gods and demons,
I confess if my samaya vows have been damaged!

The three collections and two vehicles of characteristics,
The three outer Tantras of Capacity, Kriya and Yoga,
The three inner yogas, the Tantras of Skillful Means,
And the assembly of deities of the nine vehicles—
Towards a yogi whose practice links their view and conduct,
Why would the dakinis enact their punishment?
Why would the emanations of the Powerful One's enlightened mind appear?
Without rejecting cause and effect, I will take up virtue.
I will not engage in negativity and I will shy away from its ripening.
Without casting aside the precepts and treatises,
I will link tantra, transmission, and key instructions.
Without leaving them behind or letting them fade away,
I will put them into practice as taught.

> As a powerful yogi who meditates, practices, and engages
> The Secret Mantra teachings respectfully with body, speech, and mind,
> May all my broken and damaged vows be repaired!
> Please purify all breaches of the main and subsidiary vows,
> The coarse and the subtle, all the negativity I've committed,
> And all the other ways in which I've erred!
> Bestow the supreme and mundane spiritual attainments!
>
> Though the wisdom deities are not swayed by discursive thought,
> They are surrounded by oath-bound protectresses who are under their command.
> If I have done anything against their enlightened minds, may they tolerate my shortcomings!
> If there are any longstanding obscurations, may they be purified!
> If there are any current conditions or obstacles that stand in my way, reverse them,
> And bestow the supreme spiritual attainment of purity!

This confession, which relates to the practice of the various paths, is drawn from the *Stainless Confession Tantra*.

There are various vows that need to be maintained once one enters the gate of the Dharma.[51] These range from the eight temporary vows, restrictions related to the full moon, new moon, and eighth day of the lunar month, to the four root and eight subsidiary vows taken by lay people and novices. The two hundred and fifty precepts of the fully ordained monk are also included. Here, one confesses if one has erred or done wrong concerning any of these.

Next are the vows of the solitary buddhas, whose practice relates to the twelve links of interdependent origination. Once you have taken on the vows of a solitary buddha, you must realize that samsara has no inherent existence and that all that appears and exists is like an illusion. Again, here you confess if you have erred or done wrong concerning any of these vows.

The bodhisattva vows come next. When you enter the gate of the bodhisattvas you take on various vows. There are those associated with aspiration and application bodhichitta, the relative and the ultimate, and so on. There is also the discipline of refraining from engaging in negative actions, the discipline of gathering virtuous qualities, and the discipline of working for the benefit of sentient beings, as well as the discipline associated with the twenty vows. Here, you confess if you have erred or done wrong concerning any of these.

Next are the outer traditions of the Secret Mantra—the Tantras of Capacity. Once you've entered the gate of the first of these traditions, Kriya, you should engage in the threefold purity, regard the Three Jewels and the vajra master as your gurus, and maintain your vows towards your vajra and familial siblings in the appropriate way. Mantra, mudra, and concentration should also be safeguarded and not allowed to degenerate. Here, you confess if you have done wrong, erred, or gone against any of these principles.

The second of the outer tantras is the Vehicle of Upaya. Once you've entered this system, you need to put its view and conduct into practice, as well as the entire range of mudras, mantras, and key instructions. These all need to be internalized. Here, you confess if there are any flaws that have caused these to degenerate.

When you've entered the third of these traditions, the Yoga Vehicle, the relative truth, which encompasses all that appears and exists, needs to be purified within the state of the ultimate nature of mind. The path entails visualizing the divine mandala via the five manifestations of enlightenment and then invoking the wisdom being and dissolving it into yourself as the samaya being. In addition, your own symbolic mudra is always to be maintained. Here, you confess if these have been damaged and gone unnoticed.

The three inner tantric traditions of skillful means, the first of which is Mahayoga, are covered next. When you've entered this vehicle, you must maintain the vows associated with each of the five buddha families, with the knowledge that all the phenomena of samsara and nirvana are of the nature of the five male buddhas and five female buddhas. In other words, they are of the nature of skillful means and knowledge. Here, you confess if you haven't understood this and have engaged in wrongdoing as a result.

The second inner tantra is that of Anuyoga. Once you've entered this vehicle, you must realize that the expanse and awareness are beyond coming together or parting. Furthermore, you must also understand that all that appears and exists, the inner and outer—the entire range of phenomena of the past, present, and future—are all self-aware wisdom. The mudras of the vajra and bell must also be maintained at all times. If this hasn't been realized and these vows have been corrupted, here you confess.

Third is the tradition of Atiyoga, the Great Perfection. When you enter this vehicle, you leap directly into self-occurring wisdom. This wisdom has no sense of partiality or limitation; it is changeless, neither permanent nor nothing at all. All phenomena have been perfect from the very beginning within the enlightened mind. Hence, there is nothing to accept or reject when it comes to reality itself, nor is there any need for willful action—this is the great spontaneous presence of the three kayas.

Here, you come to a decisive experience that is beyond being labeled as ground, path, or fruition, in which you never separate from the fourth time, the cycle of reality. Through this, you become completely immersed in the great universal presence of reality itself, understanding once and for all that samsara and nirvana are nothing more than the mind. Since they are ineffable, permanence and nothingness are done away with. You will then come to see that whatever you meet, whatever you encounter, is liberated from the very start. With this newfound confidence, you will behold the self-manifestation of the dharmakaya directly and become firmly rooted in a realization that transcends the intellect and in which the phenomena of appearances and mind are exhausted. The subjective wisdom that realizes the object of reality itself will well forth. In the process, samsara and nirvana will awaken as the mandala of bodhichitta.

This is the vow that is maintained from the very outset—the great vow that requires no maintenance. The vows of nonexistence, openness, and oneness are perfected within the ground.[52] Beyond number and limit, and devoid of grasper and grasped, everything is included in mind alone. Without anything left out, it is spontaneously present. This "vow with no border" is the supreme vow of the victorious ones. Here, you confess if you haven't understood this and have entertained doubts or second thoughts.

Powerful yogis who have trained themselves well in these nine vehicles and have not done anything that goes against the vows of these traditions will never be tarnished by broken precepts, negativity, or faults.

If you are not inclined to recite this extensive confession liturgy, you can practice the following abbreviated version:

> **OM**
> **In the presence of my revered gurus**
> **I openly confess my lack of provisions and possessions.**
> **In the presence of the host of yidams and deities,**

> I openly confess my rejection and acceptance of direct realization.
> In the presence of the four classes of dakinis,
> I openly confess the oaths I've made that have been corrupted.
> In the presence of the Dharma protectors and protectresses,
> I openly confess delaying the torma offering for months and years.
> In the presence of all my parents throughout the three times,
> I openly confess not having repaid your kindness.
> In the presence of my Dharma siblings and relatives,
> I openly confess the lack of loving affection that I've pledged to have.
> In the presence of the beings of the six classes of existence,
> I openly confess my lack of compassion and altruism.
> The various vows of individual liberation,
> The precepts of the bodhisattvas,
> And the mantric precepts of the masters of awareness—
> All that is to be maintained, practiced, and realized—
> Where any of these have been corrupted, I openly confess.
> Without hiding or concealing anything, I will restrain myself from now on.
> Now that the negativity and obscurations accrued
> Throughout the three times have been openly confessed,
> Purify them and grant me enlightened form, speech, and mind,
> And all the other supreme and mundane spiritual attainments!

It is said that if you apply yourself diligently to purifying negativity and obscurations with the meditation and recitation of Vajrasattva, and you confess your past karma with an intense feeling of regret and remorse, your negativity and obscurations will be purified to the point where nothing at all remains. As written in the *Verses That Illuminate the Ultimate*:

> Since the obscurations are the relative itself,
> There is no question that they can be cleared away through purification.

You should apply yourself to this process until certain signs occur that indicate that your negativity and obscurations have been purified. The various signs that can take place include various [omens that occur in dreams]: that one has bathed, for example, or that pus, blood, insects, spiders, and scorpions emerge from one's body, that one has diarrhea or vomits, gets rid of old clothes and puts on new ones, climbs upwards, flies in the sky, or travels to a flower-filled isle.

CHAPTER 5

Liberation & the Mandala Offering

The Benefits of Liberation

ONCE AGAIN, orient yourself by thinking, "I must swiftly liberate every sentient being from the ocean of samsara's suffering, and bring them all to the omniscient state of perfect buddhahood. To do so, I will put these profound teachings into practice!" With this in mind, listen well and don't let yourself get distracted.

How to Listen to a Teaching

The *Precious Wish-fulfilling Treasury* teaches how one should go about listening to a teaching:

> Take the right approach when listening
> And study the Dharma with these thirty-six qualities:
> The six ways to have appreciation, including the thought of the
>   Jewel,
> The six austerities, such as tolerating the afflictions,
> The six ways to remain unchanged by circumstances, like pursuing
>   many teachings,
> The six objectives, such as generating compassion,
> The six necessities, including knowing the particulars,
> And the six things to seek, such as seeking the Dharma.

The first six are as follows:

> Think of the guru who teaches you the Dharma as a treasury of jewels, and the Dharma as a wish-fulfilling gem. Regard lis-

tening to the Dharma as an extremely rare opportunity. Hold memorizing and contemplating the Dharma in high regard and as something meaningful. Think of the precise realization of the Dharma as something very difficult to find and regard giving up the quest for the Dharma to be like giving up divine nectar and drinking poison in its place. Think of those who listen to and ponder the Dharma as individuals who are doing what is meaningful. This is the perspective you should cultivate.

Concerning the six austerities, the same text adds:

> Endure being afflicted by heat and cold for the sake of your spiritual teacher and the Dharma. Endure the afflictions of hunger and thirst, as well as those of ridicule and taunts. Endure being afflicted by fatigue and the work of sentient beings. Endure the afflictions of giving away certain things and seeking others. Value such endurance, even at the cost of your life.

And on the six armors that allow one to remain unchanged by circumstances:

> Do not let even a spear deter your exertion when it comes to teaching and earnestly pursuing the Dharma. Take hold of a great many teachings, comprehend the meaning of the Dharma, and put it into practice. Rely upon those who take this approach and show them great respect.

In the following passage, the same text explains the six special objectives:

> You should understand all the basic virtues, and with this understanding, put them into practice in the right way. Develop great compassion for sentient beings and take hold of the entire range of sacred Buddhist teachings. Do not break the lineage of the Three Jewels, and bring sentient beings to a state of complete maturation—these are the objectives you should have.

Another text explains how to accomplish the six necessities:

It is necessary to understand the details of the Buddha's teachings once you've heard them. With this knowledge, it is necessary to do nothing inappropriate. It is necessary to teach others in the same way, and having done so, it is necessary for both you and others to attain liberation. It is necessary to refine your knowledge, and also that of others. It is also necessary to cut through the doubt of those who come from the four directions. Apply yourself to studying in these six ways.

Concerning the six things to seek, it is said:

> Seek the Dharma sincerely, without guile or deceit. Do not seek for your own benefit, but for the welfare of all. Seek with the wish to eliminate the afflictions of beings, not out of desire for wealth and fame. Seek by practicing intelligently, not out of hypocrisy. Seek without any second thoughts, and in order to cut through the doubts of all. Seek to perfect the qualities of the buddhas, free from conceit and desire. You should seek earnestly in this way.

Listen well with these thirty-six qualities.

Contemplating the Benefits of Liberation

The particular teaching you will be listening to now concerns the benefits of liberation. Contemplate this topic and train your mind in the following way: Throughout your various lifetimes, from the furthest reaches of samsara down to the present, there isn't a single form of vice you haven't accumulated, nor is there a single form of suffering you haven't experienced. Furthermore, there isn't a single being in the lower realms whose form you have not taken. The fact of the matter is that you've been concerned solely with acts that bring suffering—think about the pointlessness of it all. With an intense sense of disenchantment, contemplate the great benefits involved in working to accomplish liberation and enlightenment. Keeping these in mind, put them into practice.

The *Precious Wish-fulfilling Treasury* explains further:

> Nirvana is liberation from samsara.
> The latter, as we have seen, is pointless,
> While nirvana is the unsurpassed cool nectar;
> It is peace and it is bliss.

As shown here, samsara will bring you nothing but grief. With all its faults, it is like a pit of fire—so difficult to escape. Nirvana, on the other hand, is like a cool, enchanting forest filled with peace and bliss. Possessed of the powers, fearlessnesses, and other excellent qualities, it is permanent and stable, and devoid of aging and death.[53] So leave samsara behind and venture forth to this sacred and wondrous place, where there are no obscurations. Then apply yourself to the methods that lead others there as well.

In this context, your attitude when practicing the Dharma should be such that you consider others more important than yourself. Keep your attitude directed towards benefiting both yourself and others, for it is said that producing the virtue associated with this unique mindset involves an inconceivable number of benefits and merits. The *Prayer of Noble Excellent Conduct* states:

> If faith arises just one time,
> An extraordinary amount of merit is involved.

The Pleasures of the Higher Realms

Virtue can be linked with either merit or liberation. When linked with merit, the result is the pleasure of the higher realms. If the virtue involved is slight, one will be reborn as an ordinary human. If moderate, one will take birth as a king or wealthy householder. And if a great deal of merit has been amassed, the result will be a birth as a spiritual individual or a universal emperor.

To elaborate, the status of a universal emperor comes about through the force of the merit one has amassed in the past; it is the highest position one can attain as a human being. The seven riches of royalty come about naturally through the force of this merit. With control over the four continents, jewels and sense pleasures virtually rain down. One's subjects and retinue will be protected from the pains of poverty, hunger, and thirst, and have the power and might associated with great wealth. This all comes about as the main outcome of having engaged in virtue in the past.

This also holds for the other beings in the higher realms. The life span, glorious riches, strength, and other qualities of the demi-gods rival those of the gods and wealth deities. These all result from practicing virtue. The demi-gods live on the slopes of Mount Meru, which stretch all the way down to the golden ground. One of their cities, called the "Golden City," can compete even with the city Beautiful to Behold in the Heaven of the Thirty-three. It has a wish-fulfilling tree, ponds of divine nectar, a gathering place for the demi-gods called "Excellent Wealth," the Wonderful Flat Rock, the elephant "Snow Mountain," pleasure groves, chariots and swift horses, war elephants that are difficult to withstand, and all sorts of spontaneously present pleasures and excellent enjoyments. Again, all of this comes about due to the strength of virtuous merit.

The first of the six classes of desire realm gods are the four great kings, who live on the four terraces of Mount Meru, where they are miraculously born. As soon as they are born, sense pleasures and desirable things spontaneously and naturally appear. On top of Mount Meru, in the Heaven of the Thirty-three, is the city Beautiful to Behold, the Mansion of Victory, and other celestial palaces. All of these arise naturally through the force of merit. The ground in these places is made of jewels. There are four groves there as well: the Grove of Chariots, the Grove of Coarseness, the Grove of Union, and the Grove of Delight. They have a wish-fulfilling tree, ponds of divine nectar and other sense pleasures and desirable things. The gods just have to think of these things and they appear. Indra and the thirty-two vassal kings, along with their divine offspring, live for one thousand of their own years in these heavens. This too arises from the excellent virtue such beings accumulated in the past. These realms comprise the pleasures of the gods and humans who live on earth.

Those who have amassed even more merit end up as one of the four classes of desire realm gods that live in space. The first of these live in the magnificently arrayed heaven Free from Strife, which is located in a realm adorned with the wish-granting tree known as "Transformed by the Mind." There, baby boys and girls are born miraculously on lotuses. It is called "Free from Strife" because these beings experience no hostility or strife with the demi-gods. Since boys and girls are born there simultaneously, it is also called the "Heaven of Twins." The gods there have only to think of sense pleasures and desirable things and they appear. This all comes about from gathering the accumulation of merit.

Above this is the Joyous Heaven, located in a place with a wish-granting tree known as "Beautiful to See." This is where the regent Maitreya resides, staying in a gathering place called "Excellent Dharma." In this joyful realm, the great mass of merit these gods have accumulated causes the sound of Dharma, sense pleasures, and desirable things to occur automatically.

Above the Joyous Heaven is the class of gods that live in the Heaven of Enjoyable Manifestations, a place beautified by the wish-granting tree called "Beautiful to Look Upon." These gods conjure up all sorts of desirable things with their minds—glorious pleasures and delights that are enjoyed by both themselves and others.

Above this heaven, in a place with the wish-fulfilling tree "Ornamented with Jewels," are the gods of the Heaven of Mastery over Others' Creations. These gods have truly excellent desirable qualities, which are superior to those possessed by others. The sense pleasures and desirable things experienced by all these beings result from the merit associated with the ten virtues. When either a slight, moderate or great amount of such merit has been amassed, the result is the attainment of the pleasures of the gods and humans of the desire realm.

When a great deal of merit related to the ten virtues has been amassed and linked with a state of absorption, one will be born as a god in the form or formless realms. Those in the first class of gods live in the seventeen form realms. Of these, there are three realms associated with the first absorption. In the space of Jewel Tingka is the Heaven of the Class of Brahma.[54] Above that, in the space of Samika, is the Heaven of Brahma's Priests. And above that, in the space of Kerudza, are the gods of the Heaven of the Great Brahman. These comprise the first absorption, in which the clinging related to the enjoyment of sense pleasures has been eliminated, and one dwells in a state of one-pointed absorption.

There are three levels in the second absorption. In the space of Glorious Jewels Blazing with Light is the Heaven of Faint Light. Above that, in the space Adorned with Kékéru, is the Heaven of Boundless Light. Above that, in the space of Shrikutra, is the Luminous Heaven. These are states where one experiences the bliss and joy of unwavering and perpetual concentration.

There are also three levels in the third absorption. The Heaven of Minor Virtue is located in the space of Jewel Tingkala. Above that, in the space of Indranila, is the Heaven of Boundless Virtue. And above that, in the space of the Sun Jewel, is the Heaven of Expansive Virtue. The experience in these states is one of bliss, clarity, and nonconceptuality, where even the comings and goings of the breath are not felt.

There are eight more levels in the fourth absorption. The first of these is the Cloudless Heaven, located in the space of Thick Masses of Clouds of Jewels. Above that, in the space Adorned with Kilaka, is the Heaven of Those Born of Merit. And above that, in the space of Pervasive Beauty, is the Heaven of Great Result. According to the scriptures, this fourth absorption is said to be the purest absorption.

Above these heavens are the pure realms of five deities who are extremely accustomed to states of absorption. In the space of the Palace with Tiers of Jewels and Crystal is the Inferior Heaven. Above that is the Unafflicted Heaven, in the space of Jeweled Anther Sprout. Above that, in the space of the Utterly Beautiful, is the Heaven of Magnificent Appearance. Above that, in the space of Adorned with Blue Jewels, is the Heaven of Great Knowledge. And above that, in the space Arrayed with Jewel Beads, are the gods of the Supreme Realm. These are also referred to as "noble abodes of spontaneous absorption."

All together, these are the seventeen form realms. The unwavering concentrations and boundless positive qualities found in these realms result from the elimination of vice and the practice of virtue.

Above these are the four formless spheres. In the space of the Manifestation of Great Clouds is the Sphere of Boundless Space. The beings in this realm remain in a state of meditative concentration for 20,000 great eons. Above that is the Sphere of Boundless Consciousness, in the space of the Projected Manifest Wheel. These beings stay in a state of meditative concentration until 40,000 great eons have elapsed. Above that, in the space of the Manifest Wheel is the Sphere of Total Nothingness, where beings dwell in a state of meditative concentration for 60,000 great eons. And above that is the Sphere of Neither Existence nor Nonexistence, in the space of Stacked Lotuses. In this realm, beings dwell in a state of meditative concentration for 80,000 great eons. This is known as "the Peak of Existence."

All together, the planes of existence listed here comprise the three realms, from the Hell of Incessant Torment up to the Peak of Existence. In these realms, beings experience either suffering or pleasure as the result of the specific karma they have accumulated. For this very reason, you should have confidence in the principle of karmic causality. The realms just discussed are the perfect and excellent pleasurable results that can be had within existence, the virtues of entering the higher realms.

Liberation

The second section concerns the vehicle linked with true goodness, liberation. At this point, I will just give a brief overview of the benefits of liberation. The superior mindset of the sages—those fit for the Great Vehicle and the tremendous wave of bodhisattva activity it entails—involves extricating the mind from samsara and developing the intent to practice for both one's own benefit and that of others. It is said that this attitude brings an incalculable number of benefits. In the *King of Samadhi Sutra*, it is written:

> The merit entailed in taking seven steps towards an isolated place with an interest in the selflessness of phenomena is even greater than setting every single sentient being throughout the three realms on the path of the ten virtues.

If, as stated here, just giving rise to this mindset entails such immense benefit, why even mention what wonderful qualities will result when one develops a positive attitude, meets with an extraordinary spiritual teacher, receives vows and then actually practices the teachings?

Those of us who enter the gate of the Dharma should make the three trainings the basis for our practice and commit ourselves to the four immeasurables. We should then apply ourselves assiduously to the ten virtues and the six perfections, holding both in great esteem. In doing so, we will amass an incalculable number of benefits. The master Shantideva said:

> The appearance of a tatagata,
> Faith, a human existence,
> And the chance to make a habit of practicing virtue—
> When will I come across such rare things? [IV.15]

Furthermore, rising above the sufferings of samsara, conquering the factors that conflict with liberation, overwhelming evil with one's majestic presence, possessing the seven riches of nobility and being worthy of the veneration of gods and men, being confident and learned in the fields of teaching, debate, and composition, possessing the ten powers and four forms of fearlessness, and, finally, obtaining the supreme form adorned with the marks and signs and reaching the state of perfect buddhahood—all of this comes about due to virtue and supreme concentration.

Even on a temporary level, virtue and supreme concentration lead to the eight mundane spiritual attainments. In particular, it is said that these two will give you the strength to work for the benefit of yourself and others, the excellent skills needed to ride the steed of bodhichitta from bliss to bliss, and either the primordial dharmakaya, the sambhogakaya, or at the very least, the nirmanakaya. The dharmakaya pervades all of samsara and nirvana; it is great bliss, present from the very beginning as the continuous cycle of eternity. The sambhogakaya is the great, unobstructed play [of the dharmakaya], present and unwavering throughout the three times. The nirmanakaya possesses the two forms of wisdom and works for the welfare of samsara's sentient beings without forsaking them.

There is no question that these come from applying oneself solely to the attainment of unsurpassed enlightenment. As written in the *Way of the Bodhisattva*:

> Virtue borne in mind
> Will bring great offerings
> In every place you go,
> As the reward that results from merit. [VII.42]

Hence, the state of a perfect tatagata will be actualized and, through this, its qualities attained.

Mandala Offering
Gathering the Accumulations

Fortunate individuals will take an interest in pursuing the sublime liberation outlined above, with total trust in the three forms of enlightenment. Once this has come to pass, the next step is to set about amassing the factors that cause liberation to take place: the accumulations. By training in this way, the qualities of enlightenment will become a reality.

The instructions on the practice of mandala offering facilitate gathering these accumulations. There are two kinds of mandala involved here, the mandala of accomplishment and the offering mandala. For the first, begin by setting out an extensive range of offerings, including a perfect and complete mandala arrangement and the three supports.[55] If this isn't possible, you can visualize the field of merit in the space before you: the gurus, buddhas, and the assembly of realized bodhisattvas, as well as yidam deities, warriors, dakinis, and dharma protectors and protectresses. Then take a mandala made of jewels or another material in hand, anoint it with scented water and the five substances that come from cows, and circle it holding a flower.[56] Next, recite the following while imagining the mandala to be the golden earth:[57]

OM VAJRA BHUMI AH HUM

Then visualize a range of iron mountains at its perimeter and say:

OM VAJRA REKHA AH HUM

At the center of a circle of iron mountains and the heaps of flowers that have been set down, visualize Mount Meru. With a heap of flowers placed for each, next follow the four continents, the subcontinents and so on, down to the banner of total victory. These steps comprise the thirty-seven-element mandala, a practice that, at present, is widely practiced in both the Nyingma and Sarma schools. Imagining every one of their forms, fill the mandala with all the enjoyable things of gods and humans, without leaving a single thing out. Imagine your own body, possessions, and all the virtue you've managed to amass throughout the three times and offer them all.

This is condensed even further in the following liturgy, "A Mandala Offering to the Three Kaya Guru":

OM AH HUM

> This jewel mandala, adorned with gold and turquoise,
> I offer to the compassionate nirmanakaya guru.
> The mandala of my own body, adorned with the sense faculties,
> I offer to the sambhogakaya guru.

> The mandala of the sphere of reality, adorned with my own awareness,
> I offer to the buddha, to the dharmakaya guru.

OM GURU RATNA MANDALA PUJA MEGHA SAMUDRA SPARANA SAMAYE AH HUM

Start out by offering jewels, gold, silver, copper, iron, turquoise, coral, vaidurya, pearls, precious wish-fulfilling jewels, and all the other material riches of mankind that you actually have. Next, imagine the various desirable possessions of the gods, serpent beings, powerful spirits, and wealth gods. With a pure and altruistic mindset, offer all this to the compassionate nirmanakaya guru, showing great respect via the three gates.

Next, offer your treasured illusory body to the sambhogakaya guru. This offering includes the essences of the four major elements and the beautiful flowers of the clear elements, sense fields, and aggregates, as well as the gates of the five sense faculties. Your limbs are the four continents, surrounded by the subcontinents. Your five chakras are Mount Meru, studded with five gems. Your heart is a wish-fulfilling jewel. Your head is a treasure vase, and the eight collections are eight offering goddesses, all dancing beautifully. Freely offer all this to the sambhogakaya guru.

Finally, offer the mandala of the total perfection of the three spheres. Here, the unconditioned sphere of reality is offered. All-pervasive and entirely beyond the relative, its nature is utterly pure and it is adorned with the four types of correctly discerning awareness: the bodhisattva's awareness of equality, the unsurpassed awareness of the nirmanakaya, the awareness of ignorance, and the awareness of the true nature. In an all-encompassing, non-referential state that transcends the intellect, offer this to the dharmakaya and the assembly of the ocean of wisdom.

As shown in the following quotation from the *Great Array*, the merit entailed in offering one's body, wealth, and basic virtues within the perfection of the three spheres is impossible to measure. It states:

> Offering a mandala with a totally pure mindset
> Entails an immeasurable amount of merit.

By making such an offering, the two accumulations are perfected and the two obscurations are purified. The purpose of this offering is to achieve the fruition that culminates from this process—the dharmakaya and rupakaya. *Reciting the Names of Manjushri* states:

> Possessing merit is the accumulation of merit;
> Wisdom, the great wellspring of wisdom;
> Possessing wisdom, one knows existence and nonexistence—
> Accumulating the two accumulations, the one who gathers.

As stated here, you must gather a great mass of merit, the cause [of liberation]. Doing so involves a vast number of benefits, both temporary and ultimate. The prophecy in the following passage from the *Sutra of a Boy's Prophecy* echoes this point:

> Once, when the Blessed One was residing in Shravasti, a young boy offered the Buddha two handfuls of dirt. "Through this merit," the Buddha said, "you will become an emperor with dominion over all Jambudvipa. You will erect ten million reliquaries for the tatagatas and then become a buddha yourself."

On the other hand, if you don't gather the accumulations and purify your obscurations, you will not realize true reality. The scriptures state:

> So long as the basic virtues are incomplete,
> Supreme emptiness will not be realized.

To traverse the path of the blissful ones of the past, diligently gather the accumulations with your three gates by engaging in practices such as the ten Dharma activities. *Key Instructions on All Dharma Activities, the Tantra of the Manifest Realization* states:

> The ten gateways to the Dharma
> Are to write down its words,
> Make offerings, be generous, listen,
> Read, memorize, explain, recite,
> Contemplate, and meditate on its meaning—
> This is the path traversed by our guides.

As shown here, when using the three gates to complete the two accumulations, you need to offer a mandala and the seven branches, as well as actual physical offerings and those you imagine. All this should be offered to the blissful ones, the victorious ones and their heirs, and to the gurus and assembly of mandala deities. The accumulation of merit is what causes the extraordinary accumulation of wisdom, so make these offerings constantly and diligently.

CHAPTER 6

Faith & Guru Yoga

Faith and Liberation

THE SIXTH SECTION involves contemplating the nature of faith and, in particular, how relying on faith will allow you to be liberated from the great ocean of samsaric suffering. For those of you who are now receiving guidance on the liberating instructions of the Secret Mantra Vajra Vehicle, there are three points you should be aware of concerning the way in which such teachings should be received: (1) the nature of the master who is giving the teachings, (2) the nature of the student who is receiving them, and (3) certain traits that are needed by both.

The Nature of the Teacher

Concerning the first of these, the *Ornament of the Sutras* states:

> Follow spiritual teachers who are restrained, subdued, and entirely at peace,
> Who have superior qualities, diligence, and a wealth of scriptural knowledge,
> Those who have realized the basic nature and are skilled in teaching it to others,
> Teachers who are the very embodiment of love, those who do not grow weary.

As shown here, teachers should be peaceful and well restrained in body, speech, and mind. They should have many positive qualities, great diligence, and be learned, particularly when it comes to Buddhist scripture.

They should also be skilled in teaching profound topics. Their compassion should be great, and they should be able to tolerate difficulties for the sake of teaching the Dharma.

The Nature of the Student

As for the students, those who receive teachings should have a keen interest in the Dharma and their guru and should be enthusiastic and greatly respectful to both. This will enable them to practice the Dharma. The master Shakyaprabha said:

> Teach well those with these qualities:
> Respect for their gurus,
> Pure discipline, concentration,
> Diligence in recitation,
> Absorption, restraint, patience,
> And diligence in observing the vows.

As a student with these characteristics, you should do your best to remain untainted by negative factors, such as the faults of the vessel and the six stains. Instead, cultivate a sense of delight, respect, and faith, while eliminating sleepiness, dullness, and the other factors that obscure, as well as pride and the other afflictions. Move beyond negative mindsets that are tainted by fixating on this life alone, and focus solely on liberation.

A unique type of sincere interest and motivation must be developed in this context. Think to yourself, "I will listen to this teaching for the benefit of all sentient beings and in such a way that it benefits my mind!" When receiving teachings with this motivation, whatever studies you engage in will be immaculate and brilliant. Furthermore, since the first step in making the Dharma your path is to study, you must do so correctly. For this reason, these points are extremely important.

As written in the *Sutra That Condenses the Precious Qualities of Realized Beings*:

> Someone with a firmly established sense of delight, respect, and faith,
> Who has cleared away obscurations and afflictions and moved beyond impurity,

Who works for the welfare of others and perfects knowledge with certainty,
Someone who works in these areas with confidence—listen to such a person.

Qualities Needed by Both Teacher and Student

Next are the qualities needed by teacher and student alike. At the outset, bodhichitta should be developed by thinking to yourself, "I will attain enlightenment for the welfare of all sentient beings. To this end, I will apply myself to explaining (or listening) to the Dharma." The master should then visualize him- or herself as the primary figure of all the various classes and mandalas, the sovereign and primordial protector Samantabhadra. Students should visualize themselves as either Manjushri or Tara. Next, imagine the light of the Dharma radiating out from the mouth of the teacher and into the ears of the students, dissolving into them. Finally, both the teacher and those receiving the teachings should remain undistracted from the words of the Dharma and their meaning and listen one-pointedly.

All six perfections are present when a teacher teaches: giving a clear explanation is generosity; restraining the afflictions is discipline; being free from any sense of difficulty while teaching is patience; applying oneself to the explanation is diligence; remaining undistracted is absorption; clarifying the words of the teachings and their meaning is knowledge.

These six are also present for the students receiving the teachings: Offering a seat and mandala is generosity; keeping the area clean and restraining one's behavior is discipline; not harming any sentient being or showing malice towards them is patience; supplicating to understand the meaning of the teaching is diligence; grasping the instructions without being distracted is absorption, and asking questions to clear up doubts is knowledge. Hence, the very nature of these activities entails six perfections, or six aspects.

The benefits of explaining and listening to the Dharma are as follows: those who expound the genuine Dharma as just explained will reap the benefits associated with the generosity of giving the Dharma, the most exalted form of generosity. In all their lives, they will come to possess a treasury of teachings. The tatagatas and their heirs will be aware of them and they will always remember their past lives. Not only will they hear teachings directly from the buddhas, they will quickly attain Buddhahood themselves. These are just some of the benefits.

By receiving teachings, the obscurations of the mind will be purified and the bonds of doubt severed. One will never be apart from the sacred Dharma and will attain the ability to perfectly retain the teachings. One will no longer fall to the lower realms and will be protected by the gods. In addition to having few illnesses and adversities, buddhahood will be attained swiftly. Again, these are just some of the benefits.

As indicated in the following passage from the *Supreme Continuum*, attaining the eye of knowledge leads to the transcendence of samsara:

> Knowledge is supreme.
> And since study is its basis,
> Study is supreme as well.

And in the *Condensed Perfection of Knowledge*:

> With knowledge, one will come to know the nature of phenomena.
> This, in turn, will bring the swift transcendence of all three realms.

As stated here, explanation and study are the sole source of the Dharma. For this reason, you should be diligent in these two endeavors.

Faith

The particular teaching that concerns us here involves the great importance of contemplating the nature of faith—the root of all Dharmas—and progressing along the path having done so. The *Jewel Garland* states:

> Due to faith, one practices the Dharma,
> And due to knowledge, one truly knows.
> Of these two, knowledge is paramount,
> While faith is its prerequisite.

The *Heap of Jewels* explains:

> For those without faith,
> Positive qualities do not occur,

> Just as a green sprout won't bud
> From a seed burnt by fire.

And the *Supreme Continuum* says:

> The innate ultimate
> Is realized through faith.

Now we will go into more detail about the nature of faith. In essence, faith is an extremely lucid state of mind. It is a state of mind that engages an object that should be taken up or rejected by either engaging it or turning away.

The various types of faith are discussed in the following quote from the *Precious Wish-fulfilling Treasury*:

> With inspired faith, one either takes up or rejects causes and results.
> With interested faith, the mind earnestly engages the supreme object.
> With respectful faith, one is perfectly conscientious.
> With lucid faith, the mind beholds qualities with total lucidity.
> With the faith of conviction, doubts about the Dharma come to an end.
> With the faith of mental certainty, one has great faith
> In the supreme dharmas of study, contemplation, and meditation.

As stated here, there are six kinds of faith: (1) inspired faith, (2) interested faith, (3) respectful faith, (4) lucid faith, (5) the faith of conviction, and (6) the faith of mental certainty. Aside from being a more condensed presentation, there is no difference between the three kinds of faith and the six listed here. Interested, respectful, and lucid faith are all included in lucid faith. Inspired faith and the faith of conviction are included in the faith of conviction. The faith of mental certainty is synonymous with inspired faith because it involves the wish to cast aside suffering and its source and to attain liberation by correctly entering into the path of cessation, the true nature of phenomena.

The first of these six types is inspired faith. Inspired faith involves the wish to engage and abandon samsara and nirvana, and the subsequent joy one takes in wholesome activities. With this wish, one hopes to eliminate samsaric suffering and attain the liberation of enlightenment, as well as to engage the factors that cause these two. In the same way that someone who desires wealth hankers after money, with inspired faith, one wishes to seek out the Dharma. In other words, one desires to cast aside suffering and its source, and to enter into the path and cessation.

The signs that one is fully present to the significance of this form of faith are that one no longer takes any interest in worldly activities but instead pays attention solely to study and contemplation. As stated in the *Jewel Lamp Sutra*:

> Developing faith is the prerequisite, like a mother.
> It safeguards all positive qualities and causes them to develop.
> It clears away doubt and delivers one from the stream.
> Faith is what characterizes the city of happiness and goodness.

Interested faith entails a sense of complete delight concerning the guru and the Three Jewels, as well as an interest in engaging these objects and relying on a guru. One is interested in accomplishing buddhahood, taking the Dharma as one's path, and having the Sangha as one's companion. One engages these factors like a child following after its mother. As a sign that interested faith has taken birth in one's mind, when one sees, hears, or just remembers the precious guru who set one on the path to liberation, one will be deeply moved and supplicate him or her.

Listing its benefits, the *Jewel Lamp Sutra* states:

> If one has faith in the Buddha and Dharma,
> Is faithful towards the activities of the Buddha's heirs,
> And has faith in unsurpassed enlightenment,
> The mindset of a great being has taken birth.

In the *Sutra of the Inconceivable Secret*, it is written:

> When one has faith, the buddhas will be seen, the Dharma heard, and one will pay respect to the Sangha. One will not decline from this state and will never be apart from these, no matter where one is born.

Respectful faith is based on a lucid frame of mind and involves being conscientious and industrious, as well as physically, verbally, and mentally respectful towards one's spiritual elders. Being physically respectful entails circumambulation, making prostrations, and other forms of disciplined behavior. Verbal respect involves offering praises and speaking respectfully. With mental respect, one sees someone or something as being worthy of receiving offerings and then acts accordingly. Just as subjects venerate their king, one is diligent and acts with decorum. As a sign that this has taken birth in your being, you will be free from any expression of pride or conceit when in the presence of a spiritual elder.

Explaining the benefits of this form of faith, the *Jewel Lamp Sutra* states:

> It eliminates pride and is the root of respect.
> Faith gathers in basic virtues as if by hand.

And further, again from the *Jewel Lamp Sutra*:

> With persistent conscientiousness, restrain the sense gates, calm your mind and safeguard the minds of others as well. When consistently pursuing the Dharma with such faith and conscientiousness, there will be no danger of falling to the lower realms.

Lucid faith is directed towards the positive qualities of one's superiors. With great faith in these objects, one has a sense of clear delight, while at the same time remaining untainted by guile or deceit. "Lucid" refers to this type of vivid presence. Lucid faith has three aspects: that which concerns the apparent, relative side of virtue, that which concerns the virtue related to ultimate knowledge, and that which concerns the union of these two, the virtue of equality. Just as a ketaka gem can clear murky water, lucid faith clears away all negative mental activity. As a sign that this form of faith has taken root, one will take great delight in virtuous endeavors and no longer become involved with negativity, whether physically, mentally, or verbally. The *Jewel Lamp Sutra* explains its benefits:

> Faith creates great joy in the teachings of the victorious ones.
> Faith is what characterizes the city of happiness and goodness.
> Faith pervades all positive qualities and wisdoms.

With the faith of conviction, one will have no doubt concerning the dharmas of the ground, path, and fruition. With a correct understanding of the words of the scriptures and the logical proofs that elucidate the meaning of the ground, path, and fruition, and with a correct understanding of their actual meaning, one will engage them accordingly. This is the faith of conviction. It also involves conviction in the causes and results of samsara as factors that need to be eliminated, and in the causes and results of nirvana as factors that need to be taken up. With the faith of conviction, one is also convinced of the pointlessness of neutral activity. Engaging in virtue in this way is like engaging in farm work with the conviction that one will be able to reap the harvest of one's labors the following fall. The sign that the faith of conviction has taken birth in one's being is a sense of certainty, a conviction in the Buddha as one's teacher, in the sacred Dharma of the Great and Lesser Vehicles as the teachings, and in the two Sanghas as the retinue, as well as in the representations of these three. Its benefits are cited in the *Jewel Lamp Sutra*:

> Faith clarifies and sharpens the faculties.
> Others will not create difficulties for those with the strength of faith.
> It is the basis for the elimination of afflictions.

And in the collected teachings of the bodhisattvas:

> Faith is the desire to listen to the sacred Dharma,
> And conviction in karma and its ripening.
> Rely upon this and take delight in it.

The faith of mental certainty concerns the profound Dharma and has three aspects. It is the desire for the definitive meaning, the nature of reality. It also entails settling into the state that ensues once this has been perceived. Finally, it involves studying, contemplating, and meditating on the scriptures that teach this nature. With this kind of faith, one holds true reality in great esteem, just as if one had found gold beneath the earth. As a sign that this has taken birth, one will be driven to practice day and night. Concerning its benefits, the *Jewel Lamp Sutra* states:

> Faith is what brings the attainment of buddhahood.

And in the *Noble Chandragarbha Sutra*:

> The faith of mental certainty in the Three Jewels
> Is like a wish-fulfilling gem.

Explaining the nature of those who have this kind of faith, the *Precious Wish-fulfilling Treasury* states:

> By nature, faith is like fertile earth—it is the basis for all positive qualities
> And is what causes the accumulation of virtue to develop.
> Like a ship, faith delivers one from the ocean of existence.
> Like an escort, it protects one from the demons and afflictions.
> Like a mount, it takes one to the sanctuary of liberation.
> Like the king of gems, it fulfills all wishes.
> Like a warrior, it overwhelms all those with ill intent.
> It is the supreme treasure of all the sacred accumulations.

As written here, like fertile earth, faith allows the sprout of enlightenment to grow and flourish. The *Jewel Lamp Sutra* states:

> Like a fresh seed, faith causes qualities
> To grow in the field of enlightenment.
> With faith, seek out the qualities that are innate.

Like an oceangoing vessel, faith delivers one from the ocean of samsara. As written in the *Sutra of the Ten Dharmas*:

> Led by renunciation,
> Faith is the supreme vehicle.
> For this reason, intelligent people
> Adhere closely to faith.

Like a good escort, faith protects one from the enemy of the afflictions. The *Sutra of the Inconceivable Secret* states:

> Those with faith are born in the presence of the buddhas. Seeking out all that is virtuous, they take no interest in families, wives,

daughters, sons, and other such things. Even when young, they are uninterested in worldly love. Instead, with faith they take ordination and follow a spiritual teacher. With a virtuous mindset, they study and practice the Dharma assiduously, making it meaningful and not leaving it as mere words. They exert themselves and study widely. They do not regard the teachings they have received with a frivolous attitude but compassionately teach others what they have learned.

Like a good mount, faith takes one to the sanctuary of liberation. In the *Jewel Lamp Sutra*, it is written:

> With faith, one abandons restrictive situations
> And encounters supreme freedoms.
> With faith, one is able to transcend evil paths.
> It is the specific avenue to wisdom and that which makes it grow;
> It shows the way to the supreme path of liberation.

Since faith fulfills one's desires, it is like a precious gem. The same text states:

> Faith is a treasure, a gem, the supreme of all there is.
> It is the factor that causes one to delight in giving.
> Like a wish-fulfilling jewel, faith fulfills all needs.

Like a warrior, faith annihilates negativity. The *Sutra Requested by Sagaramati* states:

> With faith, one has the strength of sincere interest in the Buddha and so forth, the strength of practicing with conviction in the ripening of karma, the strength of not casting away bodhichitta, and the strength of stabilizing one's practice of the yidam deity. Finally, with faith, one abandons all forms of negativity and has the strength to endure all forms of harm.

If, as stated here, faith is able to eliminate states of restriction and to gather in virtue, people who have such faith are especially noble individuals and very rare. The same text states:

With faith, one will remain detached towards that which arouses passion.
It eliminates restricted states and provides the supreme opportunity.
Faith is what brings the attainment of the state of the victorious ones.
Those with faith in such qualities are rare amongst the masses of ordinary beings.

For these reasons, faith is the foremost of the seven riches. As written in the *Sutra of the Inconceivable Secret:*

> With faith, lucidity, sincere interest, and a clear mind, one will have no doubts, hesitations, or second thoughts about karma and its ripening. With sincere interest, realization, and conviction, one will know that virtuous and nonvirtuous karma ripens and does not just disappear. With this knowledge, one will not engage in negativity, even at the cost of one's own life. Instead, one will engage in the tenfold path of virtuous activity. By being generous, one will gain wealth. By being disciplined, one will be reborn in the higher realms. By studying, one will become intelligent, and with meditation, all positive qualities will develop.

For those without the good fortune to connect with the Dharma and who don't have even the slightest trace of faith, there will be innumerable problems. In brief, like the impossibility of a boulder rising to the surface of the ocean, without faith you will never arrive on the high ground of liberation. Just as a ferry with no ferryman will not be able to ford a river, without faith you won't be able to cross over the river of existence. In the same way that someone whose arms have been amputated may visit a jewel isle yet still be unable to take advantage of its riches, without faith it will be impossible to incorporate any positive qualities into your own state of being. Just as a burnt seed will produce no sprout, without faith the sprout of enlightenment will never arise. Like a blind man in a temple, if you have no faith you will never see the light of the Dharma. Like a clever man falling into the pit of samsara, without faith whatever you do will end up as a samsaric activity. In short, the problem with having no faith is that attaining the enlightenment of liberation will be impossible. As written in the *Sutra of the Ten Dharmas:*

> Wholesome qualities do not occur
> In those who have no faith.

As shown here, not having faith is a great loss, so it must be developed.

There are various objects that can serve as a basis for developing faith. Inspired faith develops by seeing the nature of samsara. Interested faith will take root once one grows weary of friends who have a negative influence. Respectful faith grows from the extraordinary support of the Jewels. Lucid faith develops from the support of the supreme object and [hearing inspiring] stories. The faith of conviction grows out of hearing about the principle of causality. The faith of contemplating the Dharma comes from hearing of the profound. Since it arises based on these objects, you must develop faith by making these factors your focal point. In the collected teachings of the bodhisattvas, it is written:

> What we refer to as "having faith" means having great faith in that which is superior; studying with a spiritual teacher; wishing to look upon realized beings; desiring to listen to the sacred Dharma; having conviction in karma and its ripening; knowing that the buddhas, bodhisattvas, the listeners, and other such beings are our spiritual teachers; having conviction in them; and, with this conviction, serving and pleasing them.

There are numerous factors that cause faith to flourish. It will flourish if you follow and have heartfelt devotion towards a sacred guru. It will flourish when accompanied by a mingling of your own state of being with the Dharma. It will flourish by reading the profound sutras and tantras. It will flourish by contemplating the uncertainty of the time of death. It will flourish through seeing and hearing anecdotes related to the principle of karmic causality. And it will flourish by doing many practice sessions while meditating and practicing the profound. The *Sutra of the Inconceivable Secret* says:

> With this, you will not engage in negative activities
> But will act in ways that are praised by realized beings.

Hence, you should develop such faith every day, using either all of these or each individually.

There are also certain problems that cause faith to diminish. These you must eliminate. To form the idea that your spiritual teacher has flaws, for example, is a sign that you've been possessed and affected by a demonic force. It is also a problem if you think that Dharma practice in general is negative or mistaken. Another such flaw is to befriend ordinary people, as is letting your diligence in practice wane. To nonchalantly engage in sense pleasures is also a problem, as is to lack devotion towards the Jewels.

To turn away from these factors, think about the positive qualities of your guru, the Jewels, and your fellow practitioners. Develop pure perception and reverence towards all Dharma practitioners. Seeing others in a negative light is a sign of your own impurity, so you should keep your own counsel. Think to yourself that this is no different from seeing a white conch as yellow. Do not befriend worldly people and try to keep the problems associated with sense pleasures in mind. In short, you need to understand that these faults cause faith to diminish and are, therefore, demons. The *Mother* states:

> Demonic, evil-minded individuals will appear before beginners and, though they have sincere interest, influence them and turn them away from the practices of the bodhisattva.

What follow are instructions on how to keep your mind continually in the company of circumstances that arouse faith. Since seeing the transitions of life and death is a condition that leads to the birth of faith, you should develop faith by thinking about all those who have died. Since the occurrence of illness, negative forces, and obstacles is a condition that leads to the birth of faith, you should develop faith by seeing them as the master's way to exhort you to practice virtue. Since faith arises when the sufferings associated with negative circumstances occur, you should develop faith with the knowledge that such experiences are leading you to enlightenment. Since hearing the life stories of the saints of the past is a condition that leads to the birth of faith, you should develop faith by practicing the Dharma and enduring hardships. Since faith arises when we hear the sutras and stories about the Buddha's past lives and learn about the great activities of the buddhas and bodhisattvas, you should develop faith by focusing on the enlightenment of the Great Vehicle. To conclude, it is extremely important to develop faith every day using all of these conditions. You should recognize their importance without letting yourself become jaded.

To develop faith in this way, you need to give rise to a sense of disgust towards the confused perceptions of samsara, like a nauseous person looking at food. Your feeling of intense devotion towards the guru and Three Jewels should be like that of a small child seeing its mother. You should study and contemplate with great diligence, like a thirsty person drinking water. Like a beggar who's found gold and turquoise, you should consider your spiritual practice extremely important. You should delight in virtuous pursuits as though you are a merchant who has arrived in an isle of gold, and you should have great faith and desire for the various vehicles as though you are going to sell the gold that you've gathered. Since these are the ways to gauge whether or not faith has arisen, it is important to cultivate these factors and not let them decline. As you do so, apply yourself to these methods for developing faith by taming your own state of being with the Dharma. Don't let yourself part ways with the Dharma!

Without faith, it doesn't matter how many other good qualities you have. They won't do you any good, just as beautiful things don't make any difference to a blind man. This is why you need to develop faith. Since it is a great loss if it declines for even a moment, you should think solely about all the marvelous qualities of the Dharma, the guru, your fellow practitioners, and the buddhas. Cultivate faith without any sense of bias or preference and make it a priority to tame your own mind.

There are six different kinds of inauthentic faith. For novice Dharma practitioners, faith may grow greater and greater when they are with their guru but be lost altogether when they are not. The faith of some individuals develops rapidly in certain circumstances but disappears when those factors are gone. Others have faith that grows stronger when they are practicing the teachings they like, or when they are stricken with illness or some other harmful factor, but do the opposite and abandon it once they get what they want or recover. Some get interested in one practice, then another, and before long end up starting many different practices, but in the end they don't accomplish any of them. Some lack the faith in which the profound Dharma and root guru are seen to be indivisible and go after whichever is most convenient. Some have faith that is always vacillating; they develop a bit of faith, but then lose it once they encounter adverse circumstances.

You should first examine the Dharma and the guru. Once you've done so, accept them. The next step is to develop faith by always being respectful towards them, without any sense of disenchantment, instability, artifice, or any other such factor. Your faith should have ten different qualities. The great masters of the past would start out with a process of detailed examination. Once they found a genuine guru and genuine teachings, their faith would then be unchanging like the king of mountains, constant like the sun, and boundless like a great ocean. It would be as tolerant as a mother, without center or edge like space, and neither too tight nor too loose, like a well-strung bow. Like the sky, such faith could not be influenced by others or lost in the face of rebuke or other such negativity, and, like a bridge or ship, with such faith these individuals would be free from weariness and fatigue. Finally, their faith would be unceasing like the flow of a river and ornamented with respect, flexibility, and politeness like an embroidered shawl. This is the kind of faith you should have.

Arousing faith in this manner involves an innumerable number of positive qualities, but to summarize, developing faith forms the basis for all wholesome phenomena. It also clears away the suffering of samsara and leads one along the path to liberation. The buddhas and bodhisattvas will always be aware of you. You will possess shame, modesty, knowledge, and a whole host of positive qualities. You will be reborn in a pure buddha realm and, in all your births, meet a sacred guru, sacred teachings, and sacred companions as soon as you are born. Divine beings who are interested in practicing the Dharma and other wholesome activities will look after you. Your sleep will be blissful and you will even dream about your guru, the Jewels, practicing the Dharma, and other positive experiences. Likewise, you will wake in a state of bliss. Whatever you wish for will come to pass. Passing away in bliss, the buddhas and bodhisattvas will lead you blissfully along the path and all your fears about the intermediate state will be gone. You will also be born wherever you desire, becoming a successor of the buddhas. Finally, you will swiftly attain the state of buddhahood. As stated in the *Jewel Lamp Sutra*:

> Even if you offer every kind of pleasure for eons
> To all sentient beings, who number as many
> As the particles of dust throughout the ten realms,
> That cannot be compared to the merit generated
> By having faith in the Buddha's teachings.
> Such faith is especially exalted and not to be found elsewhere.

There are innumerable such quotations, too many to list here.

To sum up, faith is the factor that brings the swift attainment of the wisdom of the buddhas, as stated in the Vinaya scriptures:

> Since it is difficult to uphold all the guidelines of a fully ordained monk in a perfect manner, you should faithfully follow a spiritual teacher and keep the company of those who act in a similar manner. You should abandon those who are negative influences. Seek out the sacred Dharma and contemplate its meaning. Maintain your discipline, which is like a precious jewel, and develop supreme bodhichitta. Work diligently in these pursuits and, before long, you will attain the wisdom of the buddhas.

You should focus on the six types of faith mentioned above and exert yourself with a hundredfold effort. Bring the thousand petals of faith to blossom by mingling your faith with the ten virtues and ten perfections and directing it towards the gurus throughout the ten directions, the Jewels, and the masses of sentient beings.

The Guru

Thus, fortunate individuals who desire liberation should contemplate faith and practice guru yoga. Furthermore, they should also follow a fully qualified guru, a spiritual teacher who has the specific trait of having brought the process of study, contemplation, and meditation to fruition. As stated in the *Precious Wish-fulfilling Treasury:*

> To cross over the ocean of samsara's suffering,
> Rely upon a captain, the glorious guru.

As mentioned here, samsara is vast, as it is without beginning or end. It is deep as well. No matter how deep you go, you will never touch bottom. With its violent strength, the force of karma can take you anywhere. Its stormy waves are difficult to bear, and it is filled with all manner of harmful forms of suffering. Now that you have the support of a human body, you need to board the vessel of the unsurpassed Dharma with a captain-like guru at the helm, and cross over this ocean of samsara. If you don't work hard now, you will be trapped in the midst of the lower realms of samsara and will never have an opportunity to free yourself.

Once renunciation has arisen, those who wish to cross the seas must necessarily start out by relying upon a good ship and captain. Just so, to be liberated from the boundless ocean of samsara, you need to rely on the profound Dharma and a skilled guru, one who has the qualities of accomplishment. This sacred piece of advice is considered to be of the utmost importance for those who wish to travel to the sanctuary of liberation.

There are numerous qualifications an authentic guru must have, which are summarized in the following passage from *Resting in the Nature of Mind*:

> Their enlightened form is peaceful,
> Their actions pure and faultless.
> They are skilled in cutting through doubts,
> While their speech is pleasant and stainless.
> Their enlightened minds profound and at peace,
> They are treasuries of omniscient wisdom.
> Their enlightened qualities are limitless,
> And their learning and compassion great.
> Their knowledge is incredibly vast,
> And their realization and conduct like space.
> With enlightened activities that are immeasurable,
> They bring meaning to whomever they touch.
> They are loving, indefatigable and perpetually diligent—
> Rely on such a guide, who steers beings upwards.

As stated here, qualified spiritual teachers should be able to benefit sentient beings with their many positive qualities, those of enlightened form, speech, and mind. Their knowledge and realization should be as deep as space. With their enlightened acts, they should be able to sow the seeds of liberation in whomever they come into contact with, and they should regard each being with compassion, as if that being were their only child. Finally, they should be rich in the qualities of scripture, which will allow them to turn the wheel of the Dharma by teaching whichever vehicle a particular individual happens to be inclined towards.

In addition to those already listed, there are specific qualifications a guru of the Secret Mantra should have. Listing these qualities, *Resting in the Nature of Mind* states:

> One with empowerment, vows, and samayas kept pure,
> Who has crossed over an ocean of tantric topics and key instructions,
> And mastered approach, accomplishment, application, and activity;
> One with experience and realization, having attained the warmth
> Of progress in the view, meditation, conduct, and fruition;
> Loving and skillful, thus capable of maturing and liberating disciples,
> One with an undiminished bounty of lineage blessings:
> Follow such a glorious guru, one accomplished and wise.

Further, in the great master Vimalamitra's *Mirror-like Commentary on the Magical Web*, it is written:

> Gurus should have obtained the entire range of outer and inner empowerments associated with the mandala. With pure vows and samayas, gurus should be learned when it comes to the meaning of each individual tantra and have trained in the nature of approach, accomplishment, and application. They should be realized as well, with no ignorance concerning the view. They should be experienced and well acquainted with meditation. They should have a wide range of activities at their disposal and guide their disciples with compassion. These are the eight qualities gurus should have.

My own guru, furthermore, has said that nine qualities are required. In addition to the eight just mentioned, a guru should also hold an unbroken lineage suffused with blessings. Such a guru is the source of all positive qualities. As stated in the *Buddha Avatamsaka Sutra*:

> Ah, child of the victorious ones, the positive qualities that come from associating with spiritual teachers are infinite. The reach of their compassion is as vast as space, while their mantras and concentrations are as plentiful as the stars. With their infinite compassion, they are like an immense ocean, and their noble minds are like a great river. Like a vast ocean, they are unmoved by distractions, and like Mount Meru, they never waver from

suchness. Like a great lotus, they dwell in existence yet remain untainted by its flaws. Their love is like that of one's parents, unobscured and impartial, while with their limitless qualities, they are like a mine filled with jewels. Since they liberate all that moves within samsara, they are just like the tatagatas. Their positive qualities are infinite in number and beyond reckoning.

Hence, such gurus have an infinite number of positive qualities.

Gurus with these qualities are equal to the buddhas in terms of their enlightened activities. They can also be said to be equal because they are emanations of the victorious ones. As said in the *Great Drum Sutra*:

> Do not lament, Ananda, do not grieve.
> In future times, I will manifest
> As a spiritual teacher and work
> For the benefit of you and all others.

And in the *Tantra of the Vajra Mirror:*

> Vajrasattva, the main deity of the mandala,
> The guru is the equal of all the buddhas.

As stated in the *Condensed Realization*, you should follow such a supreme and sacred guru with great faith:

> The unsurpassed essence and circumstance for maturation
> Is the spiritual teacher, the protector who guides
> And leads along the path those who have lost their way,
> Acting as a precious lamp and dispelling the darkness.
> The teacher is like the eye and consciousness for sight,
> Like a ship, delivering one from the Unfordable River,
> Or a fortress, a stronghold in the midst of a dangerous land,
> Like a supreme physician, drawing out the disease of samsara,
> An unsurpassed, sacred captain, leading you to a jewel-filled isle.
> Before setting out, you should know this for certain.

This topic is also explained in the *Precious Wish-fulfilling Treasury*:

> A guru with all the supreme qualities just explained is like the udumbara flower.
> Those who have most of them are like buddhas.
> Even those with six of these qualities are worthy of being studied with.
> In these degenerate times, finding such a guru is exceedingly rare,
> So you should follow one with great faith and respect.

As explained here, a guru who has all of these qualities is as difficult to come across as the udumbara, the king of flowers. Those who have most of these qualities are equal to the buddhas. Even those with six such qualities should be regarded as sacred and studied with accordingly.

Of these, you should primarily follow those who are learned when it comes to the path. As written in the *Sutra That Condenses the Precious Qualities of Realized Beings*:

> Always follow gurus who are learned. Why? Because the qualities of learnedness come from such gurus.

There are six reasons to follow such sacred gurus continuously. The first advises us to follow a guru because there is no one whom we can consult about the attainment of permanent happiness and enlightenment aside from a guru. As stated in the *King of Magic*:

> For sure protection against the fears of samsara
> And supreme guidance to nirvana
> There is nothing aside from the guru.

"Well," you may wonder, "are there not also buddhas, who are both skillful and compassionate?" In response, it may be said that the buddhas themselves do not come into being without a guru. They too start out by serving a guru. For this very reason, the guru is the universal source of refuge and protection. The *Condensed Realization* states:

> You should know that the guru
> Should be esteemed even more
> Than the buddhas of a thousand eras.
> Why? Because these buddhas arise
> By serving their gurus as well.

Even our very own teacher, the blessed Buddha, did not come into being without a guru. Hence, it necessarily follows that you as well should rely solely and continuously on a guru. In the *Condensed Realization*, it is written:

> Buddhas never arise without serving a master.
> I have never seen such a thing truly happening.
> And if it did, it would conflict with scripture.

And in the *Wheel of Bliss Tantra*:

> Hence, the root of all qualities
> Is said to be the vajra holder guru.
> It is impossible to achieve attainments
> That do not come from a guru.
> The occurrence of a "buddha" as well
> Is impossible without a guru.
> It is a qualified guru who will
> Lead you out of existence.

Just doing a bit of spiritual practice while remembering a guru with such supreme qualities will bring an infinite amount of merit. As stated in the *Supreme Wish-fulfilling Tantra*:

> When compared with meditating on the guru,
> One's chosen deity, at the crown of the head,
> Even placing thousands of buddhas and mandalas
> In your palm and circling the three thousandfold universe
> And then dissolving them into your heart a thousand times
> Won't equal a hundredth, not even a thousandth, of the former.
> Therefore, with mindfulness, visualize the guru
> At all times adorning the crown of your head.

And in the scriptures:

> The guru is the Buddha, the guru is Dharma,
> And just so, the guru is the Sangha as well.
> The guru is the one who does everything

And is equal to all the buddhas.
One should not abandon but practice the guru.
Specifically, if one has sincere interest and motivation,
There is no doubt that the guru will be accomplished.
The guru is Vajradhara, so they should not be seen as separate.
The divine nectar that flows from this source
Will be experienced by that very practitioner.
The end result of all spiritual attainments
Comes from pleasing a guru.

The *Condensed Realization* explains:

Meditating on the guru alone is superior
To meditating on a hundred thousand deities
For a hundred thousand eons.

And in the *Self-Presence of Great Samantabhadra Tantra*, it is taught:

Those who meditate on the kind guru,
Who comes from the Great Perfection of Ati,
In the center of their hearts, the palms of their hands,
Or upon the crowns of their heads,
Will obtain the qualities of a thousand buddhas.

THE PRACTICE OF GURU YOGA

It is inappropriate to practice guru yoga while envisioning yourself in an ordinary way. For this reason, start out by refining away any sense of impurity and recite the following:

**In a state of natural emptiness, from fixation entirely free,
I myself am visualized, fully present as the yidam deity.
On the crown of my head is a lotus, ringed with a thousand petals,
And a seat upon its anthers, made of the sun and the moon.
The guru sits at its center, the great Padmakara —**

> In essence he is Samantabhadra, the enlightened three kayas in form.
> The victors' realization and the symbols of the vidyadhara—
> These lineages are present above him, seated together in tiers.
> The oral lineage of people, of treasure teachings, and prayers,
> The lineage entrusted to dakinis, as well as all the three roots,
> Finally the siddhas and vidyadharas, both of India and Tibet—
> All now gathered here together, crowded as on market day.
> They are brilliant and majestic, blazing like a great mass of light,
> Each of their three places marked with the syllables OM, AH, and HUM.
> Light radiates out and invokes the three-kaya master of Oddiyana
> And the lineage of the teachings—every one whom I trust.
> Without a single one left out, they all dissolve inseparably,
> As I supplicate with fervent devotion and with a one-pointed mind.

To explain this liturgy: Start out by resting in a state of emptiness. Out of this, visualize yourself as the wrathful deity Hayagriva. You have one face and are red in color. In your right and left hands, respectively, you hold a club and skull cup filled with blood. Your feet are set apart from one another, and on your crown there is a green horse head. Your orange, matted hair streams upwards, your mouth gapes, and your tongue is curled back. Your four fangs are bared, and your eyes are red and bulging. Adorned with the eight charnel ground ornaments and displaying the nine magnificent dances, you are inseparably intertwined with your female counterpart, Vajravarahi.

On your crown, visualize a thousand-petaled lotus with sun and moon-disc seats. Your own root guru is seated upon them, visualized in the form of Padmakara of Oddiyana. He has one face and two arms, all the accoutrements of a nirmanakaya buddha, and is white in color with a tinge of red.

Seated upon his crown is the sambhogakaya of Oddiyana, Amitayus, along with his female counterpart. He is red in color, with one face and two arms, and is adorned with the ornamentation of a sambhogakaya buddha. On the crown of Amitayus is the dharmakaya of Oddiyana, blue in color and holding a vajra and bell. He has the appearance of Vajradhara and is in union with the white wisdom dakini. Upon his crown sit the male and female buddhas, Samantabhadra and Samantabhadri. Visualize all of these situated one above the other.

As its retinue, the dharmakaya is surrounded by an ocean of wisdom. The sambhogakaya is surrounded by the assembly of sambhogakaya bodhisattvas, including those of the lineage of the victors' realization and the symbolic lineage of the masters of awareness. Surrounding the nirmanakaya are those of the oral lineage of people, of the lineage of treasure teachings and prayers, and of the lineage entrusted to dakinis. The Indian and Tibetan masters of awareness are also present, as are the three roots and an ocean of dakinis. They are all brilliantly colored and gathered together in throngs, a mass of blessings and light.

Visualize an OM syllable at the crown of each of these figures, an AH at their throats, and a HUM in their hearts. White, red, and blue lights then radiate out from these three syllables, inviting wisdom beings from the pure realms of the natural three kayas. The wisdom beings then dissolve into them and merge inseparably. Finally, recite the following supplication one-pointedly, with sincere devotion and intense longing:

OM AH HUM

> I supplicate you, Samantabhadra and Samantabhadri,
> Grant your blessings that I may realize the innate nature of things!
> I supplicate you, the sixth buddha Vajradhara,
> Grant your blessings that I may realize self-occurring spontaneous presence!
> I supplicate you, teacher Vajrasattva,
> Grant your blessings that I may realize that things are free from arising, cessation, and all elaborations!
> I supplicate you, master of awareness Garap Dorjé,
> Grant your blessings and free this illusory body into luminosity!
> I supplicate you, wise Shri Simha,
> Grant your blessings that the ends of the four limits be reached!
> I supplicate you, master Padma and spiritual partner,
> Grant your blessings that I may be initiated into the display of awareness!
> I supplicate you, Vimalamitra and the rest of the eight Indian masters of awareness,
> Ka, Chok, Shang and the rest of the twenty-five disciples,

The hundred treasure revealers and the host of karmically linked
    guardians,
Root and lineage gurus, I supplicate you all!
Grant your blessings that experience and realization dawn as
    wisdom!

Namo
I supplicate you, lord guru, the dharmakaya buddha,
Grant your blessings and clear away the darkness of ignorance!
I supplicate you, sambhogakaya guru,
Grant your blessings that meditative concentration be born in my
    mind!
I supplicate you, compassionate nirmanakaya guru,
Grant your blessings that experience and realization be born!
I supplicate you, guru, the enlightened form of the ocean of
    victorious ones,
Grant your blessings that I may accomplish both my own and
    others' welfare
And bestow upon me the spiritual attainment of immortality!
I supplicate your enlightened speech, my guru,
Grant your blessings that my speech may gain power,
And bestow upon me the spiritual attainment of Brahma's
    melody!
I supplicate your enlightened mind, my guru,
Grant your blessings that realization may arise in my mind,
And bestow upon me the spiritual attainment of Mahamudra!
I supplicate your perfect qualities and enlightened activities,
Grant your blessings of all four empowerments
And bestow upon me the spiritual attainment of the four kinds of
    activity!

OM AH HUM

I supplicate you, supreme dharmakaya Amitabha, grant your
    blessings!
I supplicate you, Great Compassionate One, supreme
    sambhogakaya, grant your blessings!
I supplicate you, supreme nirmanakaya Padmakara, grant your

blessings!
I supplicate you, dakini Yeshé Tsogyal, grant your blessings!
I supplicate you, twenty-five masters of awareness, the king and his subjects, grant your blessings!
I supplicate you, two supreme treasure revealers and eight lingpas, grant your blessings!
I supplicate you, one hundred and eight masters of the profound treasures, grant your blessings!
I supplicate at your feet, treasure revealer Ratna Lingpa, grant your blessings!
I supplicate you, son of the victorious ones Tsewang Trakpa, grant your blessings!
I supplicate you, supreme son Ngakwang Trakpa, grant your blessings!
I supplicate you, noble master of awareness Kunga Trakpa, grant your blessings!
I supplicate at your feet, Karwang Kunga Tenzin, grant your blessings!
I supplicate you, master of mantra Padma Wangtrak, grant your blessings!
I supplicate you, compassionate Karma Chakmé, grant your blessings!
I supplicate at your feet, guru Punda Vidyadhara, grant your blessings!
I supplicate you, kind and noble root guru, grant your blessings!
I supplicate you, peaceful and wrathful mandala deities, grant your blessings!
I supplicate you, warriors, dakinis, and protectors of the teachings, grant your blessings!

How wondrous!
Complete embodiment of all the Three Jewels and three roots,
Primordially enlightened protector, unconfused and self-arisen,
Mighty king, the guru in whom all qualities are spontaneously present,
Guru Padmakara, you who are free from the fears of mortality,
O guru, my faith in you is firm, I think of you now!

With intense longing, I supplicate you from the depths of my
   heart!
May your compassion not wane, please give rise to a host of
   powerful blessings
And grant them to this faithful child at this very moment!
Grant me every single empowerment and spiritual attainment,
   without a single one left out!
Grant your blessings that the source of the illusory and confused
   appearances of this life may collapse,
That renunciation and disenchantment arise and that my mind
   wake into awareness,
That meditative experiences and the wisdom of realization be
   perfected as the essence of my own awareness.
Grant your blessings that our two minds may merge inseparably
   as one!

SARVA SIDDHI PHALA HUM AH

As you recite the preceding liturgy, remain one-pointed and undistracted as you supplicate with great respect.

Next, receive the four empowerments:

All the objects of refuge dissolve into my root guru.
From the blessings amassed at the guru's four places
Comes the light of wisdom, in the form of syllables—
A white OM, red AH, blue HUM, and green HRIH.
Dissolving into my own four places, the four obscurations
   are purified,
The four empowerments perfected, the wisdom of the four joys
   born,
And the fruition of the four forms of buddhahood attained.
The guru then enters my crown and dissolves into me.
Our minds merge indivisibly, and then my very own mind
Becomes the unborn dharmakaya, uncontrived simplicity.

AH

As you recite the liturgy, the sources of refuge begin to dissolve. The ocean of wisdom that surrounds the dharmakaya dissolves into it, receding like the rays of a setting sun. The entire retinue of the sambhogakaya dissolves as well, merging with Amitayus and his spiritual counterpart like a small stream flowing into the ocean. The nirmanakaya assembly dissolves into the nirmanakaya buddha Padmakara, like snow landing on the surface of a lake. Next, the dharmakaya buddhas Samantabhadra and Samantabhadri dissolve into the dharmakaya of Oddiyana and his spiritual counterpart. They, in turn, dissolve into Amitayus and his spiritual counterpart. These buddhas, the forms of perfect enjoyment, then dissolve into the nirmanakaya buddha Padmakara. Finally, visualize Padmakara as a mass of light, inseparable from your own root guru and the essence of the three kayas. A treasury of blessings and enlightened qualities, his body has an overwhelming presence and is blazing with light. Envision him as the very embodiment of the bestowal of the supreme wisdom empowerment.

The next step is to receive the four empowerments. Begin by visualizing the wisdom syllable OM, the essence of enlightened form, between the eyebrows of the guru's body. Accompanied by white light, the syllable emanates out and dissolves into the space between your own eyebrows. Through this, physical impurities are purified, the empowerment of the enlightened form is attained, and the wisdom of joy is born. The body and appearances are liberated into emptiness as well, and the fruitional state of nirmanakaya buddhahood is attained.

Next, at the base of the neck of the guru, visualize the wisdom syllable AH as the very essence of enlightened speech. Surrounded by red light, this syllable emanates out and dissolves into your own throat center. This purifies verbal obscurations, brings the attainment of the empowerment of enlightened speech, and arouses the wisdom of supreme joy in your state of being. In addition, the comings and goings of empty sound—ordinary speech—enter the central channel. Ordinary speech gains power and the fruition of sambhogakaya buddhahood is attained.

Once this is complete, envision a blue HUM syllable, the essence of the enlightened mind, in the endless knot of the heart center of the guru. Accompanied by blue light, it emanates out and dissolves into your own heart center. With this, all mental obscurations are purified and you obtain the empowerment of the enlightened mind. Wisdom free from joy is born in your state of being as well, and the mind is liberated into empty clarity.

Realization is born and the fruitional state of the dharmakaya is attained.

Finally, visualize a green syllable HRIH emanating from the activity chakra at the guru's navel. Surrounded by green light, it dissolves into your own navel. This, in turn, purifies cognitive obscurations, brings the attainment of the precious word empowerment, and produces the wisdom of coemergent joy in your state of being. The aggregates are liberated into rainbow light and, with the qualities of acceptance and the supreme state,[58] the fruitional state of the essence kaya is attained.

When it comes to empowerment, there are a great many divisions. This, however, is the ultimate empowerment. Hence, you shouldn't entertain any doubts or hesitations, but instead apply yourself one-pointedly to this process with faith, respect, and sincere interest. Without being distracted, practice until signs appear that mark your attainment of the strength of blessings. You should also eliminate any negative attitudes you may have by developing a sense of certainty that your guru is the very essence, the very embodiment, of all the jewels. Keeping his or her enlightened qualities in mind, arouse a feeling of boundless faith and intense devotion, enough to bring you to tears. Then supplicate and receive the four empowerments as many times as you can.

At the conclusion of this practice, the guru, the glorious embodiment of the four forms of enlightenment, moves to the crown of your head. With boundless compassion, the guru then melts into light and dissolves into you. This causes your own three gates to merge indivisibly with the three vajras, the enlightened form, speech, and mind of your guru. Finally, rest in a state of unified bliss-emptiness.

Once the session is finished, dedicate the basic virtues you've amassed to enlightenment:

> **This pure accumulation of virtue, the essence of this merit,**
> **I dedicate to all sentient beings without limitation,**
> **May they realize the nature of the secret Vajrayana**
> **And attain the state of the guru, the lord of the families!**

With this recitation, the essence of the entire range of pure virtues that have been amassed is dedicated to the welfare of all sentient beings. This unsurpassed merit is offered in such a way that there is no sense of limitation or restriction towards the infinite number of beings. Instead, we pray for *all* sentient beings. What we are essentially doing here is praying that all beings be freed from ignorance and from the 84,000 afflictions it produces. Due to this mass of confusion, we solidify things, believing we need to take up some and reject others.

We then pray that, once free from the afflictions and confusion, all beings actualize their own self-occurring wisdom, the great all-embracing empty awareness of reality itself, and further, that they directly realize the unmistaken truth, the nature of the unsurpassed and utterly secret Vajra Vehicle. Further, we pray that with this realization, they might attain the precious state of the great vajra-holder, the glorious guru who is the sovereign lord of the buddha families, or, said differently, that they might attain the precious state of the victorious one Padmakara. Keeping all this in mind, dedicate the merit while remaining in a state free from any sense of fixation or specific focal point.

Concluding Verses

༄༅། །དགོངས་བ་སན་བརྒྱུད་མཁའ་འགྲོའི་སིང་གི་བཅུད། །
ཨ་ཏི་རྫོགས་པ་ཆེན་པོའི་ཏི་ལ་ཀ །
ནམ་མཁའ་འོད་གསལ་རིག་འཛིན་དགོངས་པའི་གཏེར། །
ཤིང་རྟ་བཟང་པོས་གསལ་འདི་ཨེ་མ་མཚར། །
ཨོ་རྒྱན་གུ་ རུ་པཉྩ་ཆེན་པོ་མ་ལ། །
ཁད་པར་མཁའ་འགྲོ་ཡེ་ཤེས་མཚོ་རྒྱལ་གྱི། །
བྱིན་བརླབས་རྒྱས་རྗེས་ཨ་རི་ནུབ་སླེ་དུ། །
ཚུལ་ཁྲིམས་གཞོན་ནུས་ཨིན་ཇིའི་སྐད་དུ་བསྒྱུར། །

ཞེས་རྫོགས་ཆེན་པའི་གྲུབ་མཐར་སྨྲས་པ། ཁོ་བོ་རྫོགས་ཆེན་དཔོན་སློབ་བདུན་པར་འབོད་པ་ནས་གནང་སྤྲས་པའོ།

The innermost heart of dakinis, of the mind, symbol, and hearing lineages;
The essential drop of Ati, bindu of the Great Perfection;
Wisdom mind treasure of the vidyadhara Namkha Ösel—
Is illuminated by *The Excellent Chariot*, how wondrous indeed!

Through the blessings and compassion of Padmakara and Vimalamitra,
And especially through those of the dakini Yeshé Tsogyal,
This has now been translated into the English language
By Tsultrim Shönu in the Western land of America.

These verses were spoken spontaneously by one known as the seventh Dzogchen Ponlop Rinpoche, the lowest of Dzogchenpas. They were recorded and translated by Tsultrim Shönu [Cortland Dahl] on September 3, 2006.

Abbreviations

BT	*The Treasury of Knowledge: Systems of Buddhist Tantra.* Jamgön Kongtrül.
CCM	*dPal gsang ba'i snying po de kho na nyid nges pa'i rgyud kyi 'grel pa phyogs bcu'i mun pa thams cad rnam par sel ba.* Klong chen rab 'byams.
CG	*bsKyed pa'i rim pa cho ga dang sbyar ba'i gsal byed zung 'jug snye ma.* dGe rtse ma h'a pandita tshe dbang mchog grub.
CNT	*Chos kyi rnam grangs shes bya'i nor gling 'jug pa'i gru gzing.* mGon po dbang rgyal, editor.
CY	*Chos dbyings rin po che'i mdzod kyi 'grel pa lung gi gter mdzod.* Klong chen rab 'byams.
DK	*sDe dge bka' 'gyur.*
DMW	*Deity, Mantra, and Wisdom: Development Stage Meditation in Tibetan Buddhist Tantra.* Jigme Lingpa, Patrul Rinpoche, and Getse Mahapandita.
DON	*Byang chub sems dpa'i spyod pa la 'jug pa rtsa ba dang 'grel pa.* mKhan po kun bzang dpal ldan.
DR	*rDzogs rim chos drug bsdus don.* dPal sprul O rgyan 'jigs med chos kyi dbang po.
DT	*sDe dge bstan 'gyur.*
DZ	*The Practice of Dzogchen.* Tulku Thondup.
EM	*Empowerment.* Tsele Natsok Rangdröl (contained in *Dzogchen Essentials*).

GD	*Bla ma dgongs pa 'dus pa'i cho ga'i rnam bzhag dang 'brel ba'i bskyed rdzogs zung 'jug gi sgron ma mkhyen brtse'i me long 'od zer brgya pa.* 'Jigs med gling pa.
GS	*rDzogs pa chen po sems nyid ngal gso'i gnas gsum dge ba gsum gyi don khrid byang chub lam bzang.* Klong chen rab 'byams.
HE	*Zab mo snying thig gi gnad thams cad bsdus pa'i don khrid lag len gsal ba.* bKra shis rgya mtsho.
JL	*bsKyed rim lha'i khrid kyi rnam par bzhag pa 'og min bgrod pa'i them skas* (Dodrupchen edition). 'Jigs med gling pa.
KG	*dPal sgrub pa chen po bka' brgyad kyi spyi don rnam par bshad pa dngos grub snying po.* 'Ju mi pham rgya mtsho.
KJ	*mKhas pa'i tshul la 'jug pa'i sgo.* 'Ju mi pham rgya mtsho.
KN	*rDzogs pa chen po mkha' 'gro snying thig gi khrid yig thar lam bgrod byed shing rta bzang po.* Nges don bstan 'dzin bzang po.
KR	*bsKyed rim gyi zin bris cho ga spyi 'gros ltar bkod pa man ngag kun btus.* Kun mkhyen bstan pa'i nyi ma.
KS	*rDzogs pa chen po ngal so skor gsum dang rang grol skor gsum dang bcas pod gsum.* Klong chen rab 'byams.
LG	*gTer 'byung rin po che'i lo rgyus.* Klong chen rab 'byams.
LW	*Light of Wisdom, Vol. 2.* Padmasambhava and Jamgön Kongtrül.
MV	*dBus dang mtha' rnam par 'byed pa'i bstan bcos kyi 'grel pa 'od zer phreng ba.* 'Ju mi pham rgya mtsho.
MW	*The Treasury of Knowledge: Myriad Worlds.* Jamgön Kongtrül.
ND	*Lam zhugs kyi gang zag las dang po pa la phan pa'i bskyed rdzogs kyi gnad bsdus.* 'Jam mgon kong sprul blo gros mtha' yas.
NG	*mTshams-brag Manuscript of the rNying ma rgyud 'bum.*

NK	*rNying ma bka' ma rgyas pa.*
NO	*Yon tan rin po che'i mdzod kyi 'grel pa zab don snang byed nyi ma'i 'od zer.* Yon tan rgya mtsho.
NS	*The Nyingma School of Tibetan Buddhism.* Dudjom Rinpoche.
ON	*gSang 'grel phyogs bcu'i mun sel gyi spyi don 'od gsal snying po.* 'Ju mi pham rgya mtsho.
PA	*Pure Appearance.* Dilgo Khyentse Rinpoche.
PK	*Peking bka' 'gyur.*
PT	*Peking bstan 'gyur.*
RTZ	*Rin chen gter mdzod chen mo.* 'Jam mgon kong sprul blo gros mtha' yas (compiler).
SC	*rDzogs pa chen po mkha' 'gro snying tig gi khrid yig zab lam gsal byed.* gTer bdag gling pa.
SD	*dPal gsang ba'i snying po de kho na nyid nges pa'i rgyud kyi rgyal po sgyu 'phrul drwa ba spyi don gyi sgo nas gtan la 'bebs par byed pa'i legs bshad gsang bdag zhal lung.* Lo chen dharma shri.
SG	*Theg pa lam zhugs kyi bshags pa'i rtsa 'grel bsdus pa thar lam sgron me.* Nges don bstan 'dzin bzang po.
SS	*Srog sdom gzer bzhi'i dmigs pa gnad 'gags khams gsum rol pa tshangs pa'i sgra dbyangs.* dPal sprul O rgyan 'jigs med chos kyi dbang po.
ST	*Srog sdom gzer bzhi'i zin bris kun mkhyen brgyud pa'i zhal lung.* mKhan chen ngag dbang dpal bzang.
TC	*Theg pa'i mchog rin po che'i mdzod.* Klong chen rab 'byams.
TD	*Bod rgya tshig mdzod chen mo.* Krang dbyi sun, editor.
TK	*Shes bya kun khyab mdzod.* 'Jam mgon kong sprul blo gros mtha' yas.

TN	*The Small Golden Key.* Thinley Norbu.
TP	*Man ngag lta phreng gi 'grel pa rong zom paṇḍita chen po chos kyi bzang pos mdzad pa.* Rong zom chos kyi bzang po.
TT	*Theg pa mtha' dag gi don gsal bar byed pa grub pa'i mtha' rin po che'i mdzod.* Klong chen rab 'byams.
WC	*Zab bsang bdud rtsi'i sgo 'byed skal bzang kun dga'i rol ston.* Dil mgo mkhyen brtse.
WPT	*rDzogs pa chen po klong chen snying thig gi sngon 'gro'i khrid yig kun bzang bla ma'i zhal lung.* dPal sprul O rgyan chos kyi dbang po.
YD	*Theg pa chen po'i man ngag gi bstan bcos yid bzhin rin po che'i mdzod.* Klong chen rab 'byams.
YDD	*Theg pa chen po'i man ngag gi bstan bcos yid bzhin rin po che'i mdzod kyi 'grel pa pad+ma dkar po.* Klong chen rab 'byams.
YS	*sNying thig ya bzhi.* Klong chen rab 'byams (compiler).
YT	*Yon tan rin po che'i mdzod las 'bras bu'i theg pa'i rgya cher 'grel rnam mkhyen shing rta.* 'Jigs med gling pa.
ZD	*Zab don rgya mtsho'i sprin.* Klong chen rab 'byams.

Glossary

Absolute bodhichitta (*don dam byang sems*) – The wisdom that directly realizes EMPTINESS. [TD 1304]

Absorption (*ting nge 'dzin*) – "To truly grasp," meaning that within this mental state one is able to focus one-pointedly and continuously on a given topic or on the object one is examining. [TD 1027]

Accomplished master (*grub thob*) – An individual who has actualized the unique realizations of the path and achieved both supreme and mundane SPIRITUAL ATTAINMENTS. [TD 403]

Accumulation of merit (*bsod nams kyi tshogs*) – The accumulation of positive, virtuous activities, such as making offerings, that involve a conceptual reference point. [TD 3051]

Accumulation of wisdom (*ye shes kyi tshogs*) – The accumulation of non-referential WISDOM is the accumulation of the undefiled virtue that enacts the attainment of the DHARMAKAYA, the fruitional wisdom in which EMPTINESS is embraced by BODHICHITTA. [TD 2594]

Active wisdom (*bya grub ye shes*) – The form of WISDOM that involves the enlightened form, speech, and mind spontaneously working for the welfare of sentient beings. [YT 431]

Activity mudra (*las kyi phyag rgya*) – See FEMALE MUDRA.

Afflicted mind (*nyon yid*) – A neutral, obscured state of mind characterized by fixation on the self; this form of consciousness, which continues to function until the paths of realization have been attained, observes the UNIVERSAL GROUND CONSCIOUSNESS and continually takes it to be a self. [TK 2, 197]

AFFLICTION (*nyon mongs pa*) – A factor that upsets or disturbs the mind and body and produces fatigue. [TD 971]

AFFLICTIVE OBSCURATIONS (*nyon mongs pa'i sgrib pa*) – Thought patterns, such as avarice, that obstruct the attainment of liberation. [TD 970]

AKANISHTA ('Og min) – See SUPREME REALM.

AKSHOBYA (Mi bskyod pa) – As one member of the FIVE BUDDHA FAMILIES, Akshobya represents the VAJRA family and the principle of enlightened mind, indivisible EMPTINESS and compassion. [BT 408]

AMITABHA ('Od dpag med) – As one member of the FIVE BUDDHA FAMILIES, Amitabha represents the lotus family and the principle of enlightened speech, the source of all the Buddhist teachings. [BT 408]

AMITAYUS (Tshe dpag med) – A buddha of the lotus family associated with longevity.

AMOGHASIDDHI (Don yod grub pa) – As one member of the FIVE BUDDHA FAMILIES, Amoghasiddhi represents the karma family and the principle of ENLIGHTENED ACTIVITY, which is carried out by venerating the buddhas and working for the welfare of sentient beings. [BT 408]

AMRITA (*bdud rtsi*) – See NECTAR.

ANUTTARAYOGA TANTRA (*rnal 'byor bla na med pa'i rgyud*) – Literally, "Unsurpassed Union Tantra." The fourth and highest of the FOUR CLASSES OF TANTRA. In the NEW SCHOOLS, this system consists of the FATHER TANTRAS, MOTHER TANTRAS, and NONDUAL TANTRAS. In the NYINGMA SCHOOL, this class of tantra is equated with the THREE INNER TANTRAS of MAHAYOGA, ANUYOGA, and ATIYOGA. Ju Mipham explains the uniqueness of this system: "From the perspective of this approach, not only is the CAUSAL VEHICLE of the perfections a 'long path' but the OUTER TANTRAS are as well. In other words, this is the true 'swift path' and 'FRUITIONAL VEHICLE.' All other approaches are taught according to the mindsets of disciples to lead them to this vehicle. Here, in contrast, the ultimate, DEFINITIVE MEANING is revealed explicitly, just as it is seen by the WISDOM of the BUDDHAS." [KG 37]

ANUYOGA (*rjes su rnal 'byor*) – Literally, "Concordant Yoga." Anuyoga is the eighth of the NINE VEHICLES found in the tantric tradition of the NYINGMA SCHOOL. To enter this system, one first receives the thirty-six supreme EMPOWERMENTS, which include ten outer empowerments, eleven inner empowerments, thirteen practice empowerments and two SECRET EMPOWERMENTS. Next, one trains in the Anuyoga view until one has come to a definitive understanding of the essence of the threefold MANDALA of SAMANTABHADRA. In the meditative system of this tradition, one practices the PATHS OF LIBERATION and SKILLFUL MEANS. The former involves settling in a nonconceptual state that is in harmony with REALITY ITSELF or, in accordance with letters, reciting MANTRAS to visualize a mandala of DEITIES. The latter entails arousing coemergent WISDOM by relying upon the upper and lower gates. In terms of conduct, one understands all appearances and mental events to be the play of the wisdom of great bliss, and with this understanding, uses the direct cause of being beyond acceptance and rejection to attain the fruition of this path. Here, the fruition involves the five yogas (which are in essence the FIVE PATHS), the completion of the ten levels, and the attainment of the state of Samantabhadra. [TD 3120]

APPLICATION BODHICHITTA (*'jug pa'i byang chub kyi sems*) – To develop BODHICHITTA by actually engaging in certain activities, such as the SIX PERFECTIONS, with the express aim being to bring all sentient beings to the state of buddhahood [TD 905]. This consists of committing oneself to the cause of enlightenment, in contrast to ASPIRATION BODHICHITTA, where one commits oneself to its fruition [YT 475].

APPLICATION OF MINDFULNESS (*dran pa nyer bzhag*) – "Mindfulness" here refers to KNOWLEDGE, meaning to know the characteristics of phenomena as they are, unmistakenly. Hence, this aspect relates to INSIGHT. "Application" refers to the placement of attention one-pointedly on the analytic process that one's knowledge is engaged in. Hence, this aspect relates to TRANQUILITY. Most commonly, there are said to be four applications of mindfulness, which are the four focal points used when cultivating insight. These are (1) the application of mindfulness to the body, (2) the application of mindfulness to sensation, (3) the application of mindfulness to the mind, and (4) the application of mindfulness to phenomena. These four partially constitute the THIRTY-SEVEN FACTORS OF ENLIGHTENMENT. [TD 1322]

APPROACH AND ACCOMPLISHMENT (*bsnyen sgrub*) – The four phases of tantric practice: approach, close approach, accomplishment, and great accomplishment. Ju Mipham explains: "Approach and accomplishment encompass all the various practices that utilize the unique methods of the SECRET MANTRA tradition to achieve whatever SPIRITUAL ACCOMPLISHMENTS one desires, whether supreme or mundane." [ON 534]

ASPIRATION BODHICHITTA (*smon pa'i byang chub kyi sems*) – To commit oneself to attaining the fruitional [state of buddhahood], meaning that one is oriented towards the attainment of enlightenment and, consequently, engages in its related practices. [YT 475]

ATIYOGA (*shin tu rnal 'byor*) – Literally, "Supreme Yoga." Atiyoga is the highest of the NYINGMA tradition's NINE VEHICLES. In the textual tradition of this tantric system, Atiyoga is equated with the GREAT PERFECTION of one's self-occurring WISDOM. This wisdom is free from elaborations and not subject to any sense of partiality or limitation. As such, it is considered the very pinnacle of all the various vehicles, since it contains all of their significance. Within this Great Perfection, all the various phenomena of samsara and nirvana, all that appears and exists, arise as the play of this self-occurring wisdom, apart from which nothing exists. The fundamental basis of existence, in this tradition, is this self-occurring wisdom. In terms of the path, there are two forms of practice: the BREAKTHROUGH stage of original purity and the DIRECT LEAP stage of spontaneous presence. Through these two practices, the four visions are brought to a state of culmination and one attains the result of this process, liberation within the very ground, the attainment of the permanent state of the YOUTHFUL VASE BODY. [TD 3118]

AVALOKITESHVARA (sPyan ras gzigs) – As a YIDAM DEITY, Avalokiteshvara is considered to be the unified essence of the enlightened speech of all the BUDDHAS and the embodiment of compassion. [TD 1674]

AWARENESS MANTRA (*rig sngags*) – A MANTRA that is used to accomplish the activity of a DEITY and that emphasizes the VAJRA WISDOM of the enlightened mind. [TD 2681]

BARDO (*bar do*) – See INTERMEDIATE STATE.

BLISSFUL ONES (*bde bar gshegs pa*) – An alternate term for the BUDDHAS, who, by relying upon the path of bliss—the VEHICLE OF THE BODHISATTVAS—progress to the blissful fruition, the state of perfect buddhahood. [TD 1368]

BLOOD (*khrag*) – As a symbolic representation used in DEVELOPMENT STAGE practice, blood is often visualized filling a SKULL CUP, representing the conquering of the FOUR DEMONS. [KR 51]

BODHICHITTA (*byang chub kyi sems*) – This mindset comes about by taking the welfare of others as one's focal point and then orienting oneself with the desire to attain total and perfect enlightenment. This unique frame of mind forms the core of the GREAT VEHICLE path. It can be divided into ASPIRATION BODHICHITTA and APPLICATION BODHICHITTA. [TD 1869]

BODHISATTVA (*byang chub sems dpa'*) – Literally, "heroic being of enlightenment"—individuals who train in the GREAT VEHICLE, who are so called because they do not become discouraged in the face of the long duration it takes to attain great enlightenment, nor in giving away their own head and limbs out of generosity. [TD 1870]

BRAHMA'S MELODY (*tshangs pa'i dbyangs*) – Brahma's melody is one of the THIRTY-TWO MARKS OF THE BUDDHAS. This pure melody allows all sentient beings throughout the various realms of the universe to understand the sacred Dharma. [TD 2254]

182 / GREAT PERFECTION

Breakthrough (*khregs chod*) – Along with DIRECT LEAP, breakthrough is one of two stages of practice found in the GREAT PERFECTION's KEY INSTRUCTION CLASS. This practice is designed to liberate those prone to laziness in an effortless manner. In this approach, one first identifies, and then sustains recognition of, one's own innately pure, empty awareness. This practice is the essence of Great Perfection practice. [DZ 67]

Buddha (*sangs rgyas*) – One who has cleared away the darkness of the TWO OBSCURATIONS and in whom the two forms of KNOWLEDGE have blossomed. [TD 2913]

Causal Vehicle (*rgyu'i theg pa*) – An alternate name of the Vehicle of Characteristics, or VEHICLE OF PERFECTIONS, so called because it takes the factors that cause the attainment of perfect buddhahood, such as the thirty-seven factors of enlightenment, as the path. [TD 580]

Central channel (*rtsa dbu ma*) – The central channel is the main energetic channel in the body. It runs vertically through the center of the body. Its upper end is located at the cranial aperture on the crown of the head, while its lower end is found in the secret place (the perineum). [TD 2212]

Chakra (*'khor lo*) – (1) In terms of the energetic body, the chakras are circular conglomerations of energetic channels that are supported by the CENTRAL CHANNEL [TD 2209]. (2) As a symbolic implement used in DEVELOPMENT STAGE practice, the chakra is a circular instrument that symbolizes cutting through the AFFLICTIONS [KR 51].

Channels, energies, and essences (*rtsa rlung thig le*) – These three factors function as the support for consciousness, ensuring that the life remains stable and the life-force uninterrupted. Of these three, the channels are said to be like a house, the essences like the wealth contained therein, and the ENERGIES like their owner. [TD 2213]

Charya Tantra (*spyod rgyud*) – Literally, "Performance Tantra." The second of the THREE OUTER TANTRAS; the view of this tradition is similar to that of YOGA TANTRA, while its conduct is equated with that of KRIYA TANTRA. For this reason, it is also known as "Dual Tantra" [NS 271]. This is the second of FOUR CLASSES OF TANTRA found in the NEW SCHOOLS.

COGNITIVE OBSCURATIONS (*shes bya'i sgrib pa*) – The conceptualization of the THREE SPHERES, which obstructs the attainment of total omniscience (the state of buddhahood). [TD 2860]

COMPLETION STAGE (*rdzogs rim*) – Tantric practice is divided into two phases, the DEVELOPMENT STAGE and the completion stage. Explaining these two, Lochen Dharmashri writes: "To summarize, the development stage involves transforming impure appearances into pure ones and meditating on the MANDALA circle. In the completion stage, the aim is to realize the WISDOM of bliss–EMPTINESS." The latter, he continues, can be divided further into the conceptual completion stage and nonconceptual completion stage. He writes: "In this stage, one either meditates conceptually on the ENERGIES, CHANNELS AND ESSENCES, or nonconceptually by absorbing oneself in REALITY" [SD 325]. Ju Mipham summarizes this phase as follows: "All the various forms of completion stage practice bring about the manifest appearance of pure wisdom by bringing the karmic energies into the CENTRAL CHANNEL, though this may be brought about either directly or indirectly" [ON 417].

CONDITIONED PHENOMENA (*'dus byas*) – That which has arisen or been constructed due to the coincidence of multiple causes and conditions; the phenomena that collectively comprise the five aggregates. [TD 1408]

DAKINI (*mkha' 'gro ma*) – (1) A yogini who has attained the extraordinary SPIRITUAL ACCOMPLISHMENTS; (2) a female divinity who has taken birth in a PURE REALM or other similar location. [TD 298]

DEFINITIVE MEANING (*nges don*) – To specific disciples, it is taught that the profound nature of all phenomena is EMPTINESS, free from arising, cessation, and every other elaboration, and that the actual condition and nature of things is one of LUMINOSITY, which is beyond anything that can be thought or put into words. The definitive meaning refers

184 / GREAT PERFECTION

to this nature, as well as to the scriptures that teach it and their related commentaries. [TD 655]

DEITY (*lha*) – See YIDAM DEITY.

DESIRE REALM (*'dod khams*) – One of the THREE REALMS that comprise SAMSARA; sentient beings in this realm are attached to material food and sex, primarily because they sustain themselves through the five sense pleasures. This realm is referred to as such because it is home to desirous sentient beings. [TD 1414]

DEVELOPMENT AND COMPLETION (*bskyed rdzogs gnyis*) – The DEVELOPMENT STAGE and COMPLETION STAGE comprise the inner tantric path to liberation. According to Khenpo Ngaga: "All the various categories of TANTRA relate to the two stages of development and completion" [ST 6]. Explaining the function of these two approaches, Lochen Dharmashri writes: "The development stage purifies [the idea that] the environment and its inhabitants are real entities with their own characteristics, while the completion stage purifies the subtle clinging that can occur while meditating that these are all illusory, as is the case in development stage practice" [SD 325].

DEVELOPMENT, COMPLETION, AND GREAT PERFECTION (*bskyed rdzogs gsum*) – In the NYINGMA tradition, the system of the INNER TANTRAS is said to comprise three avenues of practice—the DEVELOPMENT STAGE, the COMPLETION STAGE, and the GREAT PERFECTION. These three, in turn, are associated with MAHAYOGA, ANUYOGA, and ATIYOGA—the THREE INNER TANTRAS. As Dilgo Khyentse explains: "Development and Mahayoga are like the basis for all the teachings, completion and Anuyoga are like the path of all the teachings, and the Great Perfection of Atiyoga is like the result of all the teachings." [WC 773]

DEVELOPMENT STAGE (*bskyed rim*) – Along with the COMPLETION STAGE, the development stage is one of two phases that constitute Buddhist practice in the INNER TANTRAS. Explaining this approach, Ju Mipham writes: "The phases of development stage practice correspond to the way in which conventional existence develops.... Practicing with this approach *purifies* the habitual patterns of samsara, *perfects* the fruition of nirvana, and *matures* the practitioner for the completion stage" [ON 416]. This practice is discussed extensively in DMW.

DHARMA (*chos*) – Most commonly, the word *dharma* is used either to refer to the BUDDHA's teachings or as a general term meaning "phenomena." As the *Great Dictionary* notes, however, this word has ten traditional usages, all of which relate to something that "holds its own essence." These ten are (1) knowable objects, (2) spiritual paths, (3) the transcendence of suffering, (4) mental objects, (5) merit, (6) life, (7) the sublime words of the Buddha, (8) temporal progression, (9) regulation, and (10) systems. [TD 825]

DHARMAKAYA (*chos kyi sku*) – One of the THREE KAYAS. When classified into two forms, the state of buddhahood is divided into the dharmakaya and RUPAKAYA (the form of reality and the embodied forms). The dharmakaya benefits oneself and results from the culmination of abandonment and realization [TD 829]. Longchenpa explains further, "By nature, the dharmakaya is the indivisible wisdom-expanse, the culminating realization that is free of every trace of impurity, like space" [TT 277].

DHARMA PROTECTOR (*chos skyong*) – A protective deity that is bound under oath to protect the Buddhist teachings. [TD 830]

DIRECT LEAP (*thod rgal*) – Along with the BREAKTHROUGH stage, direct leap is one of two phases of practice found in the GREAT PERFECTION's KEY INSTRUCTION CLASS. In contrast to breakthrough, which focuses on emptiness and original purity, the direct leap emphasizes spontaneous presence and the active manifestations of reality itself. This approach is directed towards diligent individuals who liberate themselves through meditation. [YT 689]

DISCERNING WISDOM (*so sor rtogs pa'i ye shes*) – The inner state of clarity in which all that can be known is understood in a distinct manner. [ZD 78]

Dominant result (*bdag po'i 'bras bu*) – One of a fivefold classification of results; a result whose arising is entirely dictated by a particular cause that "dominates" its corresponding result, such as when virtuous activities cause a rebirth in a positive location. [TD 1358]

Dorsem Nyingtik (*rDor sems snying thig*) – The Dorsem Nyingtik (Heart Essence of Vajrasattva) was revealed by the treasure revealer Kunkyong Lingpa in the fifteenth century. Though these teachings were originally transmitted to Padmasambhava by Garap Dorjé, Jamgön Kongtrül classified them as belonging to the Heart Essence teachings of Vairochana because the latter received this transmission directly from Padmasambhava and later revealed it as treasure in his incarnation as Kunkyong Lingpa. The root tantra of this cycle is included in RTZ, vol. 89 (shi), pp. 385-497.

Dual Tantra (*gnyis ka rgyud*) – An alternate name for **Charya Tantra**.

Dzogchen (*rdzogs chen*) – See **Great Perfection**.

Early Translation School (*snga 'gyur*) – See **Nyingma School**.

Eight charnel ground ornaments (*dur khrod chas brgyad*) – The three garments (*bgo ba'i gos gsum*): elephant, human, and tiger skin; two fastened ornaments (*gdags pa'i rgyan gnyis*): human skulls and snakes; and three smeared things (*byug pa'i rdzas gsum*): ashes, blood, and grease. [TN 84]

Eight collections of consciousness (*rnam shes tshogs brgyad*) – The six collections of consciousness plus the **afflicted mind** and the **universal ground consciousness**. [TK 1, 50]

Eight Sadhana Teachings (*sgrub pa bka' brgyad*) – **Mahayoga** is traditionally divided into two sections: the **tantra section**, which includes the *Guhyagarbha Tantra*, and the **sadhana section**. The latter division contains the Eight Sadhana Teachings, which comprise the ritual practices and instructions associated with eight divinities—five transcendent deities and three mundane deities. The five wisdom deities are MANJUSHRI Yamantaka (embodying enlightened form), Padma HAYAGRIVA (embodying enlightened speech), Vishuddha (embodying enlightened mind), Vajramrita Mahottara (embodying enlightened qualities), and VAJRAKILAYA (embodying enlightened activity). The three classes of worldly divinities are Matarah (liberating sorcery), Lokastotrapuja (mundane praises), and Vajramantrabhiru (wrathful mantra) [NS 283]. These teachings have been maintained and practiced in both the TRANSMITTED TEACHINGS and the TREASURE tradition. In the former, the primary source is a cycle titled *The Fortress and Precipice of the Eight Teachings: The Distilled Realization of the Four Wise Men*. There are a great many related teachings in the treasure tradition. The most important, however, are found in the revelations of Nyang Ral Nyima Özer, Guru Chöwang, and Rigdzin Gödem [WC 777].

EIGHT MASTERS OF AWARENESS (*rig 'dzin chen po brgyad*) – These eight masters of awareness were Indian gurus entrusted with the Eight Sadhana Teachings: Vimalamitra, Humkara, Manjushrimitra, Nagarjuna, Padmasambhava, Dhanasamskrita, Rambuguhya-Devachandra, and Shantigarbha. These individuals are also referred to as the "eight great ACCOMPLISHED MASTERS" (*grub pa'i slob dpon chen po brgyad*). Details on the lives of these masters can be found in NS 475-83.

EIGHT MUNDANE SPIRITUAL ATTAINMENTS (*thun mong gi ngos grub brgyad*) – See MUNDANE SPIRITUAL ATTAINMENTS.

EMPOWERMENT (*dbang*) – In a general sense, an empowerment is a tantric ritual that matures the student and allows them to engage in specific tantric practices. There are a great many divisions and descriptions pertaining to empowerment, such as those of the ground, path, and fruition. There are also unique empowerments associated with each tantric lineage and vehicle. Concerning the meaning of the term "empowerment," Jamgön Kongtrül explains that the original Sanskrit term has the literal meaning of "to scatter and pour." The meaning, he explains, is that empowerments cleanse and purify the psycho-physical continuum by "scattering" the obscurations and then "pouring" the potential of WISDOM into what is then a clean vessel, the purified psycho-physical continuum [TK 3, 54]. Stressing the importance of the empowerment ritual, Tsele Natsok Rangdröl writes: "Unless you first obtain the ripening empowerments, you are not authorized to hear even a single verse of the tantras, statements, and instructions. (Unauthorized) people who engage in expounding and listening to the tantras will not only fail to receive blessings, they will create immense demerit from divulging the secrecy of these teachings. A person who has not obtained empowerment may pretend to practice the liberating instructions, but, instead of bringing accomplishment, the practice will create obstacles and countless other defects" [EM 39].

EMPOWERMENT INTO THE DISPLAY OF AWARENESS (*rig pa'i rtsal dbang*) – In the ATIYOGA tradition, those with the fortune to do so may enter into the MANDALA of ULTIMATE BODHICHITTA right from the beginning, without having to rely upon the symbolic wisdom of the first three empowerments. The empowerment that allows one to do so is the empowerment into the display of awareness. Quoting the master Manjushrimitra, Jamgön Kongtrül writes: "The profound, supreme, and true empowerment / Is the attainment of the empowerment into the display of awareness. / It is an empowerment because one realizes the nature of mind." [TK 3, 103]

EMPTINESS (*stong pa nyid*) – The manner in which all phenomena are devoid of inherent existence; their true nature. In certain contexts, sixteen or eighteen forms of emptiness are listed: (1) internal emptiness, (2) external emptiness, (3) internal and external emptiness, (4) the emptiness of emptiness, (5) great emptiness, (6) ultimate emptiness, (7) conditioned emptiness, (8) unconditioned emptiness, (9) emptiness that transcends extremes, (10) emptiness without beginning or end, (11) unrelinquished emptiness, (12) natural emptiness, (13) the emptiness of all phenomena, (14) the emptiness of particular characteristics, (15) unobservable emptiness, and (16) the emptiness of the essential lack of entities. When eighteen are listed, the following two are added: (17) the emptiness of the lack of entities, and (18) emptiness of the very essence. [TD 1110]

ENERGY (*rlung*) – One element of the triad ENERGIES, CHANNELS, AND ESSENCES. This factor has the nature of the five elements and completely pervades the energetic channels. [TD 2734]

ENLIGHTENED ACTIVITY (*'phrin las*) – One aspect of the fruitional state of buddhahood. The most common presentation of enlightened activity contains four divisions: pacifying, enriching, magnetizing, and wrathful activity. To these four, a fifth division is sometimes added, that of spontaneous activity [TD 1771]. According to Ju Mipham, enlightened activity can also be divided into supreme and mundane. The former, he writes, involves "planting the seed of liberation in the minds of others by granting EMPOWERMENTS, and through MANTRAS, MUDRAS, and so forth, while the latter functions to bring others more temporary forms of happiness" [ON 559].

ESSENCE KAYA (*ngo bo nyid sku*) – As discussed in the Perfection of Knowledge literature, the essence kaya is one particular facet of buddhahood. In particular, this refers to the kaya of the perfection of the sphere of reality, in which there are two forms of purity, natural purity and incidental purity. [TD 663]

FAITH (*dad pa*) – Generally, three types of faith are discussed in the scholastic tradition: lucid faith, inspired faith, and the faith of conviction. The first entails a lucid frame of mind that arises in reference to the Three Jewels. The second concerns the desire to take up and reject the four truths. The third involves having conviction in the principle of karmic causality. [YD 607]

FATHER TANTRA (*pha rgyud*) – Father Tantra emphasizes both the methods of the DEVELOPMENT STAGE and the energetic practices of the COMPLETION STAGE. In the NEW SCHOOLS, the Father Tantra includes the five stages of the *Guhyasamaja Tantra* [ST 6]. In the NYINGMA tradition, Father Tantra is equated with MAHAYOGA, the seventh of the NINE VEHICLES [DZ 24].

FEMALE MUDRA (*phyag rgya ma*) – The secret spiritual partner of a GURU; the female embodiment of knowledge (*rig ma*) with whom a yogi of the Mantra Tradition practices. [TD 1733]

FEMALE SPIRITUAL PARTNER (*yum*) – A female YIDAM DEITY that embodies the principle of KNOWLEDGE [TD 2585]. See also MALE AND FEMALE SPIRITUAL PARTNERS.

FIVE ACTS OF IMMEDIATE RETRIBUTION (*mtshams med lnga*) – (1) To kill one's father, (2) to kill one's mother, (3) to kill a foe-destroyer, (4) to create a schism within the Buddhist community, and (5) to maliciously draw blood from the body of a buddha. [TD 2311]

FIVE BUDDHA FAMILIES (*rigs lnga*) – The five buddha families function as the support for the FIVE WISDOMS. The relationship between these two groups is as follows: The WISDOM OF THE SPHERE OF REALITY is linked with the BUDDHA family and the buddha VAIROCHANA, ACTIVE WISDOM with the karma family and the buddha AMOGHASIDDHI, the WISDOM OF EQUALITY with the jewel family and the buddha RATNASAMBHAVA, DISCERNING WISDOM with the LOTUS family and the buddha AMITABHA, and MIRROR-LIKE WISDOM with the VAJRA family and either VAJRASATTVA or AKSHOBYA. [TK 2, 80]

FIVE DEGENERATIONS (*snyigs ma lnga*) – (1) The degeneration of life span, (2) the degeneration of the afflictions, (3) the degeneration of sentient beings, (4) the degeneration of time, and (5) the degeneration of the view. [TD 1001]

FIVEFOLD CERTAINTY (*nges pa lnga*) – The five certainties of the SAMBHOGAKAYA: the certain place is the Richly Arrayed SUPREME REALM, the certain form has all the MARKS AND SIGNS of buddhahood, the certain retinue consists solely of realized BODHISATTVAS, the certain teaching is that of the GREAT VEHICLE alone, and the certain time is the duration of SAMSARA. [TD 656]

FIVE MANIFESTATIONS OF ENLIGHTENMENT (*mngon byang lnga*) – An extensive approach to development stage practice found in the MOTHER TANTRAS: Enlightenment manifesting from the visualized moon, sun, seed syllable, symbolic implements, and complete enlightened form [TK 3, 208]. This topic is discussed extensively in DMW.

FIVE PERFECTIONS (*phun sum tshogs pa lnga*) – The perfect teaching, the perfect time, the perfect teacher, the perfect place, and the perfect retinue. [TD 1718]

Five substances that come from cows (*ba byung lnga*) – Cow urine, dung, milk, butter, and curd that have not touched the ground. [TD 1802]

Five visions (*gzigs pa lnga*) – The five visions beheld by the victorious one Shvetaketu [the name of Shakyamuni as he dwelt in Tushita Heaven before taking birth for the final time]: (1) his birthplace, Kapilavastu; (2) his royal caste; (3) his descent from the Shakya clan; (4) his mother, Mayadevi; and (5) the era into which he was born, that of the fivefold degeneration. [TD 2495]

Five wisdoms (*ye shes lnga*) – According to Jigmé Lingpa, wisdom can be divided into twenty-five categories, as there are five different forms of wisdom present in each continuum of the FIVE BUDDHA FAMILIES [YT 431]. More commonly, however, five forms of wisdom are taught. Dudjom Rinpoche explains that the WISDOM OF THE SPHERE OF REALITY is that which realizes how things really are, whereas the four subsequent wisdoms—MIRROR-LIKE WISDOM, the WISDOM OF EQUALITY, DISCERNING WISDOM, and ACTIVE WISDOM—in their function of supporting and depending upon the former, comprise the wisdom that comprehends all that exists. It has also been explained that the first wisdom mentioned above refers to the ultimate, while the latter four relate to the relative [NS 140].

Foe-destroyer (*dgra bcom pa*) – One who has destroyed, or conquered, all of his or her foes, here referring to the FOUR DEMONS [TD 464]. This is the fruition of the LESSER VEHICLE.

Formless realm (*gzugs med khams*) – The four spheres of perception, from that of boundless space up to the peak of existence. In these spheres, there is no coarse form, only clear mental forms. The beings in these realms are free of attachment to form but are attached to the state of formlessness. [TD 2503]

Form realm (*gzugs khams*) – The abodes of the first through fourth states of ABSORPTION, which are located in the space above Mount Meru. The inhabitants of this realm have bodies of light that are clear by nature. Although they are free from passion, they still cling to form. [TD 2499]

Four absorptions (*bsam gtan bzhi*) – Four states of increasingly refined concentration associated with the FORM REALM.

Four classes of tantra (*rgyud sde bzhi*) – The four classes of tantra are KRIYA TANTRA, CHARYA TANTRA, YOGA TANTRA, and ANUTTARAYOGA TANTRA. These four divisions are commonly presented in the NEW SCHOOLS and include all tantric teachings. Although this classification system is also found in the NYINGMA SCHOOL, that tradition more often groups the tantras into the THREE OUTER TANTRAS and THREE INNER TANTRAS.

Four demons (*bdud bzhi*) – The demon of the AFFLICTIONS, the demon of the aggregates, the demon of the lord of death, and the demon of the divine son. [TD 1364]

Four empowerments (*dbang bzhi*) – The VASE EMPOWERMENT, SECRET EMPOWERMENT, KNOWLEDGE-WISDOM EMPOWERMENT, and PRECIOUS WORD EMPOWERMENT. [TD 1935]

Fourfold Heart Essence (*snying thig ya bzhi*) – A collection of GREAT PERFECTION teachings compiled by Longchen Rabjam. This compilation contains five primary divisions: (1) the HEART ESSENCE OF THE DAKINIS (Khandro Nyingtik), the Dzogchen teachings of Padmasambhava; (2) the Quintessence of the Dakinis (Khandro Yangtik), a collection of Longchenpa's commentaries on Padmasambhava's teachings; (3) the HEART ESSENCE OF VIMALAMITRA (Vima Nyingtik), the Dzogchen teachings of Vimalamitra; (4) the Guru's Quintessence (Lama Yangtik), a collection of Longchenpa's commentaries on Vimalamitra's teachings; and (5) The Profound Quintessence (Zabmo Yangtik), a collection of Longchenpa's commentaries that apply to both Padmasambhava and Vimalamitra's teachings.

Four forms of fearlessness (*mi 'jigs pa bzhi*) – (1) Fearlessness in the face of perfect realization, (2) fearlessness in the face of perfect abandonment, (3) fearlessness in the face of teaching obstructive phenomena, and (4) fearlessness in the face of teaching the path of certain release. [TD 2068]

FOUR FUNDAMENTAL AND NATURALLY NEGATIVE DEEDS (*rang bzhin gyi sdig pa'i rtsa ba bzhi*) – (1) Taking life, (2) stealing, (3) sexual activity, and (4) dishonestly proclaiming one's spiritual achievements. See also FOUR FUNDAMENTAL PRECEPTS.

FOUR FUNDAMENTAL PRECEPTS (*rtsa ba bzhi*) – The fundamental precepts associated with the vows of INDIVIDUAL LIBERATION: restraining from taking life, stealing, sexual activity, and dishonestly proclaiming one's own spiritual achievements. These four are the fundamental vows of ordained individuals. If they are allowed to degenerate, one's vows will be completely destroyed. [TD 2210]

FOUR GREAT LIBERATIONS (*grol ba chen po bzhi*) – (1) primordial liberation (*ye grol*), (2) self-liberation (*rang grol*), (3) naked liberation (*cer grol*), and (4) liberation from extremes (*mtha' grol*) [NS 334]. These four are explained in LW, pp. 88-89.

FOUR IMMEASURABLES (*tshad med bzhi*) – Immeasurable love, immeasurable compassion, immeasurable joy, and immeasurable equanimity; these four mindsets are held by practitioners of the Great Vehicle and are so called because one meditates by focusing on sentient beings without any sense of limitation, and because they bring an immeasurable amount of merit. [TD 2260]

FOUR JOYS (*dga' ba bzhi*) – The four joys are a common principle in both the SARMA and NYINGMA teachings on the SYMBOLIC COMPLETION STAGE. These four are listed differently depending on the context, but they are often presented as (1) joy, (2) supreme joy, (3) freedom from joy (or special joy), and (4) coemergent joy. The *Great Dictionary* explains: "Four joys are produced as BODHICHITTA descends to each of the four CHAKRAS. These four comprise a realization associated with the practice of inner heat (*gtum mo*), which involves taking control of the subtle energies. When bodhichitta descends from the crown center, joy is produced; when it descends to the throat center, supreme joy; when it descends to the heart center, freedom from joy; and when it reaches the navel center, coemergent joy." [TD 2562]

FOUR KINDS OF ENLIGHTENED ACTIVITY (*phrin las rnam pa bzhi*) – See ENLIGHTENED ACTIVITY.

FOUR MUDRAS (*phyag rgya bzhi*) – The four MUDRAS, or seals, are a focal point in the meditative tradition of YOGA TANTRA. These four are the activity seal of ENLIGHTENED ACTIVITY (karma mudra), the pledge seal of enlightened mind (samaya mudra), the dharma seal of enlightened speech (dharma mudra), and the great seal of enlightened form (MAHAMUDRA). [SG 335]

FOUR OBSCURATIONS (*sgrib pa bzhi*) – (1) The obscuration of desire, (2) the obscuration of the NON-BUDDHISTS, (3) the obscuration of the inferiority of the listeners, and (4) the obscuration of the inferiority of solitary buddhas. Alternately, the four are (1) the afflictive obscurations, (2) cognitive obscurations, (3) desirous obscurations, and (4) obstructive obscurations. A third enumeration gives (1) karmic obscurations, (2) afflictive obscurations, (3) cognitive obscurations, and (4) obscurations of meditative equipoise. [TD 612]

FOUR SEALS THAT MARK THE BUDDHA'S TEACHINGS (*bkar btags kyi phyag rgya bzhi*) – (1) All conditioned phenomena are impermanent; (2) all that is defiled is suffering; (3) all phenomena are empty and devoid of self; and (4) nirvana is peace. [TD 828]

FOUR TYPES OF GENEROSITY (*sbyin pa rnam bzhi*) – (1) The outer generosity of giving material goods; (2) dharmic generosity; (3) the generosity of protection, or fearlessness; and (4) the generosity of love, the wish that all beings achieve a state of perfect happiness. [YT 486]

FOUR WAYS OF ATTRACTING STUDENTS (*bsdu ba'i dngos po bzhi*) – (1) Practicing generosity, both in terms of the Dharma and in a material sense; (2) offering helpful advice; (3) acting meaningfully, or in accordance with the wishes of those in need of guidance; and (4) acting appropriately, i.e., in accordance with the behavior of those in need of guidance. [TD 1487]

FRUITIONAL VEHICLE (*'bras bu'i theg pa*) – An alternate term for the VAJRA VEHICLE; Ju Mipham explains: "This vehicle is referred to as such because the essential FRUITION is seen to be present within the very ground, whereas in other systems it is believed to be something that must be attained. Hence, in this system, the FRUITION is taken as the path in the present moment." [KG 40]

GLORIOUS MAGICAL WEB (*sGyu 'phrul drva ba*) – See TANTRA OF THE SECRET ESSENCE.

GREAT COMPASSIONATE ONE (*thugs rje chen po*) – A form of the BODHISATTVA AVALOKITESHVARA.

GREAT PERFECTION (*rdzogs pa chen po*) – This term is used in the tantric tradition of the NYINGMA SCHOOL, where it refers to the DHARMAKAYA (the nature of the mind lacking an essence), the sambhogakaya (self-illumination), and the nirmanakaya (pervasive compassionate resonance). Thus, in the Great Perfection, all the qualities of the THREE KAYAS are spontaneously *perfect*, and since this is the way all phenomena really are, it is *great*. [TD 2360]

GREAT VEHICLE (*theg pa chen po*) – The vehicle of the BODHISATTVAS, so called because it is superior to the LESSER VEHICLE of the LISTENERS and SOLITARY BUDDHAS in seven ways. [TD 1183]

GROUND, PATH, AND FRUITION (*gzhi lam 'bras gsum*) – The view, meditation, and fruition of each vehicle. The ground consists of coming to a definitive understanding of the view; the path involves familiarizing oneself with this through meditation; and the fruition is the attainment of enlightenment. [TD 2421]

GURU (*bla ma*) – A spiritual teacher; according to *Clarifying the Practice of the Heart Essence*, there are three types of guru: (1) the external guru who introduces one to meanings and the symbols that represent them; (2) the inner guru of understanding and experiencing the way things are; and (3) the secret, true guru of realization. The text goes on to explain, "for the novice practitioner, the outer guru is of paramount importance." [HE 16]

Hayagriva (rTa mgrin) – Literally, "Horse Neck." Hayagriva is a wrathful divinity of the LOTUS family and one of the YIDAM DEITIES of the EIGHT SADHANA TEACHINGS.

Hearing lineage (*snyan brgyud*) – Key instructions that have been transmitted orally through a succession of spiritual teachers. [TD 996]

Hearing lineage of people (*gang zag snyan brgyud*) – The transmission of teachings in the human realm [SD 70]; the lineage that has been gradually passed down since the eighth century, when the master Padmasambhava and the great scholar Vimalamitra directly taught their students the key instructions of the three yogas of the INNER TANTRAS [TD 343].

Heart Essence of the Dakinis (*mKha' 'gro snying thig*) – A collection of instructions from the NYINGMA tradition that the master Padmasambhava directly taught the DAKINI Yeshé Tsogyal and which were subsequently revealed as a TREASURE by Pema Ledrel Tsel [TD 297]. This is one division of the FOURFOLD HEART ESSENCE, a collection of Great Perfection instructions compiled by the master Longchenpa.

Heart Essence of the Vast Expanse (*Klong chen snying thig*) – The mind TREASURE of Rigdzin Jigmé Lingpa. [TD 48]

Heart Essence of Vajrasattva (*rDor sems snying thig*) – See DORSEM NYINGTIK.

Heart Essence of Vimalamitra (*Bi ma'i snying thig*) – The GREAT PERFECTION teachings of Vimalamitra, which were compiled by Longchenpa and included in the FOURFOLD HEART ESSENCE.

Hinayana (*theg pa dman pa*) – See LESSER VEHICLE.

Individual liberation (*so sor thar pa*) – The liberation from the lower realms and samsara that those who maintain discipline [practitioners of the Lesser Vehicle] attain for themselves. [TD 2959]

INNER TANTRAS (*nang rgyud*) – See THREE INNER TANTRAS.

INSIGHT (*lhag mthong*) – Along with TRANQUILITY, insight is one of the common denominators and causes of all states of ABSORPTION. It entails the observation of the specific distinguishing nature of a given object. [TD 3092]

INTERDEPENDENT ORIGINATION (*rten 'brel*) – The fact that all phenomena arise due to the interdependent relationship of their own specific causes and conditions. [KJ 18]

INTERMEDIATE STATE (*bar srid/ bar do*) – The bardo, or intermediate state, typically refers to the state that occurs between DEATH and a future rebirth. It can also, however, refer to the transitional periods that constitute the entire stream of existence, inclusive of birth, dreaming, meditation, death, REALITY itself, and transmigration. Concerning the specific COMPLETION STAGE practice that relates to this state, Dza Patrul writes (referring to the three intermediate states of death, reality itself, and transmigration): "In the first intermediate state, one brings LUMINOSITY onto the path as the DHARMAKAYA. In the second, union is brought onto the path as SAMBHOGAKAYA. And in the third, rebirth is taken onto the path as NIRMANAKAYA" [DR 445].

KAMA (*bka' ma*) – See TRANSMITTED TEACHINGS OF THE NYINGMA SCHOOL.

KARMA (*las*) – The nature of action; a mental factor that propels the mind towards a concordant object and causes it to fluctuate [TD 2769]. See also PRINCIPLE OF KARMIC CAUSALITY.

KAYA (*sku*) – An honorific term for body, which is often used to refer to the "body" or "form" of buddhahood, in all its various aspects. See also NIRMANAKAYA, SAMBHOGAKAYA, DHARMAKAYA, and ESSENCE KAYA.

KEY INSTRUCTION CLASS (*man ngag sde*) – The third and most profound division of the Great Perfection teachings, along with the Mind Class and Space Class. This category is further divided into outer, inner, secret, and extremely secret unsurpassed cycles. The latter refers to the Heart Essence teachings of the GREAT PERFECTION, primarily the HEART ESSENCE OF THE DAKINIS (the key instructions that were taught by the master of Oddiyana, Padmakara) and the HEART ESSENCE OF VIMALAMITRA (the lineage of the great scholar Vimalamitra) [TD 2056]. See also THREE CLASSES OF THE GREAT PERFECTION.

KHANDRO NYINGTIK (*mkha' 'gro snying thig*) – See HEART ESSENCE OF THE DAKINIS.

KNOWLEDGE (*shes rab*) – Knowledge is the factor that focuses on a specific entity, examines this object, and is then able to distinguish its essence and individual features, its general and specific characteristics, and whether it should be taken up or abandoned. Once perfected, it functions to dispel doubt. Knowledge is synonymous with the terms total awareness, total understanding, awakening, thorough analysis, thorough understanding, confidence, intellect, mental functioning, and clear realization. [TD 2863]

KNOWLEDGE–WISDOM EMPOWERMENT (*shes rab ye shes kyi dbang*) – The second of the THREE HIGHER, SUPREME EMPOWERMENTS, which is bestowed upon the student's mind in dependence upon the MANDALA of the FEMALE MUDRA. This purifies mental impurities and, in terms of the path, empowers the student to train in the COMPLETION STAGE. As the result of this empowerment, a causal link is formed that leads to the attainment of the DHARMAKAYA. [TD 2865]

KRIYA TANTRA (*bya rgyud*) – Literally, "Activity Tantra." The first of the THREE OUTER TANTRAS; the view of this system, in terms of the ultimate, relates to the self-purity of all phenomena, while relatively one gains SPIRITUAL ACCOMPLISHMENTS by being blessed by the pure DEITY. Practice in this tradition focuses on the WISDOM BEING and MANTRA recitation. Its conduct involves various forms of ritual purification and asceticism. [KG 34]

LESSER VEHICLE (*theg pa dman pa*) – The vehicle of the LISTENERS and SOLITARY BUDDHAS [TD 1183]. See also SUTRA VEHICLE, VEHICLE OF LISTENERS, and VEHICLE OF SOLITARY BUDDHAS.

LIBERATION (*thar pa*) – To be freed from that which binds; in terms of samsara, that which binds is KARMA and the AFFLICTIONS. Hence, these are the factors that need to be eliminated for liberation to occur. Synonyms for liberation include freedom, true goodness, immortality, the ultimate, the immaculate, complete freedom, elimination, purity and freedom, enlightenment, NIRVANA, peace, and the absence of rebirth. [TD 1153]

LINEAGE ENTRUSTED TO DAKINIS (*mkha' 'gro gtad rgya brgyud*) – In this lineage, the wisdom that has been transmitted to the TREASURE revealer is encoded in words and symbolic writing. Once the inventory of the teachings has been entrusted to its master, the teachings themselves are sealed in rocks, lakes, and chests [to be revealed at a later time by the treasure revealer him- or herself]. [NS 745]

LINEAGE OF ASPIRATIONS AND EMPOWERMENTS (*smon lam dbang bskur gyi brgyud pa*) – In this lineage, the one who conceals a treasure makes a declaration regarding its future recipient, such as, "In the future, may the individual who is the master of this particular teaching come to reveal it!" [NS 745]

LINEAGE OF TRANSMISSIONS AND PROPHECIES (*bka' bab lung bstan gyi brgyud pa*) – In this lineage, the individual who is destined to reveal a certain TREASURE is entrusted with the realization, or the genuine WISDOM, that is encoded [within the treasure itself] and is then encouraged with a prophetic statement of future events. [NS 745]

LISTENER (*nyan thos*) – An individual who has entered into the VEHICLE OF THE LISTENERS, one of the THREE VEHICLES. These are individuals who do not focus on practicing the teachings associated with the GREAT VEHICLE, but are so called because they "listen" or hear the teachings from the BUDDHA and so forth, and then repeat what they have heard to others. Hence they are also known as "those who listen and then repeat." [TD 933]

LONGCHEN NYINGTIK (*Klong chen snying thig*) – See HEART ESSENCE OF THE VAST EXPANSE.

200 / GREAT PERFECTION

LOWER EXISTENCE (*ngan 'gro*) – A general term used to refer to the three lower realms, where beings experience nothing but intense suffering as the result of the great number of nonvirtuous acts they committed in the past. [TD 646]

LOWER REALM (*ngan song*) – Synonymous with LOWER EXISTENCE. [TD 649]

LUMINOSITY (*'od gsal*) – Though the term literally means "light which is able to dispel darkness" [TD 2535], *'od gsal* is also commonly used in reference to WISDOM, the subjective counterpart to REALITY. As the practitioner progresses along the various paths and levels, the manner in which luminous wisdom perceives its object, REALITY, becomes more and more refined. [NO 4, 17]

MAGICAL WEB (*sGyu 'phrul drva ba*) – See *TANTRA OF THE SECRET ESSENCE*.

MAHAMUDRA (*phyag rgya chen po*) – (1) "Mahamudra" is the term given to the ultimate fruition, the SUPREME SPIRITUAL ACCOMPLISHMENT. (2) The term can also refer to one of the FOUR MUDRAS taught in the YOGA TANTRA tradition. In this context, the practice of Mahamudra relates to the enlightened form. As such, it eliminates the temporary confusion of the UNIVERSAL GROUND CONSCIOUSNESS and actualizes its nature, MIRROR-LIKE WISDOM. [TD 1732]

MAHAYANA (*theg pa chen po*) – See GREAT VEHICLE.

MAHAYOGA (*rnal 'byor chen po*) – Mahayoga is one of NINE VEHICLES found in the NYINGMA tantric tradition. In this system, one begins by maturing one's state of being with the eighteen supreme EMPOWERMENTS: the ten outer, beneficial empowerments; the five inner empowerments of potentiality; and the three profound, secret empowerments. In the next step, one comes to a definitive understanding of the VIEW, which relates to the indivisibility of the superior two truths. In terms of meditation, the development stage is emphasized—the THREE ABSORPTIONS form the structure for this stage of practice, while its essence consists of a threefold process: purification, perfection, and maturation. This is then sealed with the four stakes that bind the life-force. In the COMPLETION STAGE practice of this system, one meditates on the CHANNELS, ENERGIES, ESSENCES, and LUMINOSITY. Then, as the conduct, one relies upon the direct cause, which can be either elaborate in form, unelaborate, or extremely unelaborate, and then attains the fruition of this process—the completion of the FIVE PATHS (which are subsumed under the FOUR MASTERS OF AWARENESSS). This state of fruition is known as the unified state of the VAJRA HOLDER. [TD 2052]

MALE AND FEMALE SPIRITUAL PARTNERS (*yab yum*) – In the SECRET MANTRA VEHICLE, male and female DEITIES are said to embody key Buddhist principles and are visualized in this capacity. Getse Mahapandita explains: "Subjective appearances relate to the masculine principle of SKILLFUL MEANS. In contrast, the object, meaning EMPTINESS, relates to KNOWLEDGE, the feminine principle. The indivisible unity of these two is the great primordial union of all that exists." Discussing further, he writes: "Emptiness can be witnessed based on appearance, while appearances arise unhindered as the display of emptiness, which itself manifests as causality. Since the truth of this is undeniable, the two truths are in union; they do not conflict with the principle of INTERDEPENDENT ORIGINATION. You cannot attain the perfect result of NIRVANA by utilizing just one of these while abandoning the other. Therefore, the way to bring this onto the path is to meditate on the male and female deities in union, which symbolizes the indivisible union of skillful means and knowledge." [CG 50]

MANDALA (*dkyil 'khor*) – Explaining the meaning of this term, Ju Mipham writes: "*Manda* means 'essence' or 'pith,' while *la* has the sense of 'to take' or 'grasp.' Hence, together this term means 'that which forms the basis for grasping essential qualities.' Alternately, when this word is translated literally as a whole, it means 'that which is wholly spherical and entirely surrounds.'" Concerning the various types of mandala, Mipham continues: "There are three types of mandala: those of the ground, path, and fruition. The *natural mandala of the ground* refers to the universe and its inhabitants being primordially present as divinities, both in terms of the support and supported.... In terms of the path, there is the *mandala of meditation*, of which there are the two forms:

the symbolic mandala (such as paintings, lines, arrangements, and those made from colored powder) and the true mandala that is represented by these forms (enlightened form, speech, and mind) .... The *mandala of the ultimate fruition* is composed of the ENLIGHTENED FORMS and WISDOMS that occur once the path has been completely traversed and one has attained the state of SAMANTABHADRA" [ON 494].

The term "threefold mandala" is used to refer to the physical mandala of the DEITY, the verbal mandala of MANTRA, and the mental mandala of concentration [KN 94].

MANJUGHOSHA ('Jam dpal gzhon nur gyur pa) – The "Gentle, Glorious, and Youthful One"; see MANJUSHRI.

MANJUSHRI ('Jam dpal dbyangs) – The "Gentle, Glorious, and Melodic One"; a BODHISATTVA and YIDAM DEITY that personifies perfect knowledge. He is "gentle" in the sense of having totally eliminated any trace of coarse negativity, and glorious in that he is in the form of a sixteen-year-old youth at all times. [TD 888]

MANTRA (*sngags*) – Mantras are formations of syllables that protect practitioners of the VAJRA VEHICLE from the ordinary perceptions of their own minds. They also function to invoke the YIDAM DEITIES and their retinues [TD 707]. Explaining the etymology of the term, Dudjom Rinpoche writes, "*Mana*, which conveys the meaning of mind, and *traya*, which conveys that of protection, become 'mantra' by syllabic contraction, and therefrom the sense of protecting the mind is derived" [NS 257]. See also SECRET MANTRA VEHICLE.

MARKS AND SIGNS (*mtshan dpe*) – The excellent marks and signs that signify a fully realized being. [TD 2306]

MASTER OF AWARENESS (*rig pa 'dzin pa*) – In this term, "awareness" refers to deity, mantra, and the wisdom of great bliss. One who has "mastered" these three with profound and skillful means is a "master of awareness." [TD 2683]

MEDITATION (*sgom pa*) – See VIEW, MEDITATION, CONDUCT, AND FRUITION.

MIND CLASS (*sems sde*) – See **THREE CLASSES OF THE GREAT PERFECTION**.

MIND LINEAGE OF THE VICTORIOUS ONES (*rgyal ba dgongs brgyud*) – In this lineage, the victorious one **SAMANTABHADRA** transmits realization to the regents of the **FIVE BUDDHA FAMILIES**. These five, in turn, transmit this realization to their simultaneously arisen retinue, the **BODHISATTVAS** and so forth. [SD 69]

MIRROR-LIKE WISDOM (*me long lta bu'i ye shes*) – An aspect of wisdom, its self-illumination and unobstructed capacity to manifest. [ZD 78]

MOTHER TANTRA (*ma rgyud*) – In the Mother Tantra, the **COMPLETION STAGE** associated with the subtle essences is emphasized, in which case one relies either upon the body of another or one's own body. In the **NEW SCHOOLS**, the Mother Tantra includes Naropa's Six Dharmas [ST 6]. In the **NYINGMA** tradition, Mother Tantra is equated with **ANUYOGA**, the eighth of the **NINE VEHICLES** [DZ 24].

MUDRA (*phyag rgya*) – Most commonly, the term "seal," or "mudra," refers to physical gestures that embody certain Buddhist principles. According to Ju Mipham, however, the Sanskrit term *mudra* carries the meaning of "a stamp, symbol, or seal that is difficult to move beyond." Explaining further, he writes, "What this means is that these are unique factors that symbolize the enlightened form, speech, mind, and activities of realized beings. Once something has been 'sealed' with one of these, it is difficult to stray from the factor that is being represented." [ON 568]

MUNDANE SPIRITUAL ATTAINMENTS (*thun mong dngos grub*) – In addition to the **SUPREME SPIRITUAL ATTAINMENT**, there are eight mundane **SPIRITUAL ATTAINMENTS**: (1) the sword that enables one to travel through the sky and space, (2) pills that allow one to be invisible and shift shape, (3) eye salve that allows one to see any worldly form as nonexistent, (4) swift-footedness, (5) the ability to extract and sustain oneself on the essences of plants and minerals (which includes the practice of alchemy), (6) the ability to travel to celestial realms, (7) invisibility, and (8) the ability to extract treasures from the earth and provide beings with what they desire. [TD 675]

NATURAL NIRMANAKAYA (*rang bzhin sprul pa'i sku*) – According to Jamgön Kongtrül, the "natural NIRMANAKAYA" is like a reflection cast by the SAMBHOGAKAYA, and encompasses the five PURE REALMS, KAYAS, WISDOMS, Dharmas and other elements that appear to tenth-level BODHISATTVAS. In particular, this refers to the five nirmanakaya realms: the SUPREME REALM (Akanishta, the realm of the buddha family and the buddha VAIROCHANA), Complete Joy (Abhirati, the realm of the vajra family and the buddha AKSHOBHYA), the Glorious (Shrimat, the realm of the jewel family and the buddha RATNASAMBHAVA), the Realm of Bliss, or Lotus Mound (Sukhavati/Padmakuta, the realm of the LOTUS family and the buddha AMITABHA), and Accomplishment of Supreme Activity (Karmaprasiddhi, the realm of the karma family and the buddha AMOGHASIDDHI). [TK 1, 84]

NECTAR (*bdud rtsi*) – A substance that allows one to conquer death. [TD 1362]

NEW SCHOOLS (*gsar ma*) – This appellation is applied most commonly to the Sakya, Kagyü, and Gelug traditions. More specifically, it refers to those who uphold the Tantras of the SECRET MANTRA that were brought to Tibet in a period that began with the work of the great translator Rinchen Zangpo (tenth century C.E.) [TD 3008]. See also NYINGMA SCHOOL.

NINE EXPRESSIONS OF THE DANCE (*gar gyi nyams dgu*) – WRATHFUL DEITIES are said to have nine qualities: they are captivating, heroic, and terrifying (their three physical expressions); laughing, ferocious, and fearsome (their three verbal expressions); and compassionate, intimidating, and peaceful. [JL 233]

NINEFOLD EXPANSE (*klong dgu*) – A condensation of the teachings contained in the THREE CLASSES OF THE GREAT PERFECTION: (1) since the view is free from all elaborations, the expanse is beyond transition or change; (2) because the meditation consists of resting in the natural state, the expanse is free from the affirmations and negations of conceptual analysis; (3) since the fruition is present in its entirety, the expanse is inherently devoid of hope and fear; (4) because the essence is neither permanent nor nothing at all, the expanse is free from any need to be intellectually proven; (5) since the nature has no logical basis, the expanse is one of unceasing reality; (6) since it is characterized by being devoid of worldly entanglements, the expanse is freed from both appearances and mind; (7) as there is no sense of the three times within the sphere of reality, the expanse is free from transition and change; (8) since the display can arise as anything whatsoever, the expanse is unobstructed and self-manifesting; and (9) because spontaneous equality is without any bias or restriction, the expanse is one of innate freedom and imperturbable rest. [YT 626]

NINE VEHICLES (*theg pa dgu*) – The nine vehicles comprise the path of the NYINGMA SCHOOL of the Early Translations, the Ngagyur Nyingma. The first three vehicles are those of the SUTRA VEHICLE, the exoteric Buddhist teachings: (1) the VEHICLE OF THE LISTENERS, (2) the VEHICLE OF THE SOLITARY BUDDHAS, and (3) the VEHICLE OF THE BODHISATTVAS. The next set comprises the THREE OUTER TANTRAS: (4) the Vehicle of KRIYA, or Activity Tantra; (5) the Vehicle of UBHAYA, or Dual Tantra; and (6) the Vehicle of YOGA, or Union Tantra. The final set of three represents the inner tantric tradition: (7) the Vehicle of MAHAYOGA, or Great Yoga; (8) the Vehicle of ANUYOGA, or Concordant Yoga; and (9) the Vehicle of ATIYOGA, or Supreme Yoga (also known as the GREAT PERFECTION). [NS 164]

NIRMANAKAYA (*sprul pa'i sku*) – (1) A form of buddhahood that arises from the empowering condition of the SAMBHOGAKAYA; an embodied form that comes into existence and appears to both pure and impure disciples, working for the benefit of these beings in accordance with their mental predispositions. (2) A name applied to the reincarnations of great lamas. [TD 1689]

NIRVANA (*mya ngan las 'das pa*) – (1) To be liberated from suffering; (2) peace. [TD 2126]

NON-BUDDHIST (*mu stegs pa*) – Those whose religious persuasion does not involve maintaining that the Three Jewels are a source of refuge or accepting the FOUR SEALS THAT MARK THE BUDDHA'S TEACHINGS. [TD 2101]

Nondual Tantra (*gnyis med rgyud*) – The third of three divisions that comprise the ANUTTARAYOGA TANTRA; Nondual Tantra stresses the view of the PATH OF LIBERATION. In the NEW SCHOOLS, this includes the Six Applications of the Kalachakra Tantra. [ST 6]

Nyingma School (*rnying ma'i lugs*) – This tradition contains NINE VEHICLES and is also referred to as the SECRET MANTRA School of the Early Translations. The teachings of this school were first translated into Tibetan during the reign of King Trisong Deutsen (eighth century C.E.) and spread by the master Padmasambhava and his followers. [TD 992]

Nyingtik Yabshi (*snying thig ya bzhi*) – See FOURFOLD HEART ESSENCE.

Outer tantras (*phyi rgyud*) – See THREE OUTER TANTRAS.

Path of liberation (*grol lam*) – Along with the PATH OF SKILLFUL MEANS, this is one of two practical approaches found in the ANUTTARAYOGA TANTRAS. Ju Mipham explains, "In this phase of practice, one relies primarily upon the knowledge that comes from study, contemplation, and meditation, which allows one to come to a definitive understanding that all phenomena have been enlightened from the very beginning within the great MANDALA of spontaneous perfection, that they are one's own self-occurring WISDOM. By meditating on this, one progresses along the path and is liberated into great equality—the mandala of the self-appearance of the KAYAS and WISDOMS." [ON 420]

Path of skillful means (*thabs lam*) – Along with the PATH OF LIBERATION, the path of skillful means is one of two approaches to practice found in the ANUTTARAYOGA TANTRAS. Ju Mipham explains, "In this phase of practice, one relies primarily upon certain activities to force the arising of one's own self-occurring WISDOM. This results in the swift attainment of the FRUITION. To be more specific, one practices by relying upon the six CHAKRAS to enact a process of blazing and melting. This, in turn, generates the wisdom of BLISS." [ON 419]

PERFORMANCE TANTRA (*spyod rgyud*) – See CHARYA TANTRA.

PRECIOUS WORD EMPOWERMENT (*tshig dbang rin po che*) – The precious word EMPOWERMENT is one of the three higher supreme empowerments. This is bestowed upon the student's ordinary body, speech, and mind in reliance upon the MANDALA of ultimate BODHICHITTA. It purifies the impurities associated with the THREE GATES, along with their related habitual patterns. In terms of the path, it empowers the student to train in the natural GREAT PERFECTION. As its result, a causal link is formed that leads to the attainment of the ESSENCE KAYA, VAJRA WISDOM. [TD 2271]

PRIMORDIAL GROUND (*gdod ma'i gzhi*) – This is a key term in the Great Perfection tradition, where it is often used to describe the true nature of reality. As Longchenpa explains in the passage below, this ground is said to consist of three factors: essence, nature, and compassionate resonance. He explains: "The primordial ground is not restricted to samsara or nirvana, nor does it fall to any extreme. In this original state, the objective sphere of reality is pure by its very nature. It is empty and accommodating like the center of wide-open space, transparent and unmoving like the depths of a clear ocean, and clear and unobscured like the surface of a polished mirror. Present as the empty essence, clear nature, and unobstructed radiance of compassion, it is the fundamental and primordial nature of reality." [LG 18]

PRINCIPLE OF KARMIC CAUSALITY (*las rgyu 'bras*) – The causes and results associated with virtuous and negative actions, such as the fact that suffering results from engaging in negative activities. [TD 2773]

PROVISIONAL MEANING (*drang don*) – Teachings that emphasize the worldly perspective and which are given in order to guide ordinary disciples. This type of teaching employs various forms of verbal and conceptual expression to analyze and reify "individuals," "sentient beings," "the aggregates," "sense fields," and so forth, as well as their "birth," "cessation," "comings," and "goings." This also includes the Buddhist treatises and commentaries that are used as vehicles to express this level of meaning. [TD 1319]

PURE PERCEPTION (*dag snang*) – The perception that all that appears and exists, the entire universe and its inhabitants, are a PURE REALM and the play of the KAYAS and WISDOM. [TD 1237]

PURE REALM (*zhing khams*) – A pure land where BUDDHAS and BODHISATTVAS abide, such as the REALM OF BLISS. [TD 2388]

RATNASAMBHAVA (Rin chen 'byung ldan) – As one member of the FIVE BUDDHA FAMILIES, Ratnasambhava represents the buddha family of enlightened qualities, the source of all that is desirable. [BT 408]

REALITY (*chos nyid*) – (1) The character or nature of something; (2) the empty nature of things. [TD 836]

REALM OF BLISS (*bde ba can*) – The pure realm of AMITABHA. [TD 1368].

RELATIVE BODHICHITTA (*kun rdzob byang chub kyi sems*) – All forms of bodhichitta that arise from coarse conceptual designations. [TD 24]

RESULT OF DISENGAGEMENT (*bral ba'i 'bras bu*) – One division of a fivefold classification of results; the result that ensues once the power of knowledge has brought about the exhaustion of the element it is meant to eliminate, as when the afflictions are eliminated by meditating on the path of realized beings. [TD 1904]

RESULT OF INDIVIDUAL EFFORT (*skyes bu byed pa'i 'bras bu*) – One division of a fivefold classification of results; a result that depends upon the efforts of a living being or individual, such as a harvest that results from planting crops or the wealth that is gained through a business transaction. [TD 164]

RESULT THAT RESEMBLES ITS CAUSE (*rgyu mthun gyi 'bras bu*) – One division of a fivefold classification of results; a result that is identical to, or which resembles in form, its own cause, such as VIRTUE arising from virtue. These results, which are caused by both omnipresent causes and causes of equivalent status, can take two different forms, one behavioral and one experiential. The first refers to propensities that carry across lifetimes, such as having the desire to engage in negativity as a result of having done so in a previous life. The second refers to corresponding experiences, such as when one acts generously in one life and experiences wealth in a future life as a result. [TD 564]

RICHLY ARRAYED REALM (*stug po bkod pa'i zhing*) – A SAMBHOGAKAYA realm located above the seventeen levels of the FORM REALM. [TD 1103]

RIPENED RESULT (*rnam smin gyi 'bras bu*) – One division of a fivefold classification of results; a result that emerges from the ripening of either defiled VIRTUE or vice, such as the defiled, perpetuating aggregates. [TD 1574]

RUPAKAYA (*gzugs kyi sku*) – This refers to the NIRMANAKAYA, the emanated form that has attachment, and the SAMBHOGAKAYA, the form of perfect enjoyment that does not. These KAYAS manifest in an embodied manner for the benefit others. They appear to the perception of impure and pure disciples, respectively, once the referential ACCUMULATION OF MERIT has been perfected. [TD 2499]

SADHANA (*sgrub pa/ sgrub thabs*) – As Mipham explains, a sadhana is "that which enables one to attain or accomplish a desired end." In terms of tantric practice, he writes, this refers to "all the various practices that utilize the unique methods of the SECRET MANTRA tradition to achieve whatever SPIRITUAL ACCOMPLISHMENTS one desires, whether supreme or mundane." [ON 534]

SAMANTABHADRA (Kun tu bzang po) – (1) That which is virtuous and good in every way, completely perfect; (2) the SPHERE OF REALITY, the DHARMAKAYA; (3) a general term for buddhahood; (4) a particular TATAGATA; (5) a particular BODHISATTVA; and (6) the SAMBHOGAKAYA of the Bön tradition. [TD 18]

SAMANTABHADRI (Kun tu bzang mo) – The female counterpart of SAMANTABHADRA; representing WISDOM, Samantabhadri embodies the empty nature of all phenomena, the "pure spacious expanse." [NS 284]

210 / GREAT PERFECTION

SAMAYA BEING (*dam tshig sems dpa'*) – The samaya being is one of the three beings set forth in DEVELOPMENT STAGE practice. This is the deity that one visualizes in conjunction with the ritual of whichever YIDAM DEITY is being practiced [TK 3, 45]. According to Jamgön Kongtrül, the samaya being corresponds to the luminous, enlightened mind. This, in turn, is inseparable from the WISDOM BEING, the DHARMAKAYA of all buddhas [LW 62].

SAMAYA VOW (*dam tshig*) – Along with the vows of INDIVIDUAL LIBERATION found in the LESSER VEHICLE and the BODHISATTVA precepts of the GREAT VEHICLE, the samaya vows are one of three sets of vows that form the basis for Buddhist practice. These vows are associated specifically with the VAJRAYANA. Jamgön Kongtrül explains: "The word *samaya* means 'pledged commitment,' 'oath,' 'precept,' etc. Hence, this refers to a vajra promise or samaya because one is not to transgress what has been pledged. Samaya vows involve both benefit and risk because, if kept, samaya vows become the foundation for all the trainings of MANTRA. If not kept, however, all these trainings become futile." There are innumerable divisions of the samaya vows found in the various tantras. At the most fundamental level, however, one pledges to continually maintain the view of the enlightened form, speech, and mind of the buddhas. [LW 46]

SAMBHOGAKAYA (*longs spyod rdzogs pa'i sku*) – One of the FIVE KAYAS; while not wavering from the DHARMAKAYA, this form appears solely to those disciples who are noble BODHISATTVAS. It is also the basis for the arising of the NIRMANAKAYA and is adorned with MARKS AND SIGNS [TD 2818]. The sambhogakaya is the pooling of luminosity in the sphere of reality itself. Beyond the extremes of permanence and nihilism, it is the quality [of the state of buddhahood] that manifests as the spontaneously present signs and marks of perfect enlightenment [GS 541].

SAMSARA (*'khor ba*) – Literally, to revolve in a cyclic manner; the abode of the six classes of existence or, said differently, the five defiled and perpetuating aggregates. [TD 316]

SARMA SCHOOLS (*gsar ma*) – See NEW SCHOOLS.

GLOSSARY / 211

SECRET EMPOWERMENT (*gsang dbang*) – The secret EMPOWERMENT is the first of the three higher supreme empowerments (the other two being the KNOWLEDGE-WISDOM EMPOWERMENT and the PRECIOUS WORD EMPOWERMENT). This is bestowed upon the ordinary speech of the student by relying upon the MANDALA of relative BODHICHITTA of the MALE AND FEMALE SPIRITUAL PARTNERS in union. This purifies the impurities of ordinary speech. In terms of the path, this empowers one to meditate on the energetic practices and recite MANTRA. In terms of the FRUITION, a link is formed to the attainment of the SAMBHOGAKAYA and VAJRA SPEECH. [TD 3006]

SECRET MANTRA (*gsang sngags*) – Secret Mantra is the WISDOM of great bliss, which protects the mind from subtle concepts through the union of empty KNOWLEDGE and compassionate SKILLFUL MEANS. It is referred to as such because it is practiced in secret and not divulged to those who are not suitable recipients of these teachings [TD 3002]. See also SECRET MANTRA VEHICLE.

SECRET MANTRA VEHICLE (*gsang sngags kyi theg pa*) – An alternate term for the VAJRA VEHICLE. Ju Mipham explains: "This system is 'secret' insofar as the profound MANDALA of the victorious ones' enlightened form, speech, and mind is present as the innate nature of all phenomena. Nevertheless, this is inherently hidden from those who are confused and must be revealed skillfully. It is not revealed explicitly to the inferior practitioners of the lower approaches but is transmitted secretly. Hence, it is not part of the range of experience of ordinary disciples. The term 'MANTRA' indicates that, in order to practice the MANDALA of these three secrets, this nature is presented as it actually is; it is not hidden or kept secret." [KG 38]

SEVEN BRANCHES (*yan lag bdun*) – Seven practices that allow one to gather the accumulations and that function as a preliminary to practicing the Buddhist teachings [TD 2554]. These seven are (1) prostration, (2) offering, (3) confession, (4) rejoicing, (5) requesting to teach, (6) requesting to remain, and (7) dedicating merit.

SEVEN RICHES OF REALIZED BEINGS (*'phags pa'i nor bdun*) – (1) The river-like jewel of faith; (2) the flower-like jewel of discipline; (3) the ocean-like jewel of study; (4) the gem-like jewel of generosity; (5) the jewel of modesty, which is trustworthy like one's parents; (6) the crystalline jewel of the vows; and (7) the sun-like jewel of knowledge. [CNT 219]

SEVEN RICHES OF ROYALTY (*rgyal srid rin po che sna bdun*) – (1) The precious wheel, (2) the precious gem, (3) the precious queen, (4) the precious minister, (5) the precious elephant, (6) the precious supreme horse, and (7) the precious general. [TD 558]

SEVEN TREASURES (*rin chen sna bdun*) – (1) Gold, (2) silver, (3) *vaidurya*, (4) gems, (5) emerald, (6) crystal, and (7) red pearl [CNT 225]. According to TD, the seven treasures are synonymous with the SEVEN RICHES OF ROYALTY [TD 2697].

SIDDHA (*grub thob*) – See ACCOMPLISHED MASTER.

SIX LINEAGES (*brgyud pa drug*) – The six lineages of the EARLY TRANSLATION SCHOOL's TRANSMITTED TEACHINGS and TREASURES. This includes the three lineages that are common to both the Transmitted Teachings and the treasure tradition: (1) the LINEAGE OF THE VICTORS' REALIZATION, (2) the SYMBOLIC LINEAGE OF THE MASTERS OF AWARENESS, and (3) the HEARING LINEAGE OF PEOPLE, as well as three additional lineages that relate specifically to the karmically linked treasures: (4) the LINEAGE OF TRANSMISSIONS AND PROPHECIES, (5) the LINEAGE OF ASPIRATIONS AND EMPOWERMENTS, and (6) the LINEAGE ENTRUSTED TO DAKINIS [NS 745]. In Longchenpa's *A Cloud on the Ocean of Profound Reality*, the lineage of transmissions and prophecies is referred to as "the lineage of compassionate blessings" [ZD 308].

SIX PERFECTIONS (*pha rol tu phyin pa drug*) – (1) Generosity, (2) discipline, (3) patience, (4) diligence, (5) ABSORPTION, and (6) KNOWLEDGE. [TD 1698]

SIX STAINS (*dri ma drug*) – Six faults that should be eliminated when receiving teachings on the Dharma: (1) pride, (2) lack of faith, (3) disinterest, (4) distraction, (5) inward withdrawal, and (6) discouragement. [TD 1327]

SKILLFUL MEANS (*thabs*) – An activity that enables one to accomplish a given outcome easily [TD 1148]. See also PATH OF SKILLFUL MEANS and VEHICLE OF SKILLFUL MEANS.

SKILLFUL MEANS AND LIBERATION (*thabs grol*) – According to Ju Mipham, the path of ANUTTARAYOGA TANTRA can be divided either in terms of its essence or in terms of practice. The first division consists of the DEVELOPMENT and COMPLETION STAGES, and the second of the PATH OF SKILLFUL MEANS and the PATH OF LIBERATION. [ON 415]

SOLITARY BUDDHA (*rang sangs rgyas*) – These beings, in their final existence, do not rely upon a spiritual master. Instead, they analyze the REALITY of INTERDEPENDENT ORIGINATION and, on that basis, realize the selflessness of the individual as well as half of the selflessness of phenomena. In so doing, they become FOE-DESTROYERS who have achieved the actualization of solitary enlightenment [TD 2659]. See also LESSER VEHICLE.

SPACE CLASS (*klong sde*) – See THREE CLASSES OF THE GREAT PERFECTION.

SPHERE OF REALITY (*chos kyi dbyings*) – (1) EMPTINESS; (2) the empty nature of the five aggregates. [TD 840]

SPIRITUAL ATTAINMENT (*dngos grub*) – The positive result that one aims to attain by practicing a particular set of spiritual instructions [TD 675]. See also MUNDANE SPIRITUAL ATTAINMENTS and SUPREME SPIRITUAL ATTAINMENT.

SPIRITUAL PARTNER (*yab yum*) – See MALE AND FEMALE SPIRITUAL PARTNERS.

SUGATA (*bde bar gshegs pa*) – See BLISSFUL ONES.

SUKHAVATI (*bde ba can*) – See **REALM OF BLISS**. [TD 1368]

SUPREME REALM (*'og min*) – (1) The eight planes of existence associated with the fourth level of absorption; the gods born in this plane have reached the highest level of the **FORM REALM**. This realm, which is one of the five pure realms, is referred to as such because there are no other realms of embodied beings higher than this; (2) the Richly Arrayed Realm of Akanishta (Akanishtaghandavyuha), a **SAMBHOGA-KAYA** realm located above the seventeen form realms [TD 2529, 1103]. According to Longchenpa, the genuine, true Supreme Realm "cannot be measured in terms of dimensionality. Rather, it is free of all elaborations. This essence is the sacred point where the buddha's journey ends" [CCM 35].

SUTRA (*mdo*) – See **SUTRA VEHICLE**.

SUTRA VEHICLE (*mdo'i theg pa*) – The Buddhist teachings are often classified into two divisions, which represent two approaches to enlightenment—the Sutra Vehicle and the **VAJRA VEHICLE**. The former is often referred to as the "Causal Vehicle" because, in this tradition, practice consists of assembling the causes that lead to the attainment of liberation. This vehicle is further divided into the **VEHICLES OF THE LISTENERS** and **SOLITARY BUDDHAS** (which comprise the **LESSER VEHICLE**) and the **VEHICLE OF THE BODHISATTVAS** (the **GREAT VEHICLE**).

SVABHAVIKAKAYA (*ngo bo nyid sku*) – See **ESSENCE KAYA**.

SYMBOLIC LINEAGE OF THE MASTERS OF AWARENESS (*rig 'dzin brda'i brgyud*) – The succession of teachers who are introduced to the unique key instructions of the **NYINGMA SCHOOL**'s **SECRET MANTRA** via symbols and various skillful means. [TD 2685]

TANTRA (*rgyud*) – (1) A continuum that remains temporally unbroken; (2) a thread; (3) a region or district; (4) bloodline; (5) the **SECRET MANTRA** and its related texts. [TD 573]

TANTRA OF THE SECRET ESSENCE (*rGyud gsang ba snying po*) – This text, often referred to as the *Guhyagarbha Tantra*, is the most widely studied tantra in the NYINGMA SCHOOL. It was translated by Vimalamitra, Nyak Jnanakumara and Ma Rinchen Chok. The full title of this twenty-two-chapter text is *Tantra of the True Nature of Reality: The Glorious Secret Essence* [TD 574]. While this tantra is most often linked with the MAHAYOGA tradition, it is also listed as an ANUYOGA tantra in certain contexts and an ATIYOGA tantra in others, which is due to the fact that the view of this set of literature is said to correspond to that of Atiyoga, while in terms of conduct it is linked with Mahayoga. According to Ju Mipham, it is fine to classify this text as belonging to any one of the THREE INNER TANTRAS, from the perspective of emphasizing its teachings on DEVELOPMENT, COMPLETION, or GREAT PERFECTION, respectively [KG 10].

TANTRA OF CAPACITY (*thub pa'i rgyud*) – According to Rongzom Mahapandita, the Tantra of Capacity is the outer division of YOGA TANTRA, the third of the THREE OUTER TANTRAS. The inner division of Yoga Tantra is the Unsurpassed Yoga Tantra, which is subdivided into Development (MAHĀYOGA), Completion (ANUYOGA), and Great Perfection (ATIYOGA) [TP 238]. The Third Dzogchen Rinpoche, in contrast, uses this term to refer to all three outer tantras [KN 132].

TARA (sGrol ma) – A female YIDAM DEITY whose name (literally, "the Liberator") signifies her capacity to liberate beings from the eight forms of fear. [TD 625]

TATAGATA (*de bzhin gshegs pa*) – An epithet of the buddhas, referring to one who, in dependence upon the path of REALITY, abides in neither existence nor peace and has passed into the state of great enlightenment. [TD 1287]

TEN PERFECTIONS (*pha rol tu phyin pa bcu*) – (1) Generosity, (2) discipline, (3) patience, (4) diligence, (5) ABSORPTION, (6) KNOWLEDGE, (7) SKILLFUL MEANS, (8) strength, (9) aspiration, and (10) WISDOM. [TD 1698]

TEN POWERS (*stobs bcu*) – The ten powers of the TATAGATAS: (1) the power to know the correct and incorrect; (2) the power to know the ripening of KARMA; (3) the power to know the variety of individual interests; (4) the power to know the variety of individual characters; (5) the power to know both superior and inferior faculties; (6) the power to know all paths that can be traveled; (7) the power to know the meditative concentrations of total liberation, absorption, stability, and so on; (8) the power to know previous births; (9) the power to know of death, transmigration, and rebirth; and (10) the power to know of the exhaustion of defilements. [TD 1119]

Terma (*gter ma*) – See **Treasure**.

Thirty-seven factors of enlightenment (*byang phyogs so bdun*) – The thirty-seven factors of enlightenment are qualities that occur at various stages of the Buddhist path. According to Maitreya's *Distinguishing the Middle from Extremes*, these are (1) the four **applications of mindfulness** that occur on the lesser path of accumulation; (2) the four authentic eliminations that occur on the intermediate path of accumulation; (3) the four bases of miraculous power that occur on the greater path of accumulation; (4) the five faculties that occur on the first two stages of the path of connection—the stages of heat and summit; (5) the five powers that occur on the last two stages of the path of connection—the stage of acceptance and the supreme state; (6) the seven aspects of enlightenment that occur on the path of knowledge; and (7) the eightfold noble path that occurs on the path of cultivation. [MV 732]

Thirty-two marks of the buddhas (*mtshan bzang po so gnyis*) – See **Marks and signs**.

Three classes of the Great Perfection (*rdzogs chen sde gsum*) – According to Longchenpa, the first transmission of the **Great Perfection** teachings in the human realm took place between Garap Dorjé and Manjushrimitra. The former passed on his teachings in the form of 6,400,000 verses. The latter then codified his master's teachings and divided them into three categories: the **Mind Class**, **Space Class**, and **Key Instruction Class** [TC 16]. Explaining these three categories, Jigmé Lingpa writes, "There are no phenomena that exist apart from one's very own mind. Therefore, one is freed from the idea that there are things that need to be rejected. This is the Mind

Class. In addition, all forms of phenomenal existence have nowhere to go other than reality itself—the expanse of Samantabhadri. Because of this, one is freed from the extreme of needing antidotes. This is the activity-free Space Class. Finally, the profound Key Instruction Class involves being liberated from both factors that need to be rejected and antidotes by arriving at a decisive certainty concerning the true nature of things" [YT 608].

THREE COLLECTIONS (*sde snod gsum*) – The three collections contain the entire range of teachings given by the Buddha. These three are the VINAYA COLLECTION, the SUTRA Collection, and the Abhidharma Collection. Respectively, they relate to the THREE TRAININGS, those of discipline, meditation, and KNOWLEDGE. These collections contain all the words and meanings found within the twelvefold collection of sacred Buddhist writings and encompass all the various topics that can be known, from form all the way up to omniscience. [TD 1473]

THREEFOLD MANDALA – See MANDALA.

THREE FORMS OF ENLIGHTENMENT (*byang chub gsum*) – The fruition of the paths of the LISTENERS, SOLITARY BUDDHAS, and BUDDHAS. [TD 1872]

THREE GATES (*sgo gsum*) – Body, speech, and mind. [TD 595]

THREE GATES TO TOTAL LIBERATION (*rnam par thar pa'i sgo gsum*) – The three meditative concentrations that enable one to attain total liberation: (1) EMPTINESS, (2) the absence of characteristics, and (3) the absence of desire. [TD 1569]

THREE INNER TANTRAS (*nang rgyud gsum*) – In the textual tradition of the NYINGMA SCHOOL, the three inner tantras comprise the final three of this tradition's NINE VEHICLES. They are listed as the tantras of MAHAYOGA, the scriptures of ANUYOGA, and the key instructions of ATIYOGA [TD 1505]. These three divisions are also associated with the practices of DEVELOPMENT, COMPLETION, and GREAT PERFECTION. As Dilgo Khyentse explains: "Development and Mahayoga are like the basis for all the teachings, completion and Anuyoga are like the path of all the teachings, and the Great Perfection of Atiyoga is like the result of all the teachings" [WC 773].

THREE KAYAS (*sku gsum*) – The DHARMAKAYA, SAMBHOGAKAYA, and NIRMANAKAYA. [TD 125]

THREE OUTER TANTRAS (*phyi rgyud gsum*) – In the textual tradition of the NYINGMA SCHOOL, the three outer tantras are listed as KRIYA TANTRA (Activity Tantra), CHARYA TANTRA (Performance Tantra), and YOGA TANTRA (Union Tantra). These traditions are also referred to as the "Vedic Vehicles of Ascetic Practice," due to the fact that they include various ascetic practices, such as ritual cleansing and purification, that are similar to those found in the Vedic tradition of the Hindu Brahmin caste. [TD 1740]

THREE REALMS (*khams gsum*) – The DESIRE, FORM, and FORMLESS REALMS. [TD 226]

THREE ROOTS (*rtsa gsum*) – The three roots are the three inner objects of refuge: the GURU, YIDAM DEITY, and DAKINI. A guru is a qualified spiritual teacher who has liberated his or her own mind and is skilled in the methods that tame the minds of others. The yidam deities are the vast array of peaceful and wrathful deities and those associated with the EIGHT SADHANA TEACHINGS. The dakinis are those associated with the three abodes. The latter refers to VAJRAVARAHI in particular, the divine mother who gives birth to all BUDDHAS. [KN 23]

THREE SPHERES (*'khor gsum*) – Agent, act, and object. [TD 320]

THREE TRAININGS (*bslab pa gsum*) – (1) Discipline, (2) concentration, and (3) KNOWLEDGE. [TD 3056]

THREE VAJRAS (*rdo rje gsum*) – VAJRA BODY, VAJRA SPEECH, and VAJRA MIND.

THREE VEHICLES (*theg pa gsum*) – The VEHICLE OF THE LISTENERS, the VEHICLE OF THE SOLITARY BUDDHAS, and the VEHICLE OF THE BODHISATTVAS. [TD 1183]

THREE WAYS TO NOT BE ASHAMED OF ONESELF (*ma khrel gsum*) – A threefold principle related to the SAMAYA VOWS of YOGA TANTRA: (1) to not be ashamed in the presence of the YIDAM DEITY, (2) to not be ashamed in the presence of one's master and spiritual companions, and (3) to not be ashamed in the presence of one's own mind. [TC 247]

TÖGAL (*thod rgal*) – See DIRECT LEAP.

TORMA (*gtor ma*) – Torma is one of the primary offerings found in the SECRET MANTRA tradition, where, along with medicine and BLOOD, it comprises the inner offerings. Though there are various divisions of torma, the outer torma offering consists of "the choicest types of edibles heaped upon a vessel of precious substances," which, as Jamgön Kongtrül explains, embodies "the indivisibility of the SPHERE OF REALITY and WISDOM" [LW 129]. Explaining the significance of torma in different contexts, Dilgo Khyentse writes, "Generally speaking, torma should be viewed as the MANDALA in the context of APPROACH AND ACCOMPLISHMENT, as sense pleasures in the context of making offerings, as the DEITY in the context of EMPOWERMENT, and as the SPIRITUAL ACCOMPLISHMENTS at the conclusion of a practice" [WC 743].

TRANQUILITY (*zhi gnas*) – One of the common denominators and causes of all states of ABSORPTION. This form of meditation involves settling the mind one-pointedly in order to pacify the mind's tendency to be distracted outwards to external objects. [TD 2384]

TRANSMITTED TEACHINGS OF THE NYINGMA SCHOOL (*rnying ma bka' ma*) – The teachings of the NYINGMA SCHOOL have been transmitted through two lineages, the distant lineage of the Transmitted Teachings and the close lineage of the TREASURES. In the former, the teachings of MAHAYOGA, ANUYOGA, and ATIYOGA are preserved, respectively, under the headings of the *Tantra of the Magical Net*, the *Sutra of the Condensed Realization*, and MIND CLASS. [NS 396]

TREASURE (*gter ma*) – The teachings of the NYINGMA SCHOOL have been transmitted through two lineages, the distant lineage of the TRANSMITTED TEACHINGS and the close lineage of the treasures. In the latter, the teachings that are passed on consist of three primary categories, those that relate to Guru Padmasambhava, the GREAT PERFECTION, and the GREAT COMPASSIONATE ONE, AVALOKITESHVARA. [NS 396]

TRUE GOODNESS (*nges legs*) – A lasting state of happiness—liberation and omniscience. [TD 659]

TWELVE ASCETIC VIRTUES (*sbyangs pa'i yon tan bcu gnyis*) – (1) Wearing cast-off clothing, (2) wearing only three Dharma robes, (3) wearing woolen garments, (4) eating only one meal a day, (5) begging for alms, (6) not eating after noon, (7) staying in isolated places, (8) staying at the foot of trees, (9) living in exposed places, (10) staying in charnel grounds, (11) sleeping only while sitting up, and (12) staying wherever one finds oneself. [TD 2023]

TWELVE LINKS OF INTERDEPENDENT ORIGINATION (*rten 'brel yan lag bcu gnyis*) – The internal process of interdependent origination, i.e., the twelve links of interdependent origination that relate to the emergence of the sentient beings that inhabit the universe. These twelve consist of the three links that propel, the four links that are propelled, the three links that are to be established, and the two links that are established. [TD 1075]

TWENTY VOWS (*sdom pa nyi shu*) – The twenty vows involve restraining from committing the twenty root downfalls that conflict with BODHICHITTA. They include (1-5) five things that can easily happen to a king, (6-10) five downfalls that can easily happen to ministers, (11-18) eight things that can easily befall the beginner, and (19-20) the two factors that cause one to lose the vows of ASPIRATION and APPLICATION, or RELATIVE, BODHICHITTA [SG 334]. The first eighteen downfalls are explained in the *Akashagarbha Sutra* as well as in Shantideva's *Compendium of Instructions*.

TWO ACCUMULATIONS (*tshogs gnyis*) – The accumulation of merit and the accumulation of wisdom. The first of these involves a conceptual reference point and consists of wholesome endeavors, such as acts of generosity [TD 3051]. The second is the accumulation of non-referential WISDOM, which refers to the accumulation of the undefiled VIR-

TUE that enacts the attainment of the DHARMAKAYA, the fruitional wisdom in which EMPTINESS is embraced by BODHICHITTA [TD 2594].

TWOFOLD BENEFIT (*don gnyis*) – One's own benefit and that of others. [TD 1302]

TWOFOLD SELFLESSNESS (*bdag med gnyis*) – The selflessness of the individual and the selflessness of phenomena. [TD 1358]

TWO FORMS OF WISDOM (*ye shes gnyis*) – The wisdoms of meditative equipoise and post-meditation. [TD 2595]

TWO OBSCURATIONS (*sgrib pa gnyis*) – The AFFLICTIVE OBSCURATIONS and COGNITIVE OBSCURATIONS. [TD 612]

UBHAYATANTRA (*gnyis ka rgyud*) – Dual Tantra; an alternate name of CHARYA TANTRA.

UNEXCELLED YOGA (*rnal 'byor bla na med pa*) – See ANUTTARAYOGA TANTRA.

UNIVERSAL GROUND CONSCIOUSNESS (*kun gzhi'i rnam shes*) – This primary mental process is unobscured, neutral, and functions as the foundation for the infusion of habitual tendencies. It functions as the basis for the entire range of karmic maturation, as well as for the seeds that are implanted within it, and is the awareness of the essence of objects. [TK 2, 194]

VAIROCHANA (rNam par snang mdzad) – As one member of the FIVE BUDDHA FAMILIES, Vairochana represents the buddha family of enlightened form, the foundation of all positive qualities. [BT 408]

VAJRA (*rdo rje*) – (1) That which is unchanging and indestructible; (2) an ancient Indian symbol that, of SKILLFUL MEANS and KNOWLEDGE, is used to symbolized knowledge; (3) one of the twenty-seven coincidences in Tibetan astrology; (4) an abbreviation of the Tibetan word for diamond [TD 1438]. In VAJRAYANA practice, this SYMBOLIC

IMPLEMENT is associated with a number of important principles. Generally speaking, it is linked with the male principle, compassion, skillful means, and the great bliss of unchanging REALITY [YT 671].

VAJRA BODY (*sku rdo rje*) – As one of the THREE VAJRAS, the vajra body is the KAYA of indivisible appearance and EMPTINESS—the purification of ordinary form. [TD 122]

VAJRADHARA (rDo rje 'chang) – Vajradhara is considered the sovereign lord of all buddha families and the teacher of the TANTRAS. It is also said that this is the form Shakyamuni took when teaching the SECRET MANTRA. [TD 1439]

VAJRA HELL (*rdo rje dmyal ba*) – A term used in the SECRET MANTRA tradition to refer to the Hell of Incessant Torment. [TD 1442]

VAJRA HOLDER (*rdo rje 'dzin pa*) – (1) Great VAJRADHARA; (2) VAJRAPANI; (3) a master of the SECRET MANTRA; (4) Indra. [TD 1440]

VAJRAKILAYA (rDo rje phur pa) – A YIDAM DEITY associated with the principle of enlightened activity from the EIGHT SADHANA TEACHINGS.

VAJRA MASTER (*rdo rje slob dpon*) – A vajra master is a GURU who either grants EMPOWERMENT into a MANDALA of the SECRET MANTRA or who teaches its liberating instructions. [TD 1442]

VAJRA MIND (*thugs rdo rje*) – One of the THREE VAJRAS; according to Jamgön Kongtrül, vajra mind is linked with the DHARMAKAYA and the union of bliss and EMPTINESS. [LW 37]

VAJRAPANI (Phyag na rdo rje) – Vajrapani is the condensation of the enlightened mind of all the BUDDHAS and the embodiment of their strength, might, and power. [TD 1734]

VAJRASATTVA (rDo rje sems dpa') – Vajrasattva is a YIDAM DEITY who is considered the sovereign lord of the hundred buddha families. He is white in appearance and sits in the vajra posture. With his right hand, he holds a VAJRA at his heart, and with his left, a bell at his hip. [TD 1442]

VAJRA SPEECH (*gsung rdo rje*) – One of the THREE VAJRAS; according to Jamgön Kongtrül, vajra speech is linked with the SAMBHOGAKAYA and the union of LUMINOSITY and EMPTINESS. [LW 36]

VAJRAVARAHI (rDo rje phag mo) – Literally, "Indestructible Sow." A semi-wrathful female YIDAM DEITY; the female counterpart of Chakrasamvara ('Khor lo bde mchog) [TD 1440]. The divine mother who gives birth to all BUDDHAS [KN 23].

VAJRA VEHICLE (*rdo rje theg pa*) – Following the LESSER VEHICLE and the GREAT VEHICLE, the Vajra Vehicle is the third and highest vehicle in the Buddhist tradition. In particular, it contains the teachings on Buddhist TANTRA. Ju Mipham explains the significance of this appellation: "In this system, one does not accept or reject illusory, relative phenomena. Instead, the relative and ultimate are engaged as an indivisible unity and one's own three gates are linked with the nature of the THREE VAJRAS. Therefore, this vehicle is "vajra-like" insofar as these elements are seen to be indivisible and the very embodiment of primordial enlightenment, in which there is nothing to accept or reject, hence the term 'Vajra Vehicle'" [KG 39]. See also VEHICLE OF SKILLFUL MEANS, FRUITIONAL VEHICLE, and SECRET MANTRA VEHICLE.

VAJRA WISDOM (*ye shes rdo rje*) – Vajra wisdom is linked with the SVABHAVIKAKAYA and the union of AWARENESS and EMPTINESS. [LW 36]

VAJRAYANA (*rdo rje theg pa*) – See VAJRA VEHICLE.

VASE EMPOWERMENT (*bum dbang*) – The vase empowerment is a maturing EMPOWERMENT that is common to both the OUTER TANTRAS and INNER TANTRAS. In the latter, a MANDALA (either one made from colored powders or painted on canvas) is used to bestow the various subdivisions of this empowerment upon the student. These include the water, crown, and other sections. This process purifies physical impurities and, in terms of the path, empowers one to practice the DEVELOP-

MENT STAGE. In terms of fruition, a causal link is formed that leads to the attainment of the VAJRA BODY—the NIRMANAKAYA. [TD 853, 2865]

VEHICLE OF PERFECTIONS (*phar phyin gyi theg pa*) – An alternate name for the SUTRA VEHICLE.

VEHICLE OF SKILLFUL MEANS (*thabs kyi theg pa*) – An alternate term for the VAJRA VEHICLE. Ju Mipham explains the significance of this appellation: "This approach is referred to as such due to the four characteristics of its SKILLFUL MEANS, which are great, easy, many, and swift. With the key points of this path, afflictive and pure phenomena are not engaged from the perspective of needing to be accepted or rejected. As this is the case, they do not obscure. In addition, its methods are great, insofar as they lead to the perfection of the TWO ACCUMULATIONS. In other systems, such skillful means do not exist." [KG 38]

VEHICLE OF THE BODHISATTVAS (*byang chub sems dpa'i theg pa*) – This vehicle is first entered by taking the vows of ASPIRATION BODHICHITTA and APPLICATION BODHICHITTA. Its view involves realizing the TWOFOLD SELFLESSNESS, while its meditation consists of meditating on the THIRTY-SEVEN FACTORS OF ENLIGHTENMENT. Its conduct consists of training in the FOUR WAYS OF ATTRACTING STUDENTS and the SIX PERFECTIONS. The fruition of this vehicle is twofold: on a temporary level, there are ten levels that are attained, while its ultimate fruition is the attainment of the level of universal illumination [the state of buddhahood] [TD 1874]. See also BODHISATTVA and SUTRA VEHICLE.

VEHICLE OF THE LISTENERS (*nyan thos kyi theg pa*) – In this vehicle, one starts out by accepting to adhere to one of the seven types of discipline associated with the vows of INDIVIDUAL LIBERATION and to keep this discipline from degenerating. In terms of the view, one recognizes that all the phenomena included within the five aggregates are devoid of a personal self, yet one still holds to the idea that the two subtle, indivisible phenomenal selves truly exist. The meditation consists of TRANQUILITY and INSIGHT, the former referring to the nine ways to settle the mind and the latter to meditating on the sixteen aspects of the four noble truths. In terms of conduct, Listeners maintain the TWELVE ASCETIC VIRTUES. The fruition of this vehicle entails attaining the levels of the stream-enterer, the once-returner, the non-returner, and the foe-destroyer. Each of these contains two further divisions, abiding and remaining, making eight in total [TD 933]. See also LISTENER and SUTRA VEHICLE.

VEHICLE OF THE SOLITARY BUDDHAS (*rang sangs rgyas kyi theg pa*) – On this path, one realizes the character of INTERDEPENDENT ORIGINATION, both in its normal progression and also in reverse order, doing so without relying upon a spiritual teacher. This realization brings about a realization of the selflessness of the individual and the elimination of AFFLICTIVE OBSCURATIONS [TD 2659]. See also SOLITARY BUDDHA and SUTRA VEHICLE.

VEHICLE OF UPAYA (*u pa ya yi theg pa*) – See CHARYA TANTRA.

VIEW, MEDITATION, CONDUCT, AND FRUITION (*lta sgom spyod 'bras*) – These four factors encompass all the various elements involved in Buddhist practice. Jamgön Kongtrül explains, "Though there are a great many divisions when it comes to view, meditation, and conduct, they can all be applied to the individual mind. The view is absolute conviction in its actual nature, while meditation means to apply this to one's own state of being. Conduct involves linking whatever arises with this view and meditation and, finally, the fruition is the actualization of the true nature of reality." [ND 6]

VIMA NYINGTIK (*Bi ma'i snying thig*) – See HEART ESSENCE OF VIMALAMITRA.

VINAYA COLLECTION (*'dul ba'i sde snod*) – One section of a threefold division that constitutes the Buddhist teachings; this scriptural division emphasizes the training of supreme discipline. [TD 1407]

VIRTUE (*dge ba*) – The opposite of negativity; positive endeavors or good conduct; a phenomenon that is classified as having a definite mode of maturation, insofar as its result is [always] pleasant. [TD 450]

WISDOM (*ye shes*) – Inborn knowing; the empty and clear awareness that is self-occurring within the mind streams of all sentient beings. [TD 2593]

WISDOM BEING (*ye shes sems dpa'*) – The wisdom being is one of the three beings set forth in DEVELOPMENT STAGE practice, and that which is visualized in the heart center of the SAMAYA BEING. Dza Patrul explains, "At the heart center of each of the assembly of deities you are meditating on, visualize a wisdom being that resembles the deity it inhabits, though without ornamentation and implements" [SS 422]. While this is the most common presentation, according to Kongtrül, meditating on the wisdom being can occur in other forms as well. It can involve visualizing a form that resembles the samaya being, yet it can also entail meditating on a DEITY with a form, color, face, and arms that are different from those of the samaya being, or meditating on a symbolic implement that arises from the seed syllable [TK 3, 209]. This topic is discussed extensively in DMW.

WISDOM OF EQUALITY (*mnyam nyid ye shes*) – The aspect of WISDOM in which one internalizes the fact that all phenomena are equal, in the sense that they are all devoid of characteristics. [YT 431]

WISDOM OF THE SPHERE OF REALITY (*chos dbyings ye shes*) – The aspect of wisdom that is empty in essence and unchanging. [ZD 78]

YIDAM DEITY (*yi dam*) – Yidams are the deities, BUDDHAS, and BODHISATTVAS that form the unique support for tantric practice [TD 2565]. Concerning the ultimate nature of the yidam deity, Jigmé Lingpa writes, "You must realize that it is your own mind, with its EIGHTFOLD COLLECTION of consciousness, that arises as the KAYAS and WISDOM of the deity" [JL 235]. This topic is discussed extensively in DMW.

YOGA TANTRA (*rnal 'byor rgyud*) – Yoga Tantra is the last of the THREE OUTER TANTRAS. In this system, emphasis is placed on the internal process of ABSORPTION. In terms of the path, there are two forms of practice: the practice of SKILLFUL MEANS and the practice of KNOWLEDGE. In the first, one practices DEITY YOGA in conjunction with the FOUR MUDRAS. In the latter, one realizes the inner REALITY of the mind and actualizes DISCERNING WISDOM. To supplement this internal process, external forms of ritual purification are also practiced. [SG 335]

YOGA VEHICLE (*yo ga'i theg pa*) – See YOGA TANTRA.

YOUTHFUL VASE BODY (*gzhon nu bum sku*) – "Youthful vase body" is a concept unique to the tradition of the Great Perfection. It refers to the realization of Samantabhadra, the identity of which encompasses the ocean of wisdoms and kayas and possesses six particular characteristics. These six refer to the external illumination of consciousness turning inwards and the state of inner illumination that follows. The inner illumination of the great, primordial ground and space of being (1) manifests in its own natural state, (2) emerges from the ground, (3) is differentiated, (4) is liberated through differentiation, (5) does not come from somewhere else, and (6) remains in its own place. [TD 2432]

Notes

1 Though the lineage transmission described here is the most common, each cycle of Great Perfection teachings has its own unique presentation. According to the histories of the Heart Essence of the Dakinis, for example, Shri Simha is said to have received the Great Perfection teachings directly from the nirmanakaya buddha Garap Dorjé. This version of the lineage history is explained in more detail by Ngetön Tenzin Zangpo in the translation that follows.
2 The source cited here for the three ways of counting the Fourfold Heart Essence is the *Immaculate Oral Instructions,* the Nyingtik teachings of Jamgön Kongtrül the Great.
3 A fifth collection, titled the Profound Quintessence, is also included in the Fourfold Heart Essence. The Profound Quintessence contains Longchenpa's commentaries that relate to both the Heart Essence of the Dakinis and the Heart Essence of Vimalamitra.
4 The order of topics included here is outlined in *Structure of the Heart Essence of the Dakinis Practice*. Different traditions place these contemplations in a different order, and the number of topics is also subject to change, though they typically number between four and seven topics. The most well-known example of this progression is the four contemplations that change the mind.
5 Though there are many different classifications of the "rainbow body," most commonly this refers to a level of spiritual attainment in which the yogi/yogini's body dissolves into light at the time of death, leaving only hair and fingernails behind.
6 Though this is not mentioned in the text I consulted, it must be the Second Ponlop Rinpoche, Pema Sangak Tenzin (1731-1805), who taught the Third Dzogchen Rinpoche, judging by their respective dates.
7 Experiential guidance (*nyams khrid*) is a particular form of instruction in which a student receives a brief teaching on a particular point and then integrates the teaching via meditation before moving on to the next point.
8 The inventory (*kha byang*) of the Heart Essence of the Dakinis lists these sixty-five as follows: "The twenty-three main and subsidiary texts in the cycle of the *Tantra That Liberates Upon Wearing*, the twenty-three main and subsidiary texts in the cycle of empowerments, the five main and subsidiary texts in the cycle of practical instructions, the five main and four subsidiary texts in the cycle of supportive teachings, and the two main and three subsidiary texts on the intermediate states. These comprise the complete collection. Gathered together, these sixty-five texts make up the entire set of instructions of the Heart Essence of the Dakinis" (YS, vol. 10, pp. 1-10).
9 Though this topic is not always addressed in the preliminary practices, the liturgy mentioned here includes a brief section on the vows; see pages 77–90.
10 In the Ancient Translation School, the principle of primordial enlightenment is embodied by the dharmakaya buddhas Samantabhadra and Samantabhadri (Kun tu bzang po/mo).

These two figures, depicted in union, embody the very nature of reality, the inseparability of self-occurring wisdom and emptiness. As the principle of self-occurring wisdom, Samantabhadra is said to be the "progenitor," or the "father," of all buddhas, in the sense that all buddhas are grounded in *yeshé*, the wisdom present in every moment of experience. Likewise, Samantabhadri is referred to as the "mother of all buddhas," for buddhahood is the culmination of the understanding that all phenomena are empty by nature. In the New Translation schools, the Kagyü, Sakya, and Gelug lineages, the principle of primordial buddhahood is represented by the buddha Vajradhara.

11 All of the titles mentioned here are different ways of classifying and/or codifying the teachings of the Great Perfection. For a more detailed presentation, see CY, page 751.

12 The *Essence Tantra That Liberates Upon Wearing* is one of six texts that form the core of Heart Essence of the Dakinis. These six are collectively referred to as the *Six Essence Tantras That Liberate Upon Wearing*. The term "liberation through wearing" refers to one of six types of liberation: (1) liberation through hearing, (2) liberation through wearing, (3) liberation through seeing, (4) liberation through remembering, (5) liberation through tasting, and (6) liberation through touching.

13 The passage quoted here is from *History of the Lineage Gurus of the Great Perfection, Heart Essence of the Dakinis*. The bulk of Ngetön Tenzin Zangpo's explanation on the lineage history of the Heart Essence of the Dakinis is also from this text.

14 Terdak Lingpa's commentary adds, at this point, that the treatise that clarifies these texts is The Quintessence: A Wish-fulfilling Jewel, which is an alternate title of the Guru's Quintessence. See glossary entry for the Fourfold Heart Essence for more details.

15 The lineage succession listed here is that of Dzogchen Monastery, an important center for study and practice in the Nyingma tradition. The historical heads of this monastery are the Dzogchen Rinpoches, the Dzogchen Ponlop Rinpoches, and the Dzogchen Gemang Rinpoches. See translator's introduction for more details.

16 Pema Rigdzin was the first Dzogchen Rinpoche. He studied with many renowned teachers, including the great Fifth Dalai Lama and Karma Chakmé, and attained mastery of both the Mahamudra and Dzogchen teachings. In 1684, he established Dzogchen Monastery in Eastern Tibet, which eventually became one of the six main monasteries of the Nyingma tradition.

17 The lama referred to here is the first Dzogchen Ponlop Rinpoche, Namkha Ösel (? – 1726). This renowned master received teachings from both Nyingma and Kagyü teachers before meeting his root guru, the first Dzogchen Rinpoche, Pema Rigdzin. Namkha Ösel was known especially for his mastery of the Heart Essence of the Dakinis teachings. He is said to have given yearly teachings on this topic at the retreat center of Dzogchen Monastery, The Sanctuary of the Great Secret Definitive Meaning.

18 Terdak Lingpa includes the following line from the same text: "Then bestow the empowerment into the display of awareness." [SC 519]

19 In the Great Perfection tradition, the stages and significance of empowerment are explained in a slightly different manner than in the general tantric approach. Khenpo Yönga explains: "The stages of empowerment associated with the key instructions of Atiyoga, the pinnacle of all vehicles, are as follows: Without having to rely upon the symbolic wisdom of the third empowerment, those who have the karmic potential to enter into the mandala of ultimate bodhichitta are empowered into the display of awareness right from the outset. The master Manjushrimitra said:

> The profound, supreme and true empowerment is the attainment
> Of the empowerment into the display of awareness.

Hence, it is the realization of reality that is referred to as "empowerment"—
The crowning bestowal of the wisdom empowerment.

In addition, according to the Key Instruction Class, the four empowerments can be classified as follows: the elaborate vase empowerment, the unelaborate secret empowerment, extremely unelaborate knowledge-wisdom empowerment, and the utterly unelaborate word empowerment. There are a great many further classifications that can be made in terms of what is purified by each, what does the purifying, and so forth, but, in brief, we can say that these four purify the impurities of the body, speech, mind, and the ignorance of knowable phenomena, respectively. They also create the potential for attaining the enlightened form, speech, mind, and innate luminosity. They empower one to practice the development stage associated with the Atiyoga path, inner heat, the meditation on the union of bliss and emptiness, and the realization of originally pure wisdom and spontaneously manifest nature. These empowerments form the basis for the perfection of the four paths of training, as well as the total completion of the end result—all the qualities of the mandala of eternal adornments, the enlightened form, speech, mind, and wisdom of the protector Vajradhara. It should be understood that though these four are similar to the empowerments found commonly in the Anuttarayoga Tantra, they have a unique significance." [NO 151]

20 This rather enigmatic statement relates to the various ways of explaining the essential nature of a vow. In contrast to the two Hinayana philosophical systems, which hold that this essential nature lies in the form aggregate, the Cittamatra tradition explains this differently. Jamgön Kongtrül writes: "Since they accept [the primacy] of the universal ground consciousness, the Vijnaptivadins [the Cittamatra school] hold that physical karma, including vows, are actually part of the mental continuum. If the essence of a vow were held to be mind alone, its continuity would remain uninterrupted even during states of distraction, unconsciousness, and so forth. If, on the other hand, its essence is merely a habitual pattern, then even if a cause for relinquishing [one's vow] were encountered, [one's vow] would not be lost. Hence, [the essential nature of a vow] is held to be the continuum of the mind associated with the abandonment [of vice], as well as the seeds of the habitual patterns that are placed in the universal ground consciousness." [TK 2, 20]

21 Typically, the term "unique preliminary practices" refers to certain practices that are specific to the Vajrayana tradition—refuge, bodhichitta, the hundred-syllable mantra, mandala offering, and guru yoga. In this context, however, the term refers to practices that are unique to the Great Perfection. This includes the outer and inner "separation" practices as well as the physical, verbal, and mental preliminaries. These topics are explained in the second volume of *The Excellent Chariot*.

22 A text written by Longchen Rabjam in the fourteenth century that encompasses the entire range of Sutra and Tantra. This thirteen-chapter text is accompanied by an autocommentary entitled *The Great Chariot*. Ngetön Tenzin Zangpo quotes extensively from this text, as well as from another text by Longchen Rabjam titled *The Precious Wish-fulfilling Treasury*.

23 The Tibetan term for Buddha, *sangs rgyas* (pronounced "sang-gyé"), literally means "one who has purified and blossomed."

24 This refers to the last six of the Nyingma tradition's nine vehicles: the three outer tantras—Kriya, Carya, and Yoga—and the three inner tantras—Mahayoga, Anuyoga, and Atiyoga. See glossary entries for these terms for more details.

25 Shang-shang birds (Tib. *shang shang*): the torso and head of the shang-shang are human, while the lower part of its body is bird-like. They have both wings and human arms, and

in their hands hold two ritual cymbals which they play as they fly. On Tibetan teaching thrones, they are depicted standing, with wings outstretched and hands holding cymbals aloft.

26 For an extensive explanation of the significance of Padmasambhava's appearance, see Patrul Rinpoche, *Words of My Perfect Teacher*, pp. 314-16.

27 The Tibetan term for non-Buddhist (*mu stegs pa*) literally means "forder." This word is often used in a pejorative sense to refer to non-Buddhist Indian religions and philosophical schools, though it also implies certain similarities between some of these traditions and Buddhism.

28 A *tsa-tsa* is a small molded image, usually of a religious personage, deity, or Buddhist reliquary. These images are typically produced by Buddhist practitioners in great quantities as a way to accumulate merit.

29 This is a reference to the two phases of tantric practice, development stage (*bskyed rim*) and completion stage (*rdzogs rim*). See glossary for detailed descriptions of these two stages.

30 In addition to the quote included here, Khenpo Kunzang Paldan's commentary on the *Way of the Bodhisattva* includes the following passage from the same tantra: "First, develop bodhichitta. Then, meditate on yourself as Tara and imagine your right ear to be a lotus. Meditate on your teacher as Manjushri; light rays emanate from your master's mouth and actually dissolve into the lotus of your ear. Meditate on all beings as female deities, and at the end of the session meditate a few moments on nonconceptual emptiness." [DON 181]

31 The practice of ransoming the lives of animals involves buying an animal that is to be killed and either releasing it into the wild or keeping it, if it happens to be a domesticated animal.

32 The four "spheres of perception" are synonymous with the four formless realms.

33 This rather technical discussion is pointing out that virtue will produce a different result depending upon the mental state with which it is linked. If one engages in virtuous activities while simultaneously cultivating the states of meditative concentration collectively known as the "four absorptions," the result of this activity will be a rebirth as a god in the form realms. Similarly, when practicing virtue and cultivating the four formless absorptions, the corresponding result will be a rebirth in the four formless realms, which are experientially equivalent to these four absorptions. In this process, virtue functions to propel one into these meditative states, while the states themselves are accessed via meditation.

34 This is a reference to the main preliminary practices of Dzogchen Monastery (*sngon 'gro thar lam dkar po*).

35 These verses are from Shantideva's *Way of the Bodhisattva*, III.23-24. They are the most common recitation used when receiving the bodhisattva vows. There are two traditions associated with these vows, one stemming from Nagarjuna and another from Asanga. In the tradition of Nagarjuna, the vows for the two types of bodhichitta are received simultaneously once these verses have been recited three times. In Asanga's lineage, these two are received successively. In either case, according to Khenpo Kunzang Paldan, it is important to generate a feeling of confidence that one has actually received these vows once they have been recited three times. Khenpo Kunzang Paldan also notes that while it is preferable to receive these vows from a living master, it is also permissible to do so while visualizing the field of merit. [DON 674]

36 These eighteen downfalls are explained in the *Akashagarbha Sutra*, as well as in Shantideva's *Compendium of Instructions*.

37 The phrase "tantras, scriptures, and key instructions" can be interpreted to apply generally

to the Buddhist teachings or, as is often the case, specifically to the three inner tantras of the Nyingma school—Mahayoga, Anuyoga, and Atiyoga.
38 "The Archer" is an epithet of the Indian mahasiddha Saraha.
39 The three paths referred to here, as evident from the preceding verse in the *Jewel Garland*, are the aggregates, the concept of the self, and karma. These form the basis for one another and create a perpetual cycle of birth and death.
40 Longchen Rabjam.
41 Gemini is another name for the heaven named "Yama," "Free from Conflict." According to Jamgön Kongtrül, this name derives from the fact that "the gods here are born together in pairs." [TK 1, 16]
42 In the Tibetan medical tradition, illness is thought to be caused by imbalances and disturbances in the body's four elements—earth, water, fire, and air.
43 One day in the heavens is much longer than a human day. One hundred human years, for example, equals a single day in the Heaven of the Thirty-three, the second of the desire realm's heavens.
44 In a short commentary on this text, "the six times" is said to refer to six days, during which one takes eight vows [SG 331]. This could also refer to the three sessions that are practiced in the morning and the three practiced at night.
45 The "six branches" most likely refer to six aspects of committing one of the "root proscriptions" just mentioned. If six aspects are present, such as having a negative motivation and no regret after having committed such an act, one has committed a downfall, but it is still reparable. On the other hand, if seven such factors are present, one's vows will have been irreparably violated. A discussion of this can be found in TK 2, 90.
46 Fully ordained monks observe two hundred and fifty-three precepts: (1) the four violations, (2) the thirteen residuals, (3) the thirty downfalls related to abandonment, (4) the ninety downfalls rectified merely through confession, (5) the four to be individually confessed, and (6) the one hundred and twelve negativities. [SG 332]
47 According to Dudjom Rinpoche, the three purities are those of the external world, the beings who inhabit it, and the psycho-physical continuum. [NS 276]
48 These four vows are explained in great detail in Longchen Rabjam's text *gNas lugs rin po che'i mdzod* (translated by Richard Barron as *The Precious Treasury of the Way of Abiding*).
49 The eight classes of gods and demons are eight types of non-human beings who were able to receive and practice the teachings of the Buddha; alternately, they are invisible, worldly spirits who can either help or harm humans. On the subtle level, they are said to be the impure manifestation of the eight types of consciousness.
50 While each of the vehicles has its own particular view and conduct, these two are singled out in this context because Upatantra links the view of Yogatantra with the conduct of Kriyatantra. See NS 271 for a discussion of this topic.
51 The following explanation, and the preceding liturgy, contain a great many references to the various approaches, systems, and lineages of the Buddhist tradition, and to the vows of these approaches in particular. Three good sources of information on these topics are Jamgön Kongtrül's *Treasury of Knowledge: Buddhist Ethics*, Sakya Pandita's *A Clear Differentiation of the Three Codes*, and Dudjom Rinpoche's *Perfect Conduct: Ascertaining the Three Vows*.
52 Though there are only three listed here, typically the vows of this tradition are listed as nonexistence, openness, spontaneous presence, and oneness. These four vows are explained in great detail in Longchen Rabjam's *gNas lugs rin po che'i mdzod* (translated by Richard Barron as *The Precious Treasury of the Way of Abiding*).

53 "Powers" and "fearlessnesses" here refer to the "ten powers" and "four forms of fearlessness." See glossary entries for these two categories for more details.
54 In this section, the author has written certain names in Sanskritized Tibetan. These names have been left untranslated and rendered phonetically. Tibetan names in this section have been translated into English, as is done throughout the text.
55 The three supports are those of enlightened form (a statue of the Buddha, for example), enlightened speech (such as a sacred text), and enlightened mind (such as a stupa).
56 According to Patrul Rinpoche, there are three grades of mandala. "The material out of which the mandala should be made," he writes, "depends on your means. The best kind of mandala base would be made of precious substances such as gold or silver. A medium quality one would be made of brass or some other fine metal. At worst, you could even use a smooth flat stone or a piece of wood." [WPT 285]
57 The visualization used in the following practice is based on the traditional Buddhist cosmology. For an extensive presentation of this cosmology, see the second chapter of Jamgön Kongtrül's *Treasury of Knowledge: Myriad Worlds*.
58 Acceptance (*bzod pa*) and supreme state (*chos mchog*) are the last two of four stages on the path of connection (*sbyor lam*). As such, they are the highest states that can be attained while still in samsara.

Texts Cited

THE FOLLOWING list, arranged alphabetically by English title, gives the Tibetan and in some cases Sanskrit originals for the titles translated. It includes texts cited in the Foreword, Introduction, and Notes. For texts cited in *The Excellent Chariot*, in most cases only abbreviated titles were given by the author. To track down the source of these passages, therefore, one must link the abbreviated titles with the full titles found in various collections of Buddhist literature. Although we have done our best to correctly identify them, it is possible that this list may contain inaccurate references.

8,000 Verse Perfection of Knowledge Sutra (*'Phags pa shes rab kyi pha rol tu phyin pa khri brgyad stong pa zhes bya ba theg pa chen po'i mdo*; *Ārya aṣṭādaśasāhasrikā prajñāpāramitā nāma mahāyāna sūtra*). DK: 0010, sher phyin, ka-ga.

Advice on Impermanence (*Mi rtag pa'i don gyi gtam*; *Anityārthaparikathā*). By Hṛṣīkeśa [dGa' ba'i dbang po]. DT: 4174, spring yig, nge.

Akashagarbha Sutra (*'Phags pa nam mkha'i snying po zhes bya ba theg pa chen po'i mdo*; *Ārya ākāśagarbha nāma mahāyāna sūtra*). DK: 0260, mdo sde, za.

Application of Mindfulness (*'Phags pa dam pa'i chos dran pa nye bar bzhag pa*; *Ārya saddharmān usmṛtyupasthāna*). DK: 0287, mdo sde, ya-sha.

Array of Samayas Tantra (*Dam tshig chen po'i rgyal po dam tshig bkod pa'i rgyud*). NG: 97, vol. 4 (nga), text 13, Atiyoga.

Buddha Avatamsaka Sutra (*Sangs rgyas phal po che zhes bya ba shin tu rgyas pa chen po'i mdo*; *Buddha avatamsaka nāma mahāvaipulya sūtra*). DK: 0044, phal chen, ka-a.

A Bunch of Flowers (*'Phags pa me tog gi tshogs zhes bya ba theg pa chen po'i mdo*; *Ārya kusumasaṃcaya nāma mahāyāna sūtra*). DK: 0266, mdo sde, 'a.

Clarifying the Practice of the Heart Essence (*Zab mo snying thig gi gnad thams cad bsdus pa'i don khrid lag len gsal ba*). Written by bKra shis rgya mtsho. RTZ: vol. 90 (si), pp. 1-96.

A Cloud on the Ocean of the Profound Reality (*Zab don rgya mtsho'i sprin*). Klong chen rab 'byams. YS: vol. 8, pp. 1-488.

Collection of Purposeful Sayings (*Ched du brjod pa'i tshom*; *Udanavarga*). A compilation of verses from the Collected Teachings of the Buddha, compiled by Dharmatrata. DT: 4099, mngon pa, tu.

Collection on Impermanence (*Mi rtag pa'i tshom*). One section of the *Ched du brjod pa'i tshom*; see *Collection of Purposeful Sayings*.

Commentary on the Unsurpassed Continuum (*Theg pa chen po'i rgyud bla ma'i bstan bcos kyi rnam par bshad pa*; *Mahāyānottaratantraśāstravyākhyā*). Written by Asaṅga [Thogs med]. DT: 4025, sems tsam, phi.

Compendium of Instructions (*bSlab pa kun las btus pa'i tshig le'ur byas pa*; *Śikṣāsamuccayakārikā*). Written by Śāntideva [Zhi ba lha]. DT: 3939, dbu ma, khi.

Condensed Perfection of Knowledge (*'Phags pa shes rab kyi pha rol tu phyin pa sdud pa tshigs su bcad pa*; *Ārya prajñāpāramitā sañcaya gāthā*). DK: 0013, sher phyin, ka. Also known as *Sher phyin sdud pa*.

Condensed Realization. See *Sutra of the Condensed Realization*.

Dense Array of Ornaments Sutra (*'Phags pa rgyan stug po bkod pa zhes bya ba theg pa chen po'i mdo*; *Ārya ghanavyūha nāma mahāyāna sūtra*). DK: 0110, mdo sde, cha.

Delineation of Karma (*Las rnam par 'byed pa*; *Karmavibhaṅga*). DK: 0338, mdo sde, sa.

Distinguishing the Middle from Extremes (*dBus dang mtha' rnam par 'byed pa*; *Madhyāntavibhāga*). Composed by Maitreya [Byams pa] and transcribed by Asaṅga [Thogs med]. DT: 4021, sems tsam, phi.

Dorsem Nyingtik (*rDo rje sems pa'i snying thig*). RTZ: vol. 89, 385-568.

Essence Tantra That Liberates Upon Wearing (*bTags grol snying po'i rgyud*). The primary tantra of Heart Essence of the Ḍākinīs. YS: vol. 10, pp. 16-17.

Essence of the Oral Lineage (*rNa rgyud thig le*). Bibliographic data unknown.

The Excellent Chariot (*rDzogs pa chen po mkha' 'gro snying thig gi khrid yig thar lam bgrod byed shing rta bzang po*). By Nges don bstan 'dzin bzang po. Chengdu, China: Si khron mi rigs dpe skrun khang, 1997.

Flower Ornament Sutra (*'Phags pa sdong po bkod pa'i mdo*; *Ārya gaṇḍhavyūha sūtra*). Section 45 of the *Buddha Avatamsaka Sutra*, pages 117.1.5-315.1.1. See entry for *Buddha Avatamsaka Sutra*.

Fortunate Eon Sutra (*'Phags pa bskal pa bzang po zhes bya ba theg pa chen po'i mdo*; *Ārya bhadrakalpikā nāma mahāyāna sūtra*). DK: 0094, mdo sde, ka.

Four Hundred Stanzas (*bsTan bcos bzhi brgya pa zhes bya ba'i tshig le'ur byas pa*; *Catuḥśataka śāstra kārikā nāma*). Written by Āryadeva ['Phags pa lha]. DT: 3846, mdo 'grel, tsha.

Fundamental Vinaya (*'Dul ba gzhi*; *Vinayavastu*). DK: 0001, 'dul ba, ka-nga.

Gathering the Accumulations of Enlightenment (*Byang chub kyi tshogs bsdu ba*). Bibliographic data unknown.

Great Array (*bKod pa chen po*). Bibliographic data unknown. NS cites this text as belonging to the Heart Essence of Vimalamitra cycle. There is, however, no text with this title in that collection.

Great Chariot (*Shing rta chen po*). KS: vol. 1, pp. 113-730.

Great Commentary on the 8,000 Verse Perfection of Knowledge (*'Phags pa shes rab kyi pha rol tu phyin pa brgyad stong pa'i bshad pa mngon par rtogs pa'i rgyan gyi snang ba zhes bya ba*; *Āryāṣṭasāhasrikāprajñāpāramitā vyākhyān ābhisamayālaṃkāra loka nāma*). By Haribhadra [Seng ge bzang po]. DT: 3791, mdo 'grel, cha.

Great Drum Sutra (*'Phags pa rnga bo che chen po'i le'u zhes bya ba theg pa chen po'i mdo*; *Ārya mahābherīhārakaparivarta nāma mahāyāna sūtra*). DK: 0222, mdo sde, dza.

Guru's Quintessence (*Bla ma yang thig*). YS: vols. 1-2.

Heap of Jewels Sutra (*dKon mchog brtsegs pa chen po'i chos kyi rnam grangs le'u stong phrag brgya pa*; *Ārya mahāratnakūṭa dharmaparyāya śatasāhasrika grantha*). PK: 0760, dkon brtsegs, tshi.

Heart Essence of the Dakinis (*mKha' 'gro snying thig*). YS: vols. 10-11.

Heart Essence of Vimalamitra (*Bi ma snying thig*). YS: vols. 3-6.

Hevajra Tantra (*Kye'i rdo rje zhes bya ba rgyud kyi rgyal po*; *Hevajra tantra rāja nāma*). DK: 0417, rgyud, nga.

History of the Lineage Gurus of the Great Perfection, Heart Essence of the Dakinis (*rDzogs pa chen po mkha' 'gro snying tig gi bla ma brgyud pa'i lo rgyus*). YS: vol. 10, pp. 11-16.

Hundred Actions (*Las brgya tham pa*; *Karmaśataka*). DK: 0304, mdo sde, ha-a.
Immaculate Oral Instructions (*rDzogs pa chen po gsang ba snying thig ma bu'i bka' srol chu bo gnyis 'dus kyi khrid yig dri med zhal lung*). NK: vol. wa, pp. 115-281.
Jataka Tales: The Past Lives of the Buddha (*sKyes pa'i rabs kyi rgyud*; *Jātakamālā*). Written by Āryaśura ['Phags pa dpa' bo]. DT: 4150, skyes rabs, hu.
Jewel Garland (*rGyal po la gtam bya ba rin po che'i phreng ba*; *Rāja parikathā ratnāvali*). Written by Nāgārjuna [Klu sgrub]. DT: 4158, spring yig, ge.
Jewel Lamp Sutra (*'Phags pa dkon mchog ta la la'i gzungs zhes bya ba theg pa chen po'i mdo*; *Ārya ratnolka nāma dhāraṇī mahāyāna sūtra*). DK: 0847, gzungs, e.
Karma Nyingtik (*Karma snying thig*). RTZ: vol. 86, 423-470.
Key Instructions on All Dharma Activities, the Tantra of the Manifest Realization (*Chos spyod thams cad kyi man ngag mngon par rtogs pa'i rgyud*). According to Alak Zenkar Rinpoche, this tantra is an uncategorized tantra that is found neither in the bKa' 'gyur nor in the rNying ma rgyud 'bum. At present, it is only partially extant.
Khandro Nyingtik (*mKha' 'gro snying thig*). See *Heart Essence of the Dakinis*.
Khandro Yangtik (*mKha' 'gro yang thig*). See *Quintessence of the Dakinis*.
King of Magic (*sGyu 'phrul rgyal po*). There are a number of tantras contained in the *Collected Tantras of the Nyingma School* that could be referred to by this appellation. Most likely, this is either *rGyud kyi rgyal po chen po sgyu 'phrul snying po bkod pa* or *gSang ba'i snying po de kho na nyid nges pa*, both of which are located in vol. 21 (zha) of the *mTshams brag Edition*.
King of Samadhi Sutra (*'Phags pa chos thams cad kyi rang bzhin mnyam pa nyid rnam par spros pa ting nge 'dzin gyi rgyal po zhes bya ba theg pa chen po'i mdo*; *Ārya sarvadharmasvabhāvas amatāvipañcita samādhirāja nāma mahāyāna sūtra*). DK: 0127, mdo sde, da.
King of Tantras: the Supreme Empowerment of the Hundred Syllables of Vajrasattva (*rDo rje sems dpa'i yi ge brgya pa dbang mchog rgyal po'i rgyud*). NG: 327, vol. 13 (pa), Atiyoga.
King Who Creates All (*Kun byed rgyal po*). NG: 1, vol. 1 (ka), Atiyoga.
Lama Yangtik (*Bla ma yang thig*). See *Guru's Quintessence*.
Lamp for the Path to Enlightenment (*Byang chub lam gyi sgron ma*; *Bodhipathapradīpa*). Composed by Atiśa [A ti sha]. DT: 3947, dbu ma, khi.
Last Testament (*Sangs rgyas kyi 'das rjes gsum pa*). YS: vol. 3, 287-304; vol. 10, pp. 74-89
Letter to a Friend (*bShes pa'i spring yig*; *Suhṛllekha*). Written by Nāgārjuna [Klu sgrub]. DT: 4496, jo bo'i chos chung, gi.
Letter to a Student (*Slob ma la springs pa*; *Śiṣyalekha*). By Candragomin [Go mi dge bsnyen]. DT: 4183, spring yig, nge.
Liberation of the Brahmin Gyalwey Drökyi Kyechey (*'Phags pa sdong po bkod pa'i mdor 'phags pa bram ze rgyal ba'i drod kyi skye mched kyi rnam par thar pa*). One section of the *Gandavyuha Sutra*, the last section of the *Avatamsaka Sutra*. See *Buddha Avatamsaka Sutra*.
Luminous (*'Phags pa gzhi thams cad yod par smra ba'i dge tshul gyi tshig le'ur byas pa'i 'grel pa 'od ldan*; *Ārya mūlasarvāstivādi śrāmaṇerakārikā vṛttiprabhāvatī*). DK: 4125, 'dul ba, shu.
Magical Vajra (*sGyu 'phrul rdo rje*). Uncertain; this may refer to *rDo rje sems dpa'i sgyu 'phrul dra ba las gsang ba snying po de kho na nyid bstan pa rol pa chen po'i rgyud*. NG: 425, vol. 21 (zha), Mahāyoga.
Meeting of Father and Son Sutra (*'Phags pa yab dang sras mjal ba zhes bya ba theg pa chen po'i mdo*; *Ārya pitā putra samāgama nāma mahāyāna sūtra*). From the Ratna-kūta Sūtra, PK: 760, vol. 23, dKon brtsegs IV, zhi.
Middle-length Perfection of Knowledge (*Shes rab kyi pha rol tu phyin pa stong phrag nyi shu lnga pa*; *Pañcaviṃśatisāhasrikā prajñāpāramitā*). DK: 3787, mdo 'grel, ka. Also referred to as *Yum bar ma* and *Yum 'bring ba*.

Mirror-like Commentary on the Magical Web (*sGyu 'phrul drva ba me long lta bu'i 'grel pa*). This may refer to *gSang ba snying po'i 'grel chung piṇḍartha*, by Vimalamitra [Dri med bshes gnyen], which is contained in NK, vol. 80.

Ninefold Expanse (*Byang chub kyi sems kyi rgya mtsho klong dgu'i rgyud*). NG: 69, vol. 3 (ga), Atiyoga.

Noble Candragarbha Sutra (*'Phags pa zla ba'i snying po shes rab kyi pha rol tu phyin pa theg pa chen po'i mdo*; *Ārya candragarbha prajñāpāramitā mahāyāna sūtra*). DK: 0027, sher phyin, ka.

Noble Siṃhanādika Sutra (*'Phags pa seng ge'i sgra bsgrags pa zhes bya ba theg pa chen po'i mdo*; *Ārya Siṃhanādika nāma mahāyāna sūtra*). DK: 0209, mdo sde, tsha.

Ornament of the Sutras (*Theg pa chen po mdo sde'i rgyan gyi tshig le'ur byas pa*; *Mahāyānasūtrāl aṃkārakārikā*). DK: 4020, sems tsam, phi.

Parinirvana Sutra (*'Phags pa yongs su mya ngan las 'das pa chen po'i mdo*; *Ārya mahāparinirvāṇa nāma mahāyāna sūtra*). DK: 0119-0121, mdo sde, nya-tha.

Pema Nyingtik (*Padma'i snying thig*). Alternate name for Heart Essence of the Dakinis.

Prayer of Noble Excellent Conduct (*'Phags pa bzang po spyod pa'i smon lam gyi rgyal po*; *Ārya bhadracārya praṇidhānarāja*). DK: 1095, gzugs, wam.

Precious Wish-fulfilling Treasury (*Theg pa chen po'i man ngag gi bstan bcos yid bzhin rin po che'i mdzod*). By Klong chen rab 'byams. Vol. 7 of *mDzod bdun*. 1983. Gangtok: Sherab Gyaltsen and Khyentse Labrang (based on the Oddiyāna Institute edition of Tarthang Rinpoche).

Principles of Elucidation (*rNam par bshad pa'i rigs pa*; *Vyākhyāyukti*) By Vasubandhu [dByig gnyen]. DT: 4061, sems tsam, shi.

Profound Quintessence (*Zab mo snying thig*). YS: vols. 12-13.

The Pure Path to Liberation (*sNgon 'gro chos spyod thar lam dkar po*). By Punda bity'a dha ra (Padma rig 'dzin). Kathmandu, Nepal: Nitartha Input Center, n.d.

Quintessence: A Wish-fulfilling Jewel (*Yang thig yid bzhin nor bu*). Alternate name for the Guru's Quintessence.

Quintessence of the Dakinis (*mKha' gro yang thig*). YS: vols. 7-9.

Reciting the Names of Manjushri (*'Jam dpal ye shes sems dpa'i don dam pa'i mtshan yang dag par brjod pa*; *Mañjuśrījñānasattvasya paramārtha nāma saṃgīti*). DK: 0360, rgyud, ka.

Request of Siṃhanādika (*'Phags pa byams pa'i seng ge sgra chen po*). Section 23 of the *Ratna-kūta*, PK: 760, dKon brtsegs I, zi. See *Heap of Jewels Sutra*.

Resting in the Nature of Mind (*rDzogs pa chen po sems nyid ngal gso*). Klong chen rab 'byams. KS: vol. 1, pp. 1-111. A thirteen-chapter text written by Longchen Rabjam in the fourteenth century that encompasses the entire range of Sutra and Tantra. This is accompanied by a commentary by the same author entitled the *Great Chariot* (*Shing rta chen po*).

Sangwa Nyingtik (*gSang ba snying thig*). Alternate title of Heart Essence of Vimalamitra.

Secret Heart Essence (*gSang ba snying thig*). Alternate title of Heart Essence of Vimalamitra.

Self-Presence of Great Samantabhadra Tantra (*lTa ba thams cad kyi rgyal po kun tu bzang po che ba la rang gnas pa'i rgyud*). NG: 93, vol. 4 (nga), Atiyoga.

Seventy Stanzas on Refuge (*gSum la skyab 'gro bdun cu pa*; *Triśaraṇa gamana saptati*). Written by Candrakīrti [Zla ba grags pa]. DT: 3971, dbu ma, gi.

Six Essence Tantras That Liberate Upon Wearing (*bTags grol snying po'i rgyud drug*). YS: vol. 10, pp. 16-25.

Stainless Confession Tantra (*Dam tshig thams cad kyi nyams chag skong ba'i lung lnga bshags pa thams cad kyi rgyud dri ma med pa'i rgyal po*). NG: 415, vol. 20 (wa), Mahāyoga.

Structure of the Heart Essence of the Dakinis Practice (*mKha' gro snying tig gi lag 'grig*). YS: vol. 11, pp. 105-111.

Supreme Continuum (*Theg pa chen po rgyud bla ma'i bstan bcos*; *Mahāyānottaratantraśāstra*). Taught by Maitreya [Byams pa] and transcribed Asaṅga [Thogs med]. DT: 4024, sems tsam, phi.

Supreme Scripture (*'Dul ba lung bla ma/'Dul ba gzhung bla ma*; *Vinaya uttaragrantha*). DK: 0007, 'dul ba, na.

Supreme Wish-fulfilling Tantra (*Yid bzhin mchog gi rgyud*). Bibliographic data unknown. This may be an alternate title for the *Great Array* (*bKod pa chen po*). YDD: p. 146 cites a text called *bKod pa chen po yid bzhin mchog gi rgyud*. Whether or not this is the so-called *A ti bkod pa chen po* (cited above as the *Great Array*), however, is unclear.

Sutra of a Boy's Prophecy (*Khye'u lung bstan pa'i mdo*). Bibliographic data unknown. This most likely is a subsection of a large Great Vehicle sutra.

Sutra of Advice to the King (*rGyal po la gdams pa zhes bya ba theg pa chen po'i mdo*; *Rājadeśa nāma mahāyāna sūtra*). DK: 0214, mdo sde, tsha.

Sutra of Going for Mindfulness in the Dharma (*Chos dran 'gro ba'i mdo*). This most likely refers to *Chos rjes su dran pa*; *Dharmānusmṛti*. DK: 0280, mdo sde, ya.

Sutra of Maitreya's Way (*'Phags pa byams pa 'jug pa zhes bya ba theg pa chen po'i mdo*; *Ārya maitreyaprasthāna nāma mahāyāna sūtra*). DK: 0198, mdo sde, tsa.

Sutra of Subahu (*dPung pa bzang po'i mdo*). This may refer to *dPung bzang gis zhus pa zhes bya ba'i rgyud*; *Ārya suvāhuparipṛcchā nāma tantra*. DK: 0805, rgyud, wa. Alternately, this may be a subsection of a larger sutra.

Sutra of the Condensed Realization (*Sangs rgyas kun gyi dgongs pa 'dus pa'i mdo chen po*). NG: 373, vol. 16 (ma), Anuyoga.

Sutra of the Good Night (*'Phags pa mtshan mo bzang po zhes bya ba'i mdo*; *Ārya bhadrakarātrī nāma sūtra*). DK: 0313, mdo sde, sa.

Sutra of the Inconceivable Secret (*'Phags pa de bzhin gshegs pa'i gsang ba bsam gyis mi khyab pa bstan pa zhes bya ba theg pa chen po'i mdo*; *Ārya tathāgatācintyaguhya nirdeśa nāma mahāyāna sūtra*). Section 3 of the *Ratna-kūṭa*. PK: 760, dkon brtsegs I, tshi, vol. 22. See *Heap of Jewels Sutra*.

Sutra of the Ten Dharmas (*'Phags pa chos bcu pa zhes bya ba theg pa chen po'i mdo*; *Daśadharmaka nāma mahāyānasūtra*). PK: 0760, dkon brtsegs, tshi.

Sutra of the Vast Display (*'Phags pa rgya cher rol pa zhes bya ba theg pa chen po'i mdo*; *Ārya lalita vistara nāma mahāyāna sūtra*). DK: 0095, mdo sde, kha.

Sutra of the White Lotus of Compassion (*'Phags pa snying rje pad ma dkar po zhes bya ba theg pa chen po'i mdo*; *Ārya karuṇāpuṇḍarīka nāma mahāyāna sūtra*). DK: 0112, mdo sde, cha.

Sutra of the Wise and the Foolish (*'Dzangs blun zhes bya ba'i mdo*; *Damamūko nāma sūtra*). DK: 0341, mdo sde, a.

Sutra of Totally Pure Discipline (*Tshul khrims yongs su dag pa'i mdo*). This most likely refers to *Tshul khrims yang dag par ldan pa'i mdo*; *Śīlasaṃyukta sūtra*. DK: 0303, mdo sde, sa.

Sutra of Varahi's Realization (*Phag mo'i rtogs brjod pa'i mdo*; *Sūkarika avadāna nāma sūtra*). DK: 0345, mdo sde, am.

Sutra on Individual Liberation (*So sor thar pa'i mdo*; *Prātimokṣasūtra*) DK: 0002, 'dul ba, ca.

Sutra Requested by Akshayamati (*'Phags pa blo gros mi zad pas zhus pa zhes bya ba theg pa chen po'i mdo*; *Ārya akṣayamati paripṛcchā nāma mahāyāna sūtra*). Section 44 of the *Ratna-kūṭa*. PK: 760, vol. 24. See *Heap of Jewels Sutra*.

Sutra Requested by Ananda (*Kun dga' bo'i zhus pa'i mdo*). Bibliographic data unknown. This is most likely a subsection of a larger sutra.

Sutra Requested by Kashyapa. One chapter of the *Heap of Jewels Sutra*.

Sutra Requested by King Chandra (*rGyal po zla bas zhus pa'i mdo*). Bibliographic data unknown. This may be an alternate title for the *Noble Candragarbha Sutra*, though it most likely is a subsection of a larger Great Vehicle sutra.

Sutra Requested by Rashtrapala (*Yul 'khor skyong gis zhus pa'i mdo*; *Rāṣṭrapāla paripṛcchā nāma mahāyāna sūtra*). DK: 0166, mdo sde, ba.

Sutra Requested by Ratnachuda (*'Phags pa gtsug na rin po ches zhus pa zhes bya ba theg pa chen po'i mdo*; *Ratnacūḍaparipṛcchā nāma mahāyānasūtra*). DK: 0110, mdo sde, cha.

Sutra Requested by Sagaramati (*'Phags pa blo gros rgya mtshos zhus ba zhes bya ba theg pa chen po'i mdo*; *Ārya sāgaramati paripṛcchā nāma mahāyāna sūtra*). DK: 0152, mdo sde, pha.

Sutra Requested by Shri Datta (*dPal sbyin gyis zhus pa'i mdo*). Bibliographic data unknown. This is most likely a subsection of a larger sutra.

Sutra Requested by Subahu (*'Phags pa lag bzangs kyis zhus pa zhes bya ba theg pa chen po'i mdo*; *Ārya subāhu paripṛcchā nāma mahāyāna sūtra*). Section 26 of the *Ratna-kūṭa*. See *Heap of Jewels Sutra*.

Sutra Requested by the Girl Ratna (*Bu mo rin chen gyi zhus pa'i mdo*) Alternate title of *'Phags pa theg pa chen po'i man ngag ces bya ba theg pa chen po'i mdo*; *Ārya mahāyānopadeśa nāma mahāyāna sūtra*. DK: 0169, mdo sde, ba.

Sutra Requested by the King of Nagas Sagara (*'Phags pa klu'i rgyal po rgya mtshos zhus pa zhes bya ba theg pa chen po'i mdo*; *Ārya sāgaranāgarājaparipṛcchā nāma mahāyāna sūtra*). DK: 0153, mdo sde, pha.

Sutra That Condenses the Precious Qualities of Realized Beings (*'Phags pa chos yang dag par sdud pa zhes bya ba theg pa chen po'i mdo*; *Ārya dharmasaṃgīti nāma mahāyāna sūtra*). DK: 0238, mdo sde, zha.

Tantra of Penetrating Sound (*Srin po che 'byung bar byed pa sgra thal 'gyur chen po'i rgyud*). NG: 290, vol. 12 (na), Atiyoga.

Tantra of Precious Empowerment (*dBang bskur bla ma rin po che'i rgyud*). NG: 236, vol. 9 (ta), Atiyoga.

Tantra of Self-Arising Awareness (*Rig pa rang shar chen po'i rgyud*). NG: 286, vol. 11 (da), Atiyoga.

Tantra of the Array of Lamps (*sGron ma rnam par bkod pa'i rgyud*). This is most likely an alternate title of the *Ye shes mar me'i rgyud*. NG: 325, vol. 13 (pa), Atiyoga.

Tantra of the Assembly of Blissful Ones (*bDe gshegs 'dus pa'i rgyud*). The text cited here is most likely from a collection of texts in the Mahāyoga section of NG, the primary tantra of which is entitled *bCom ldan 'das bde bar gshegs pa thams cad 'dus pa zhes bya ba rtsa ba'i rgyud kyi rgyal po chen po*. NG: 452, vol. 24 (ya), Mahāyoga.

Tantra of the Boundless Ocean of Great Power (*dBang chen rgya mtsho mtha' yas pa'i rgyud*). Bibliographic data unknown.

Tantra of the Clear Expanse (*rGyud kyi rtse rgyal nyi zla 'od 'bar mkha' klong rnam dag rgya mtsho klong gsal rgyud*). NG: 270, vol. 10 (tha), Atiyoga.

Tantra of the Full Array (*rGyud rnam bkod*). A series of texts in vols. 5 and 6 of the Collected Tantras of the Nyingma School, which includes *rDzogs pa chen po nges don 'dus pa'i rgyud lta ba thams cad kyi snying po rin po che rnam par bkod pa*. NG: 140, vol. 6 (cha), Atiyoga.

Tantra of the Hundred Syllables of Vajrasattva (*rDo rje sems dpa' yi ge brgya pa'i rgyud*). NG: 328, vol. 13 (pa), Atiyoga.

Tantra of the Secret Essence (*Tantra thams cad kyi rtsa bar gyur pa sgyu 'phrul drwa ba gsang ba snying po de kho na nyid nges pa rtsa ba'i rgyud*). NG: 218 vol. 14 (pha), Mahāyoga.

Tantra of the Sun and Moon's Union (*Nyi ma dang zla ba kha sbyor ba chen po gsang ba'i rgyud*). NG: 298, vol. 12 (na), Atiyoga.

Tantra of the Vajra Mirror (*rDo rje sems dpa' snying gi me long gi rgyud*). NG: 292 vol. 12 (na), Mahāyoga.
Tent of the Lotus Heart (*Padma'i snying gur*). Bibliographic data unknown.
Tent of the Moon's Essence (*Zla'i snying gur*). Bibliographic data unknown.
Ten Wheels of Kshitigarbha Sutra (*'Dus pa chen po las sa'i snying po'i 'khor lo bcu pa zhes bya ba theg pa chen po'i mdo*; *Daśachakra kśitigarbha nāma mahāyāna sūtra*). DK: 0239, mdo sde, zha.
Torch of the Three Methods (*mTshan yang dag par brjod pa'i 'grel pa tshul gsum gsal bar byed pa'i sgron ma zhes bya ba*; *Nāma saṃgītivṛtti trinayaprakāzakaraṇadīpa nāma*). Author unknown. PT: 3364, rgyud 'grel, hi.
Treasury of Higher Dharma (*Chos mngon pa'i mdzod kyi tshig le'ur byas pa*; *Abhidharma kośa kārikā*). Written by Vasubandhu [dByig gnyen]. DT: 4089, mngon pa, ku.
Treasury of Magic (*sGyu 'phrul gyi bang mdzod*). Bibliographic data unknown.
Treasury of Songs of Realization (*Do ha mdzod kyi glu*; *Dohakośagiti*). Written by Saraha [Sa ra ha]. DT: 2224, wi.
Two-Part Tantra (*rGyud brtag pa gnyis*). See *Hevajra Tantra*.
Untangling the Vinaya (*'Dul ba lung rnam 'byed/'Dul ba rnam par 'byed pa*; *Vinaya vibhaṅga*). DK: 0003, 'dul ba, ca.
Verses That Illuminate the Ultimate (*Don dam gsal ba'i tshigs bcad*). Bibliographic data unknown.
Vima Nyingtik. See *Heart Essence of Vimalamitra*.
Vinaya Minutia (*'Dul ba phran tshegs kyi gzhi*; *Vinaya kṣudraka vastu*). DK: 0006, 'dul ba, tha.
Way of the Bodhisattva (*Byang chub sems dpa'i spyod pa la 'jug pa*; *Bodhisattva caryāvatāra*). Written by Śāntideva [Zhi ba lha]. DT: 3871, mdo 'grel, la.
Wheel of Bliss Tantra (*'Khor lo bde ba'i rgyud*). Bibliographic data unknown.
White Lotus of the Sacred Dharma Sutra (*Dam pa'i chos padma dkar po zhes bya ba theg pa chen po'i mdo*; *Saddharma puṇḍarīka nāma mahāyāna sūtra*). DK: 0113, mdo sde, ja.
Zabmo Nyingtik (*Zab mo snying thig*). Alternate title of *Profound Quintessence*.

Bibliography

Tibetan Language Collections

sDe dge Black bka' 'gyur. Si tu chos kyi 'byung-gnas (editor). Chengdu, China: n.p., 199-?.

sDe dge bstan 'gyur. Delhi, India: Delhi Karmapae Chodhey, Gyalwae Sungrab Partun Khang, 1985.

rNying ma bka' ma rgyas pa. bDud 'joms 'jigs bral ye shes rdo rje (compiler). Kalimpong, India: Dupjung Lama, 1982-1987.

sNying thig ya bzhi. Klong chen rab 'byams (compiler). Reprint of the A 'dzom 'brug pa chos sgar edition. Darjeeling: Talung Tsetrul Pema Wangyal, 1976.

mTshams brag Manuscript of the rNying ma rgyud 'bum. Thimphu, Bhutan: National Library, Royal Government of Bhutan, 1982.

rDzogs pa chen po ngal so skor gsum dang rang grol skor gsum dang bcas pod gsum. Klong chen rab 'byams. Scanned edition of the prints from A 'dzom 'brug pa chos sgar. New York: Tibetan Buddhist Resource Center, 1999.

Rin chen gter mdzod chen mo. 'Jam mgon kong sprul blo gros mtha' yas (compiler). Paro, Bhutan: Ngodrup and Sherab Drimay, 1976.

Tibetan Language Texts

Kun mkhyen bstan pa'i nyi ma. bsKyed rim gyi zin bris cho ga spyi 'gros ltar bkod pa man ngag kun btus. Delhi, India: Chos Spyod Publications, 2000.

Krang dbyi sun, editor. Bod rgya tshig mdzod chen mo. Chengdu, China: Si khron mi rigs dpe skrun khang, 1988.

Klu sgrub. rGyal po la gtam bya ba rin po che phreng ba. DT: 4158, spring yig, ge.

―――. bShes pa'i springs yig slob dpon chen po 'phags pa klu sgrub kyis mdza' bo rgyal po bde spyod bzang po la bskur ba. Compiled and edited by C.T. Dorjé. Delhi, Prominent Publishers, 2001.

Klong chen rab 'byams. Khrid yig nor bu lugs. YS: vol. 7, pp. 287-311.

―――. Khrid yig rin po che gser gyi phreng ba. YS: vol. 7, pp. 322-394.

―――. Khrid yig sangs rgyas mnyam sbyor. YS: vol. 12, pp. 197-253.

―――. Ngal gso skor gsum gyi spyi don legs bshad rgya mtsho. KS: vol. 3, pp. 131-244.

―――. dNgos gzhi 'od gsal snying po'i don khrid. YS: vol. 1, pp. 333-450 and vol. 2, pp. 1-143.

―――. Chos dbyings rin po che'i mdzod kyi 'grel pa lung gi gter mdzod. Gangtok, Sikkim: Sherab Gyaltsen and Khyentse Labrang, 1983.

―――. gTer 'byung rin po che'i lo rgyus. YS: vol. 7, pp. 16-120.

―――. Theg pa chen po'i man ngag gi bstan bcos yid bzhin rin po che'i mdzod. Gangtok, Sikkim: Sherab Gyaltsen and Khyentse Labrang, 1983.

―――. *Theg pa chen po'i man ngag gi bstan bcos yid bzhin rin po che'i mdzod kyi 'grel pa pad+ma dkar po*. Gangtok, Sikkim: Sherab Gyaltsen and Khyentse Labrang, 1983.

―――. *Theg pa mtha' dag gi don gsal bar byed pa grub pa'i mtha' rin po che'i mdzod*. Gangtok, Sikkim: Sherab Gyaltsen and Khyentse Labrang, 1983.

―――. *Theg pa'i mchog rin po che'i mdzod*. Gangtok, Sikkim: Sherab Gyaltsen and Khyentse Labrang, 1983.

―――. *dPal gsang ba'i snying po de kho na nyid nges pa'i rgyud kyi 'grel pa phyogs bcu'i mun pa thams cad rnam par sel ba*. NK: vol. 26, pp. 1-629.

―――. *rDzogs pa chen po sems nyid ngal gso'i 'grel pa shing rta chen po*. KS: vol. 1, pp. 113-730.

―――. *rDzogs pa chen po sems nyid ngal gso'i gnas gsum dge ba gsum gyi don khrid byang chub lam bzang*. KS: vol. 2, pp. 441-546.

―――. *Zab don rgya mtsho'i sprin*. YS: vol. 8, pp. 1-488.

dKon mchog 'jigs med dbang po. *mDo rgyud bstan bcos du ma nas 'byung ba'i chos kyi rnam grangs shes ldan yid kyi dga' ston*. Kathmandu, Nepal: Padma Karpo Translation Committee, 2000.

bKra shis rgya mtsho. *Zab mo snying thig gi gnad thams cad bsdus pa'i don khrid lag len gsal ba*. RTZ: vol. 90 (si), pp. 1-96.

Khrag 'thung bdud 'joms rdo rje. *gNas lugs rang byung gi rgyud rdo rje'i snying po*. Beijing: Mi rigs dpe skrun khang, 2004.

mKhan chen Ngag dbang dpal bzang. *Srog sdom gzer bzhi'i zin bris kun mkhyen brgyud pa'i zhal lung*. Publication data unknown.

mKhan po Kun bzang dpal ldan. *Byang chub sems dpa'i spyod pa la 'jug pa rtsa ba dang 'grel pa*. New Delhi: S.I. Publications, 2002.

Gu ru bkra shis. *bsTan pa'i snying po gsang chen snga 'gyur nges don zab mo'i chos kyi byung ba gsal bar byed pa'i legs bshad mkhas pa dga' byed ngo mtshar gtam gyi rol mtsho*. Paro: Ugyen Tempai Gyaltsen, 1979.

dGe rtse ma h'a pandita tshe dbang mchog grub. *bsKyed pa'i rim pa cho ga dang sbyar ba'i gsal byed zung 'jug snye ma*. In *sgrub pa bka' brgyad kyi bskyed rdzogs zab chos thun min skor*, pp. 138-236. Odiyan: Dharma Publishing, 2004.

mGon po dbang rgyal, editor. *Chos kyi rnam grangs shes bya'i nor gling 'jug pa'i gru gzing*. Chengdu, China: Si khron mi rigs dpe skrun khang, 2000.

Nges don bstan 'dzin bzang po. *Theg pa lam zhugs kyi bshags pa'i rtsa 'grel bsdus pa thar lam sgron me*. Included in *rDzogs pa chen po mkha' 'gro snying thig gi khrid yig thar lam bgrod byed shing rta bzang po*. Chengdu, China: Si khron mi rigs dpe skrun khang, 1997.

―――. *rDzogs pa chen po mkha' 'gro snying thig gi khrid yig thar lam bgrod byed shing rta bzang po*. Chengdu, China: si khron mi rigs dpe skrun khang, 1997.

'Jam dgon kong sprul blo gros mtha' yas. *Theg pa'i sgo kun las btus pa gsung rab rin po che'i mdzod bslab pa gsum legs par stong pa'i bstan bcos shes bya kun khyab*. Kathmandu, Nepal: Padma Karpo Translation Committee, 2000.

―――. *rDzogs pa chen po gsang ba snying thig ma bu'i bka' srol chu bo gnyis 'dus kyi khrid yig dri med zhal lung*. NK: vol. wa, pp. 115-281.

―――. *Lam zhugs kyi gang zag las dang po pa la phan pa'i bskyed rdzogs kyi gnad bsdus*. Publication data unknown.

'Jigs med gling pa. *bsKyed rim lha'i khrid kyi rnam par bzhag pa 'og min bgrod pa'i them skas*. Gangtok, Sikkim: Dodrupchen Monastery, n.d.

―――. *De bzhin gshegs pas legs par gsungs pa'i gsung rab rgya mtsho'i snying por gyur pa rig pa 'dzin pa'i sde snod dam/ snga 'gyur rgyud 'bum rin po che'i rtogs pa brjod pa 'dzam gling tha gru khyab pa'i rgyan*. In *'Jigs med gling pa'i gsung 'bum*, vol. 13 (pa). Paro, Bhutan: Lama Ngodrup and Sherab Demy, 1985.

———. *Bla ma dgongs pa 'dus pa'i cho ga'i rnam bzhag dang 'brel ba'i bskyed rdzogs zung 'jug gi sgron ma mkhyen brtse'i me long 'od zer brgya pa*. Paro, Bhutan: Lama Ngodrup and Sherab Demy, 1985.

———. *rDzogs pa chen po klong chen snying tig gi gdod ma'i mgon po'i lam gyi rim pa'i khrid yig ye shes bla ma*. *rDzogs chen skor gsum*, pp. 241-419. Kathmandu: Bla ma phrin las dgon, 1999.

———. *Yon tan rin po che'i mdzod las 'bras bu'i theg pa rgya cher 'grel rnam mkhyen shing rta*. Kathmandu, Nepal: Shechen Monastery, n.d.

'Ju mi pham rgya mtsho. *mKhas pa'i tshul la 'jug pa'i sgo*. China: mTsho sngon mi rigs dpe skrun khang, 2003.

———. *dPal sgrub pa chen po bka' brgyad kyi spyi don rnam par bshad pa dngos grub snying po*. Chengdu, China: Si khron mi rigs dpe skrun khang, 2000.

———. *dBus dang mtha' rnam par 'byed pa'i bstan bcos kyi 'grel pa 'od zer phreng ba zhes bya ba*. In *'Jam mgon 'ju mi pham rgya mtsho'i gsung 'bum rgyas pa sde dge dgon chen par ma*, vol. 4, pp. 659-784. Paro, Bhutan: Lama Ngodrup and Sherab Demy, 1984.

———. *gSang 'grel phyogs bcu'i mun sel gyi spyi don 'od gsal snying po*. Chengdu, China: Si khron mi rigs dpe skrun khang, 2000.

gNyags dzny'ana ku m'ara (translator). *Dam tshig thams cad kyi nyams chag skong ba'i lung: bshags pa thams cad kyi rgyud dri ma med pa'i rgyal po*. NG: 415, vol. 20 (wa), Mahāyoga. Also: NK: vol. 13 (pa), pp. 5-126.

gNyis su med pa'i rdo rje [Advayavajra]. *Do ha mdzod kyi dka' 'grel* (*Dohakośapañjikā*). DK: 2256, wi.

gTer bdag gling pa. *rDzogs pa chen po mkha' 'gro snying tig gi khrid yig zab lam gsal byed*. YS: vol. 7, pp. 507-635.

Dil mgo mkhyen brtse 'Gyur med theg mchog bstan pa'i rgyal mtshan. *rDzogs pa chen po klong chen snying gi thig le'i rtsa gsum spyi dang bye brag gi dbang bskur gyi phreng ba bklag chog tu bkod pa zab bsang bdud rtsi'i sgo 'byed skal bzang kun dga'i rol ston*. In *Klong chen snying thig rtsa pod*, vol. 5. Kathmandu, Nepal: Shechen Publications, n.d.

Padma dkar po. *Chos mngon pa mdzod kyi bshad pa 'grel pa lugs*. Kathmandu: Padma Karpo Translation Committee, 2005.

Padma las 'brel rtsal. *mKha' 'gro snying thig gi kha byang*. YS: vol. 10, pp. 1-10.

———. *mKha' 'gro snying thig gi lag 'grig*. YS: vol. 11, pp. 105-110.

———. *mKha' 'gro snying thig gi lo rgyus*. YS: vol. 10, pp. 69-74.

———. *bTags grol gyi rgyud drug*. YS: vol. 10, pp.16-25.

———. *bTags grol don khrid*. YS: vol. 10, pp. 82-106.

———. *Thod rgal khyad par dbang lnga*. YS: vol. 10, pp. 284-287.

———. *Pra khrid chos thun khrid kyi zhag grangs*. YS: vol. 10, pp. 290-293.

———. *Zhus len bdun rtsi gser phreng*. YS: vol. 11, pp. 1-34.

———. *Sangs rgyas kyi 'das rjes gsum pa*. YS: vol. 10, pp.74-82.

Punda bity'a dha ra [Padma rig 'dzin]. *sNgon 'gro chos spyod thar lam dkar po*. Kathmandu, Nepal: Nitartha Input Center, n.d.

dPal sprul O rgyan chos kyi dbang po. *bsKyed rim lha'i khrid kyi dka' gnad cung zad bshad pa*. In *dPal sprul gsung 'bum*, vol. nga. Sikkim: Sonam Kazi, 1970-71.

———. *rDzogs pa chen po klong chen snying thig gi sngon 'gro'i khrid yig kun bzang bla ma'i zhal lung*. In *dPal sprul O rgyan 'jigs med chos kyi dbang po'i gsung 'bum*, vol. 7. Chengdu, China: Si khron mi rigs dpe skrun khang, 2003.

———. *rDzogs rim chos drug bsdus don*. In *dPal sprul O rgyan 'jigs med chos kyi dbang po'i gsung 'bum*, vol. 4. China: Si khron mi rigs dpe skrun khang, 2003.

Bi ma la mi tra. *Shin tu spros med kyi dbang 'khor 'das ru shan dbye ba'i lag len pra khrid*. YS: vol. 5, pp. 278-282.

dByig gnyen [Vasubandhu]. *Chos mngon pa'i mdzod kyi bshad pa*. ACIP edition, n.d.

Mi 'gyur dpal sgron. *rDzogs pa chen po a ti zab don snying po'i khrid dmigs zin bris su spel ba kun bzang dgongs rgyan*. RTZ: vol. si.

Yon tan rgya mtsho. *Yon tan rin po che'i mdzod kyi 'grel pa zab don snang byed nyi ma'i 'od zer*. Kathmandu, Nepal: Sechen Monastery, n.d. (computer version)

Rong zom chos kyi bzang po. *Man ngag lta phreng gi 'grel pa rong zom paṇḍita chen po chos kyi bzang pos mdzad pa*. NK: vol. 23, pp. 177-277.

Lo chen Dharma shri. *dPal gsang ba'i snying po de kho na nyid nges pa'i rgyud kyi rgyal po sgyu 'phrul drwa ba spyi don gyi sgo nas gtan la 'bebs par byed pa'i legs bshad gsang bdag zhal lung*. Kathmandu, Nepal: Shechen Publications, n.d.

Sa ra ha [Saraha]. *Do ha mdzod kyi glu* (*Dohakośagīti*). DT: 2224, wi.

English Language Works

Della Santina, Peter. *Causality and Emptiness: The Wisdom of Nāgārjuna*. Singapore: Buddhist Research Society, 2002.

Dilgo Khyentse Rinpoche. *Pure Appearance*. Translated by the Vajravairochana Translation Committee. Halifax: Vajravairochana Translation Committee, 2002.

Dudjom Lingpa. *Buddhahood Without Meditation*. Translated by Richard Barron. California: Padma Publishing, 2004.

_____. *The Vajra Essence*. Translated by B. Alan Wallace. Austin: Palri Parkhang, 2004.

Dudjom Rinpoche. *The Nyingma School of Tibetan Buddhism: Its Fundamentals and History*. Translated by Gyurme Dorjé and Matthew Kapstein. Boston: Wisdom Publications, 1991.

_____. *Perfect Conduct: Ascertaining the Three Vows*. Trans. Khenpo Gyurme Samdrub and Sangye Khandro. Boston: Wisdom Publications, 1996.

Goldstein, Melvyn (editor). *The New Tibetan-English Dictionary of Modern Tibetan*. Los Angeles: University of California Press, 2001.

Jamgön Kongtrül. *Creation and Completion: Essential Points of Tantric Meditation*. Translated by Sarah Harding. Boston: Wisdom Publications, 1996.

_____. *The Treasury of Knowledge: Buddhist Ethics*. Translated by Kalu Rinpoche Translation Group. Ithaca, New York: Snow Lion Publications, 1998.

_____. *The Treasury of Knowledge: Myriad Worlds*. Translated by Kalu Rinpoche Translation Group. Ithaca, New York: Snow Lion Publications, 2003.

_____. *The Treasury of Knowledge: Systems of Buddhist Tantra*. Translated by Kalu Rinpoche Translation Group. Ithaca, New York: Snow Lion Publications, 2005.

Jigme Lingpa, Patrul Rinpoche, and Getse Mahapandita. *Deity, Mantra, and Wisdom: Development Stage Meditation in Tibetan Buddhist Tantra*. Translated by the Dharmachakra Translation Committee. Ithaca, New York: Snow Lion Publications, 2007.

Kangyur Rinpoche. *Treasury of Precious Qualities*. Translated by the Padmakara Translation Group. Boston: Shambhala Publications, 2001.

Khamtrul Rinpoche. *Dzogchen Meditation*. Translated by Gareth Sparham. Dharamsala, India: Library of Tibetan Works and Archives, 2004.

Khenpo Kunpal. *Drops of Nectar: Śāntideva's Bodhicāryavatara According to the Tradition of Patrul Rinpoche*. Translated by Andreas Kretschmar. Internet publication: http://www.tibet.dk/pktc/bodhicaryavatara.htm, 2003.

Longchen Rabjam. *The Precious Treasury of the Basic Space of Phenomena*. Translated by Richard Barron. Junction City, California: Padma Publishing, 2001.
_____. *The Precious Treasury of the Way of Abiding*. Translated by Richard Barron. Junction City, California: Padma Publishing, 1998.
_____. *A Treasure Trove of Scriptural Transmission*. Translated by Richard Barron. Junction City, California: Padma Publishing, 2001.
Nagarjuna. *Nagarjuna's Letter to a Friend*. Translated by the Padmakara Translation Group. Ithaca, New York: Snow Lion Publications, 2005.
Nāgārjuna. *Saint Nāgārjuna's Letter to King Gautamiputra*. Edited and compiled by Dr. C. T. Dorji. Delhi: Prominent Publishers, 2001.
Ngawang Pelzang. *A Guide to the Words of My Perfect Teacher*. Translated by the Padmakara Translation Group. Boston: Shambhala Publications, 2004.
Norbu, Thinley. *The Small Golden Key*. Boston: Shambhala Publications, 1983.
Nyoshul Khenpo Jamyang Dorjé. *A Marvelous Garland of Rare Gems*. Junction City, California: Padma Publishing, 2005.
Padmasambhava, et al. *Crystal Cave*. Translated by Erik Hein Schmidt. Kathmandu, Nepal: Rangjung Yeshe Publications, 1990.
Padmasambhava and Jamgön Kongtrül. *Light of Wisdom, Vols. I, II, and IV*. Translated by Erik Hein Schmidt. Kathmandu, Nepal: Rangjung Yeshe Publications, 1986.
Patrul Rinpoche. *Words of My Perfect Teacher*. Translated by the Padmakara Translation Group. San Francisco: HarperCollins, 1994.
Pearcy, Adam. *A Compendium of Quotations*. Internet publication: http://lotsawahouse.org/school, 2004.
_____. *A Mini-Modern Mahāvyutpatti*. Internet publication: http://lotsawahouse.org/school, 2005.
Rigdzin, Tsepak. *Tibetan-English Dictionary of Buddhist Terminology*. Dharamsala, India: Library of Tibetan Works and Archives, 1993.
Sakya Pandita Kunga Gyaltshen. *A Clear Differentiation of the Three Codes*. Albany: State University of New York Press, 2002.
Shabkar Tsokdruk Rangdrol, et al. *The Flight of the Garuda*. Translated by Erik Hein Schmidt. Kathmandu, Nepal: Rangjung Yeshe Publications, 1993.
Śāntideva. *A Guide to the Bodhisattva Way of Life*. Translated from the Sanskrit and Tibetan by Vesna A. Wallace and B. Alan Wallace. Ithaca: Snow Lion Publications, 1997.
Shantideva. *The Way of the Bodhisattva*. Translated by the Padmakara Translation Group. Boston: Shambhala Publications, 1997.
Thondup, Tulku. *Masters of Meditation and Miracles*. Boston: Shambhala Publications, 1996.
_____. *The Practice of Dzogchen*. Ithaca, New York: Snow Lion Publications, 1989.
Tsele Natsok Rangdrol. *The Circle of the Sun*. Translated by Erik Hein Schmidt. Kathmandu, Nepal: Rangjung Yeshe Publications, 1990.
_____. *Empowerment*. Translated by Erik Hein Schmidt. Kathmandu, Nepal: Rangjung Yeshe Publications, 1993.
Tulku Urgyen Rinpoche. *Vajra Heart*. Translated by Erik Hein Schmidt. Kathmandu, Nepal: Rangjung Yeshe Publications, 1988.
_____. *Vajra Speech*. Translated by Erik Hein Schmidt. Kathmandu, Nepal: Rangjung Yeshe Publications, 2001.
Van Schaik, Sam. *Approaching the Great Perfection*. Boston: Wisdom Publications, 2004.
Yeshe Tsogyal. *The Lotus-Born: The Life Story of Padmasambhava*. Translated by Erik Pema Kunsang. Boston: Shambhala Publications, 1993.

Index

Glossary entries are marked in bold type

afflictions, **178**
  as an obstacle to study, 5, 91
  as the cause of suffering, 94-95
  basis for eliminating, 148
Akanishta, *See* Supreme Realm
Akshobya, 89, **178**
Alak Zenkar Rinpoche, xi
Amitabha, 89, **178**
Amoghasiddhi, 90, **178**
animals, 105-106

Blazing Mountain Charnel Ground, ix
bodhicitta, 57-62, **181**
  absolute, **177**
  precepts of, 79-84
  relative, **208**
  safeguarding from degeneration, 74
breakthrough, xv, **182**
buddha, 27, 63, **182**
  samaya vow of, 88
Buddha Shakyamuni, ix

Chakyungwa Ngakwang Padma, 10
Charnel Ground of the Wild Jungle, 9
Chimpu Rimochen, 10
Chökyi Gyatso, 10
compassion, 62, 73-74
completion stage, xv, **183**
Cool Grove Charnel Ground, ix
covetousness, 71

dakini, **183**
  taking refuge in, 28
Dalai Lama, fifth (1617-82), xv
Dangma Lhungyal (11th-12th centuries), x

death, 51, 64
dedication of merit,
  See merit, dedication of
demi-gods, 108, 131
desire realm, 131, **184**
development stage, xv, **184**
Dharma, **185**
  benefits of teaching and studying, 143
  divisions of, 27
  samaya vow of, 88
  taking refuge in, 27
dharmakaya, **185**
  meaning of, viii
  taking refuge in, 28
Dilgo Khyentse Rinpoche (1910-91), xi
direct leap, xv, **185**
discipline
  as basis for attaining liberation, 79
  as one of the six perfections, 74
  fault of lacking, 78
  over-emphasizing, 78
  three forms of, 82, 84, 87
Dorsem Nyingtik, xi
downfalls, 83
Drimé Özer, *See* Longchen Rabjam
Drupwang Pema Rigdzin, *See* Dzogchen Rinpoche I
Dza Patrul, *See* Patrul Rinpoche
Dzogchen Gemang Tulku, xvi
Dzogchen Monastery, xi, xv–xvii
  preliminary practices of, xvii, 77
Dzogchen Ponlop Rinpoche I (Namkha Ösel, d. 1726), xi, xvi, 10
Dzogchen Rinpoche I (Pema Rigdzin, 1625-97), xi, 3, 10

250 / GREAT PERFECTION

Dzogchen Rinpoche III (1759-1792), xvi–xvii
Dzogchen Shakya, 10
Dzogchen Sonam Wangpo, 10

empowerment, 13-15, **187**
   four, 13, **192**
   into the display of awareness, **188**
   knowledge-wisdom, **198**
   precious word, **207**
   receiving (in guru yoga), 167
   secret, **211**
   ultimate, 169
   vase, **223**
   vows of, *See* samaya vows
emptiness, 74, **188**
enlightened activity, **189**
   embodiment of, 28
equanimity, 62, 73
essence, nature, and compassion, 28, 207
Excellent Chariot, xii-xiii, xvii–xviii

faith, **189**
   factors that conflict with, 153
   faults of lacking, 151
   function of, 149
   inauthentic, 154
   nature of, 145
   positive qualities of, 155
   six kinds of, 145-48
   ways to develop, 152
five buddha families, **190**
   and the Great Perfection lineage, ix
   samaya vows of, 89
five perfections, 9, **190**
form realms, 132, **191**
formless realm, 133, **191**
four immeasurables, 62, 73, **193**
four ways of attracting students, 60, **194**
Fourfold Heart Essence, xi, **192**
freedoms and endowments, 19-27, 63
   impermanence of, 45
   reason for teaching, 17

Garap Dorjé, ix , 9
generosity, 60, 74, 89, 143, **194**
gods, 109, 131-33
Great Perfection, vii-viii, xiii-xiv, **195**

different meanings of the term, vii
lineage of, viii-x, 7-11
main practices of, xv
Three Classes of, ix, **216**
guru, 156-62, **195**
   importance of studying with, 37, 156
   not acting disrespectfully towards, 85
   qualifications of, 37-39, 141, 157
   samaya vow of, 89
   taking refuge in, 28
Guru Rinpoche, *See* Padmasambhava
Guru Yeshé Rabjam, 10
guru yoga, xv, 162-170
Guru's Quintessence, xi
Gyalsé Lekpa (1290-1366), 9
Gyalsé Shenpen Tayé (1800-1869/70), xvi

harsh speech, 71
Hayagriva, 28, **196**
   as visualized in guru yoga, 163
Heart Essence of the Dakinis, x-xviii, **196**
   lineage of, viii-x, 7-11
   presentation of samaya vows in, 87
Heart Essence of Vimalamitra, x, **196**
heaven, 131-33
hell, 99-103
hundred-syllable mantra, 115

impermanence, 17, 44-56

Jigmé Lingpa (1730-98), xvi
Jinpa Zangpo, 10
Jnanasutra, x
joy, 62, 73

karma, 53, 63-77, **197, 207**
Karmapa, third, *See* Rangjung Dorjé
Key Instruction Class, ix-x, **197**
Khandro Nyingtik, See Heart Essence of the Dakinis
Khenpo Künpal (1872-1943), xv
Khenpo Ngaga (1879-1941), xv
Khenpo Pema Vajra (18th century), xv
Khenpo Petsé Rinpoche (1931-2002), xv
Khenpo Shenga (1871-1927), xv
killing, 71, 77
knowledge, **198**
   as one of the six perfections, 74

perfection of, 76
three-fold, 11
Kongpo Dzogchenpa, xi

liberation, **199**
  benefits of, 127
lineage
  entrusted to dakinis, **199**
  mind, 11, **203**
  of aspirations and empowerments, **199**
  of coded verse, 9
  of the Great Perfection, viii-x, 7-11
  of transmissions and prophecies, **199**
  oral, 11, **196**
  symbolic, 11, **214**
Longchen Rabjam (1308-1363), xi, xviii, 10
love, 62, 73
lying, 71, 77

malice, 71
mandala, **201**
  of the body, 137
  of the total perfection of the three
    spheres, 137
  three-fold, 90
mandala offering, 135-39
Manjushri, **202**
  visualizing while receiving teachings, 43
Manjushrimitra, ix-x
Mantra Vehicle, *See* Vajra Vehicle
merit
  accumulation of, **177**
  dedication of, 169-70
Mind Class, ix, **203**
Mipam (1846-1912), xv

Namkha Ösel, *See* Dzogchen Ponlop
  Rinpoche I
nirmanakaya, ix, **205**
  natural, **204**
Nyingtik Yabshi, *See* Four-fold Heart
  Essence

obscurations
  afflictive, **178**
  cognitive, **183**
  four, **194**
  two, **221**

original purity, viii, xv

Padma Rigdzin, *See* Dzogchen Rinpoche I
Padmakara, *See* Padmasambhava
Padmasambhava
  and the Great Perfection lineage, x-xi, 9
  as a source of refuge, 28
  as visualized when taking refuge, 31
Patrul Rinpoche (1808-87), x, xv
Pema Ledrel Tsel (1292-1316), x-xi, 9-10
Pema Rigdzin, *See* Dzogchen Rinpoche I
Pema Tötreng Tsel, *See* Padmasambhava
Pöba Tulku (1900/7-1959), xv
pointless speech, 71
Ponlop Rinpoche, *See* Dzogchen Ponlop
precious human existence, 19-27, 44
Precious Wish-fulfilling Treasury, xviii
preliminary practices, 17
  importance of, xii
  overview of, xiv-xv
Princess Pemasel (8th century), xi, 9
Pure Path to Liberation, xvii, 77

Quintessence of the Dakinis, xi, 192

Rangjung Dorjé (1284-1339), xi
Ratnasambhava, 89, **208**
reality, 28, **208**
refuge, 27-35, 88
Resting in the Nature of Mind, xviii
result
  dominant, 68, 71, **186**
  of disengagement, **208**
  of individual effort, **208**
  ripened, 68, 71, **209**
  that resembles its cause, 69, 71, **208**
Rigdzin Nyima Drakpa (1647-1710), xvi
Rigdzin Tsewang Norbu (1698-1755), xi
Rinchen Lingpa, 9

Samantabhadra, 3-4, 28, **209**
  and the Dzogchen lineage, viii, 7-9
  visualized when giving a teaching, 39
Samantabhadri, 9, **209**
  visualized when giving a teaching, 39
samaya vows, 15, 84-90, **210**
sambhogakaya, **210**
  as visualized when taking refuge, 31

meaning of, viii
  taking refuge in, 28
samsara, 210
  contemplating the suffering of, 93
  reversing the causes and results of, 75
Samtenpa, 10
Sangha, 27-28
  samaya vow of, 88
sending and taking, contemplation of, 59
Seven Nails, x
sexual misconduct, 71, 77
Shechen Rabjam Rinpoche I (1650-1704), xvi
Shri Simha, ix-x, 9
Siljin Charnel Ground, x
Six Experiences of Meditation, x
Six Methods of Resting, x
six mother monasteries, xi, xv
  six perfections, 39-40, 42-43, 74-75, 143, 212
six stains, 5, 6, 92, 212
skillful means, 76, 213
Sonam Rinchen, 10
Sosa Ling Charnel Ground, ix-x, 9
Space Class, ix, 216
spirits, 103-105
stealing, 71
student
  qualifications of, 40-44, 142
suffering, 93-112
Supreme Realm, viii, 133, 204, 214

Taklung Tramo Rock, 9
tantra, 214
  Anuttarayoga, 178
  Capacity, 215
  Charya, 182
  Father, 189
  Four Classes of, 192
  Kriya, 198
  Mother, 203
  Nondual, 206
  Three Inner, 217
  Three Outer, 218
  Ubhaya, 221
  Yoga, 226
Tara, 43, 215
tögal, *See* direct leap

Three Classes of the Great Perfection, ix, 216
three flaws of the vessel, 5, 91
Three Jewels, 27, 88
three roots, 28, 218
Three Statements that Strike the Vital Point, ix
trekchö, *See* breakthrough
two accumulations, 136, 220

Vairocana, 90, 221
Vairochana (translator), x
Vajra Vehicle, 63, 90, 223
Vajradhara, 28, 222
Vajrasattva, ix, 7, 9, 112-16, 222
Vajravarahi, 9, 28, 223
Vajrayana, *See* Vajra Vehicle
Vehicle of Perfections, 63, 224
Vehicle of Transformative Methods, 90
vice, 69-71
Vima Nyingtik, See Heart Essence of Vimalamitra
Vimalamitra, x
virtue, 67-70, 72-74
  dedication of, 169
  result of, 68, 130
vows, 77-90
  bodhisattva, *See* bodhisattva vows
  refuge, 34
  samaya, *See* samaya vows
vows of individual liberation, 77-78, 87

wisdom, 226
  accumulation of, 177
  active, 177
  discerning, 185
  five, 191
  mirror-like, 203
  of equality, 226
  of the sphere of reality, 226
  two forms of, 221
  vajra, 223
wrong view, 71

Yeshé Tsogyal, 9
yidam deity, 28, 89, 226

Zhotong Tidrö, 9

The Heart Essence Series

THE HEART ESSENCE SERIES contains translations of seminal writings on the Great Perfection. Beginning with the works of the Heart Essence of the Dakinis and the Heart Essence of Vimalamitra, two cycles that lie at the core of the Great Perfection lineage, the Rimé Foundation hopes to provide scholars, teachers, and practitioners of these profound teachings with accurate and readable translations of the most important Great Perfection texts. Our projects are carried out with the blessings and guidance of leading masters of the Great Perfection lineage.

Current Volumes:
- *Great Perfection: Separation and Breakthrough* – The second half of the Third Dzogchen Rinpoche's *Excellent Chariot*, which includes extensive explanations of the unique Great Perfection preliminary practices and instructions on the breakthrough stage of Heart Essence practice

Future volumes include:
- *Gateway to the Great Perfection: The Longchen Nyingtik Preliminaries* – Jigmé Lingpa's writings on the Great Perfection preliminary practices, including an extensive commentary on the seven-point contemplation of the Heart Essence of Vimalamitra
- *Heart Essence of the Dakinis: Core Teachings on the Great Perfection* – The most important texts from the Heart Essence of the Dakinis, including the *Three Last Testaments* and the *Six Essence Tantras That Liberate Upon Wearing*
- *Heart Essence of the Dakinis: Origins of the Great Perfection* – A collection of texts on the history and contents of the Heart Essence of the Dakinis cycle
- *Clarifying the Profound Path* – An important commentary on the Heart Essence of the Dakinis by Terdak Lingpa

The Rimé Foundation

THE TIBETAN WORD *Rimé* (pronounced "ree-may") literally means "without bias." This term has most recently been linked with a spiritual movement that began in Eastern Tibet roughly one hundred and fifty years ago. Like all religions and cultures, Tibetan Buddhism has seen its share of sectarian strife and turmoil. The Rimé movement aimed to counter this tendency by promoting an atmosphere of harmony and good will between the various Buddhist schools and lineages of Tibet. Rimé is not a school or sect of Buddhism, but a unique approach to spiritual practice. Adherents of this outlook are often rooted in one spiritual tradition. At the same time, however, they maintain a respect for, and willingness to learn from, other approaches. The Rimé ideal, then, is not to create one "universal approach" to spirituality, but rather to honor the differences between lineages, sects, and religions, and to foster an environment of mutual support and harmony.

The vision of the Rimé Foundation is a world in which wisdom and compassion are the guiding forces in our individual and collective lives, and in which the traditions that enable us to cultivate virtue are honored, practiced, and preserved for future generations. Our mission is to facilitate this process by preserving the spiritual heritage of Tibet, providing access to its texts, teachers, and practices, and fostering the growth of a diverse and tolerant spiritual community.

Our programs include:
- Translating classic Tibetan literature into the English language
- Bringing fully qualified Tibetan spiritual teachers into our communities to live and teach, with a special emphasis on the upper Midwestern United States
- Offering grants and support to dedicated spiritual practitioners in our community to enable them to engage in spiritual study and retreat

For more information about our organization and programs, or to support our projects, please visit us online at www.rimefoundation.org or email info@rimefoundation.org.